Workbook

MIDDLE GRADES

MATH*Thematics*

Book 2

The STEM Project

McDougal Littell

A HOUGHTON MIFFLIN COMPANY

Evanston, Illinois • Boston • Dallas

McDougal Littell: www.mcdougallittell.com
Middle School Mathematics: www.mlmath.com

ISBN 0-618-21249-3

Printed in the United States of America.

4 5 6 7 8 9-MDO- 04 03

Contents

MODULE 1   LABSHEET **1A**

Homework Frequency Table (Use with Questions 14–18 on page 6.)

Directions

- Make a tally mark (I) in the *Tally* column to represent each of your classmates' answers to Question 13. Include your own answer.

- Count the tally marks in each category and write the total in the *Frequency* column.

Time spent on homework	Tally	Frequency
did not usually have homework		
did not do assignments		
one half hour or less		
one hour		
two hours		
more than two hours		

Homework Bar Graph (Use with Questions 15–18 on page 6.)

Directions Use the data from the frequency table above to complete the bar graph. The bars have been started for you along the vertical axis. Remember to include labels or a scale along each axis.

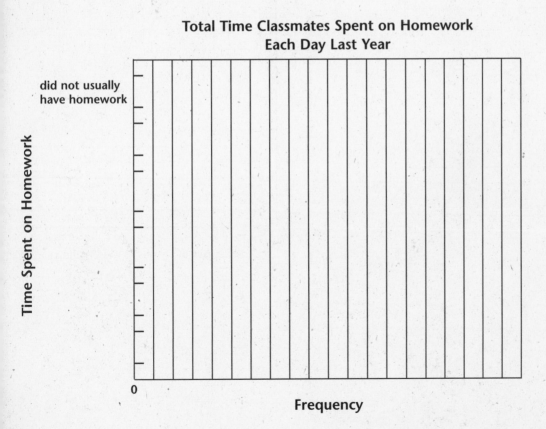

Total Time Classmates Spent on Homework Each Day Last Year

MODULE 1   **LABSHEET** (2A)

Building Patterns (Use with Questions 10 and 12 on pages 15–16.)

Directions For each pattern:

- Model the shape sequence for the first 5 terms with square tiles (or draw pictures).

- Use your models and any patterns you notice to complete the table. Make a graph of the first 5 terms of the sequence.

- Write a word sentence that explains how to find the total number of squares if you know the number of stories in the building or the number of squares in the tower.

Pattern 1   1-story building   2-story building   3-story building

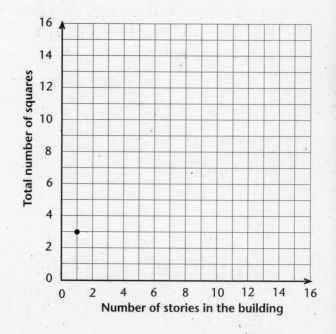

Number of stories in the building	Total number of squares
1	3
2	
3	
4	
5	
10	
90	

Word Sentence:

Patterns 2 and 3 are on Labsheet 2B.

MODULE 1   **LABSHEET** **2B**

Building Patterns continued (Use with Questions 10 and 12 on pages 15–16.)

Pattern 2   1 square in tower   2 squares in tower   3 squares in tower

The tower is shaded.

Number of squares in the tower	Total number of squares
1	4
2	5
3	
4	
5	
10	
90	

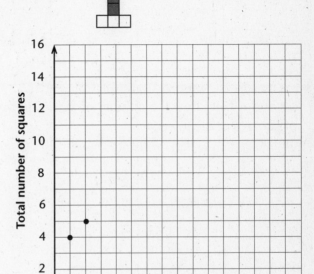

Word Sentence:

Pattern 3   1-story building with tower   2-story building with tower   3-story building with tower

Number of stories in the building	Total number of squares
1	4
2	
3	
4	
5	
10	
90	

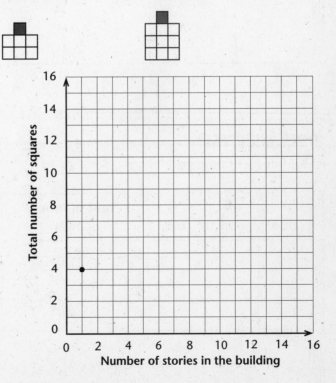

Word Sentence:

MODULE 1 **LABSHEET 3A**

Game Board (Use with *Setting the Stage* on page 26 and
with Question 11(b) on page 29.)

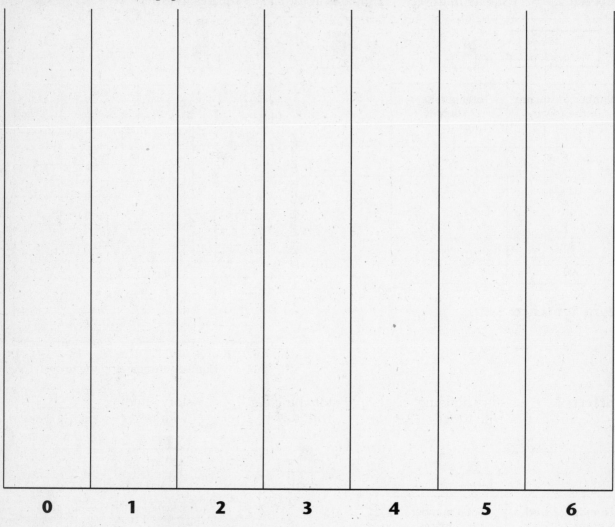

| 0 | 1 | 2 | 3 | 4 | 5 | 6 |

Frequency Table (Use with *Setting the Stage* on page 26 and with
Question 11(b) on page 29.)

Game	Tally of rolls	Total number of rolls
1		
2		
3		

MODULE 1

Results of 18 Rolls (Use with Questions 5, 7(a) and (b), 8, and 9 on pages 27–29.)

Difference	Tally	Frequency	Fraction of rolls
0			
1			
2			
3			
4			
5			
6			
Total number of rolls →		18	

Results of 72 Rolls (Use with Questions 8–10 on page 29.)

Difference	Group frequencies				Total frequency	Experimental probability
	My group	Group 1	Group 2	Group 3		
0						
1						
2						
3						
4						
5						
6						
			Total number of rolls →		72	

MODULE 1   **LABSHEET** (3C)

Rolling One Number Cube (Use with Question 13 on page 30.)

Directions Follow the steps below to complete the table showing the *Results of Rolling One Number Cube*.

- Find the theoretical probability of each outcome and record it in the last column of the table.

- Find the sum of the theoretical probabilities of the six outcomes and record it in the table.

- Take turns rolling a number cube 30 times. Keep a tally of your results. Record the frequency of each outcome for your group.

- Record the results from four other groups in the table. Then add the frequencies to get a total frequency of each outcome for 150 rolls.

- Find the experimental probability of each outcome based on the frequencies for 150 rolls.

Results of Rolling One Number Cube									
		Frequencies for 30 rolls					Frequency for 150 rolls	Probabilities	
Outcome	Tally	My group	Group 1	Group 2	Group 3	Group 4		Experimental	Theoretical
1									
2									
3									
4									
5									$\frac{1}{6}$
6									
Sum of theoretical probabilities →									

MODULE 1   LABSHEET **3D**

Difference Chart (Use with Questions 16–18 on page 32.)

Directions Suppose you roll a red number cube and a blue number cube. Complete the *Difference Chart* below to show what difference results from each roll. An example is shown. Then answer the questions below.

a. Which difference occurs most often in the chart? Which occurs least often?

b. How many boxes are there to fill in on the chart (including the ones filled in for you)?

c. What fraction of the boxes contain a difference of 4?

d. What is the theoretical probability of rolling a difference of 4?

e. What fraction of the boxes contain a difference of 6?

f. What is the theoretical probability of rolling a difference of 6?

Blue / Red	1	2	3	4	5	6
1					(5 – 1) 4	
2	1					
3						
4			(4 – 3) 1			
5						
6						

Difference Game Theoretical Probability Table

(Use with Questions 17 and 18 on page 32.)

Directions Complete the table at the right by finding the theoretical probability of each difference shown in the *Difference Chart* above. Then find the sum of the theoretical probabilities.

Theoretical Probabilities for the *Difference Game*
$P(0) =$
$P(1) =$
$P(2) =$
$P(3) =$
$P(4) = \frac{4}{36}$, or $\frac{1}{9}$
$P(5) =$
$P(6) =$
Sum =

MODULE 1   **LABSHEET** (5A)

Last-Card Table (Use with Questions 13 and 14 on page 54 and Exercise 6 on page 57.)

Directions Use the table below and follow the directions in Questions 13 and 14 on page 54 to extend your solution to the Last Card Problem.

Number of cards	1	2	3	4	5	6	7	8	9	10	11	12	13	14	15	16	17	18	19	20
Number on last card	1	2	2	4	2	4	6	8	2	4	6	8	10	12	14					

Number of cards	21	22	23	24	25	26	27	28	29	30	31	32	33
Number on last card													

Two Assessment Scales (Use with Question 16 on page 55.)

Directions Use a marker to draw a segment along each scale to the point that describes your group's work for Question 12 on page 43 of Section 4.

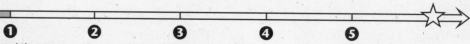

If your score is in the shaded area, explain why on the back of this sheet and stop.

The star indicates that you excelled in some way.

?→! Problem Solving

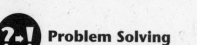

❶ I did not understand the problem well enough to get started or I did not show any work.

❷ I understood the problem well enough to make a plan and to work toward a solution.

❸

❹

❺ I made a plan, I used it to solve the problem, and I verified my solution.

Connections

❶ I attempted or solved the problem and then stopped.

❷

❸ I found patterns and used them to extend the solution to other cases, or I recognized that this problem relates to other problems, mathematical ideas, or applications.

❹

❺ I extended the ideas in the solution to the general case, or I showed how this problem relates to other problems, mathematical ideas, or applications.

MODULE 1   **LABSHEET** 5B

Problem Solving Scales for Exercises 1 and 2 (Use with Exercise 3 on page 56.)

▭ *If your score is in the shaded area, explain why on the back of this sheet and stop.*

☆ *The star indicates that you excelled in some way.*

 Problem Solving

❶ ❷ ❸ ❹ ❺ ☆➡

I did not understand the problem well enough to get started or I did not show any work.

I understood the problem well enough to make a plan and to work toward a solution.

I made a plan, I used it to solve the problem, and I verified my solution.

 Problem Solving

❶ ❷ ❸ ❹ ❺ ☆➡

I did not understand the problem well enough to get started or I did not show any work.

I understood the problem well enough to make a plan and to work toward a solution.

I made a plan, I used it to solve the problem, and I verified my solution.

....

Two Assessment Scales for Exercise 4 (Use with Exercise 5 on page 57.)

▭ *If your score is in the shaded area, explain why on the back of this sheet and stop.*

☆ *The star indicates that you excelled in some way.*

 Problem Solving

❶ ❷ ❸ ❹ ❺ ☆➡

I did not understand the problem well enough to get started or I did not show any work.

I understood the problem well enough to make a plan and to work toward a solution.

I made a plan, I used it to solve the problem, and I verified my solution.

 Connections

❶ ❷ ❸ ❹ ❺ ☆➡

I attempted or solved the problem and then stopped.

I found patterns and used them to extend the solution to other cases, or I recognized that this problem relates to other problems, mathematical ideas, or applications.

I extended the ideas in the solution to the general case, or I showed how this problem relates to other problems, mathematical ideas, or applications.

Math Thematics, Book 2 **9**

MODULE 1 LABSHEET 6A

Three Assessment Scales (Use with Exercise 18 on page 67.)

 If your score is in the shaded area, explain why on the back of this sheet and stop.

☆ The star indicates that you excelled in some way.

 ## Problem Solving

❶　❷　❸　❹　❺　☆→

❶ I did not understand the problem well enough to get started or I did not show any work.

❸ I understood the problem well enough to make a plan and to work toward a solution.

❺ I made a plan, I used it to solve the problem, and I verified my solution.

 ## Representations

❶　❷　❸　❹　❺　☆→

❶ I did not use any representations such as equations, tables, graphs, or diagrams to help solve the problem or explain my solution.

❸ I made appropriate representations to help solve the problem or help me explain my solution, but they were not always correct or other representations were needed.

❺ I used appropriate and correct representations to solve the problem or explain my solution.

 ## Connections

❶　❷　❸　❹　❺　☆→

❶ I attempted or solved the problem and then stopped.

❸ I found patterns and used them to extend the solution to other cases, or I recognized that this problem relates to other problems, mathematical ideas, or applications.

❺ I extended the ideas in the solution to the general case, or I showed how this problem relates to other problems, mathematical ideas, or applications.

Name _____   Problem _____

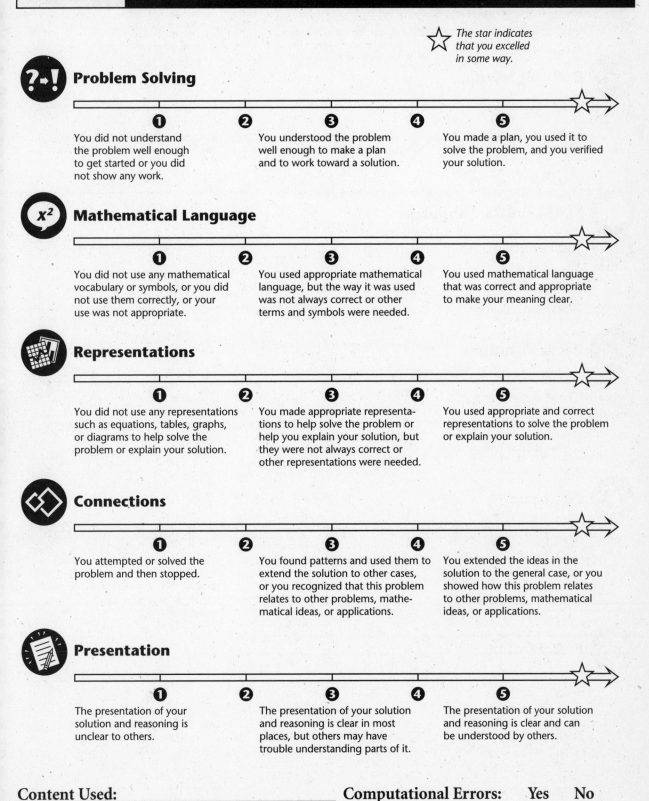

The star indicates that you excelled in some way.

Problem Solving

❶   ❷   ❸   ❹   ❺

1 You did not understand the problem well enough to get started or you did not show any work.

3 You understood the problem well enough to make a plan and to work toward a solution.

5 You made a plan, you used it to solve the problem, and you verified your solution.

Mathematical Language

❶   ❷   ❸   ❹   ❺

1 You did not use any mathematical vocabulary or symbols, or you did not use them correctly, or your use was not appropriate.

3 You used appropriate mathematical language, but the way it was used was not always correct or other terms and symbols were needed.

5 You used mathematical language that was correct and appropriate to make your meaning clear.

Representations

❶   ❷   ❸   ❹   ❺

1 You did not use any representations such as equations, tables, graphs, or diagrams to help solve the problem or explain your solution.

3 You made appropriate representations to help solve the problem or help you explain your solution, but they were not always correct or other representations were needed.

5 You used appropriate and correct representations to solve the problem or explain your solution.

Connections

❶   ❷   ❸   ❹   ❺

1 You attempted or solved the problem and then stopped.

3 You found patterns and used them to extend the solution to other cases, or you recognized that this problem relates to other problems, mathematical ideas, or applications.

5 You extended the ideas in the solution to the general case, or you showed how this problem relates to other problems, mathematical ideas, or applications.

Presentation

❶   ❷   ❸   ❹   ❺

1 The presentation of your solution and reasoning is unclear to others.

3 The presentation of your solution and reasoning is clear in most places, but others may have trouble understanding parts of it.

5 The presentation of your solution and reasoning is clear and can be understood by others.

Content Used: _____   Computational Errors: Yes   No

Notes on Errors: _____

STUDENT	SELF-ASSESSMENT SCALES

 If your score is in the shaded area, explain why on the back of this sheet and stop.

☆ *The star indicates that you excelled in some way.*

 Problem Solving

①   **②**   **③**   **④**   **⑤**   ☆➡

I did not understand the problem well enough to get started or I did not show any work.

I understood the problem well enough to make a plan and to work toward a solution.

I made a plan, I used it to solve the problem, and I verified my solution.

 Mathematical Language

①   **②**   **③**   **④**   **⑤**   ☆➡

I did not use any mathematical vocabulary or symbols, or I did not use them correctly, or my use was not appropriate.

I used appropriate mathematical language, but the way it was used was not always correct or other terms and symbols were needed.

I used mathematical language that was correct and appropriate to make my meaning clear.

 Representations

①   **②**   **③**   **④**   **⑤**   ☆➡

I did not use any representations such as equations, tables, graphs, or diagrams to help solve the problem or explain my solution.

I made appropriate representations to help solve the problem or help me explain my solution, but they were not always correct or other representations were needed.

I used appropriate and correct representations to solve the problem or explain my solution.

 Connections

①   **②**   **③**   **④**   **⑤**   ☆➡

I attempted or solved the problem and then stopped.

I found patterns and used them to extend the solution to other cases, or I recognized that this problem relates to other problems, mathematical ideas, or applications.

I extended the ideas in the solution to the general case, or I showed how this problem relates to other problems, mathematical ideas, or applications.

 Presentation

①   **②**   **③**   **④**   **⑤**   ☆➡

The presentation of my solution and reasoning is unclear to others.

The presentation of my solution and reasoning is clear in most places, but others may have trouble understanding parts of it.

The presentation of my solution and reasoning is clear and can be understood by others.

MODULE 1 SECTION 1   **PRACTICE AND APPLICATIONS**

For use with Exploration 1

Use the bar graph for Exercises 1–10.

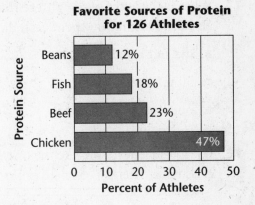

Favorite Sources of Protein for 126 Athletes

1. **a.** Who was surveyed?

   b. What information is displayed in the graph?

2. **a.** What source of protein did most athletes choose as their favorite?

   b. What source of protein did the fewest athletes choose as their favorite?

3. What do the numbers on the horizontal axis mean?

4. The bar for athletes who chose beans as their favorite source of protein is about how many times as long as the bar for athletes who chose beef? chicken?

5. How many athletes responded to the survey?

6. In this survey, is 18% of the athletes *more than* or *less than* 18 athletes?

7. Compare the bars for beans and fish. What does your comparison tell you about the percent of athletes who prefer fish to beans?

8. Compare the bars for beans and chicken. What does your comparison tell you about the percent of athletes who prefer chicken to beans?

9. Compare the bars for beans and beef. What does your comparison tell you about the percent of athletes who prefer beans to beef?

10. Almost half of the athletes surveyed chose chicken as their favorite source of protein. About how many athletes chose chicken?

(continued)

MODULE 1 SECTION 1 — PRACTICE AND APPLICATIONS

For use with Exploration 2

11. What is the letter of the phrase that best represents the average amount of time you spent each day last year exercising?

    a. did not usually exercise   **b.** 20 minutes

    c. 30 minutes   **d.** 45 minutes

    e. one hour   **f.** more than one hour

12. Use a frequency table like the one shown below to collect data about classmates, friends, or relatives for the question in Exercise 11.

Exercise Frequency Table

Time spent exercising	Tally	Frequency
usually did not exercise		
20 minutes		
30 minutes		
45 minutes		
one hour		
more than one hour		

13. Use the data in the *Exercise Frequency Table* to make an *Exercise Bar Graph* that has horizontal bars.

14. How did you choose the scale for the horizontal axis of the *Exercise Bar Graph*?

15. How did you find the most frequent answer to Exercise 11 from the *Exercise Frequency Table*? from the *Exercise Bar Graph*?

16. How is your *Exercise Bar Graph* like the bar graph shown below?

Average Time Seventh Graders at Elmwood Middle School Spent Exercising Each Day

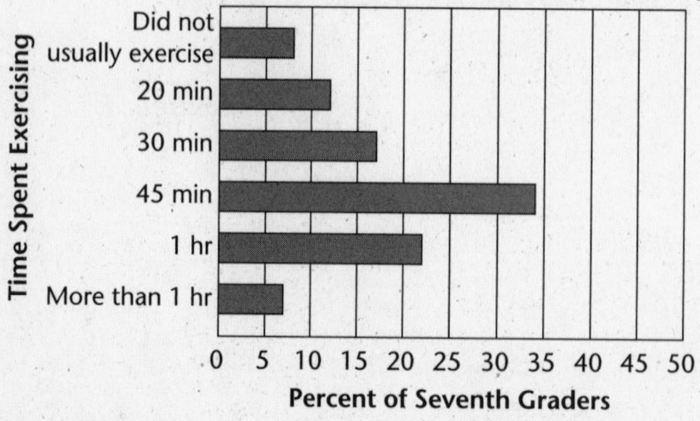

MODULE 1 SECTION 2   PRACTICE AND APPLICATIONS

For use with Exploration 1

Use the table for Exercises 1–3.

Term number	1	2	3	4	5	6	...	10	...	90
Shape sequence	⊞	⊞	⊞	⊞	?	?	?	...	?	...
Number sequence	2	4	6	8	?	?	...	?	...	?

1. How are the number sequence and the shape sequence related?

2. **a.** Draw a picture to model the 5th term of the shape sequence.

   b. What is the 5th term of the number sequence?

3. **a.** What pattern can you use to predict the 6th term of the shape sequence?

   b. Predict what the 6th term of the number sequence will be.

   c. Predict the 10th and 90th terms of the number sequence.

4. Write an equation for each word sentence. Use t for the term and n for the term number.

   a. The term is seven times the term number.

   b. The term is two less than the term number.

   c. The term is six more than the term number.

   d. The term is one fourth the term number.

5. For each sequence, make a table, draw a graph, and write an equation. Then predict the 10th term.

   a. 6, 12, 18, 24, ...   **b.** 28, 26, 24, 22, ...

6. The formula for the volume of a cube is $V = s^3$, where $V =$ the volume of the cube and $s =$ the length of an edge of the cube. Cynthia makes a jewelry box in the shape of a cube to give to her mother. The length of one side of the cube is 3 in.

   a. What is the volume of the jewelry box?

   b. What is the area of the top surface of the jewelry box?

(continued)

MODULE 1 SECTION 2 — PRACTICE AND APPLICATIONS

For use with Exploration 2

7. Write each product in exponential form.

   a. $2 \cdot 2 \cdot 2 \cdot 2 \cdot 2$ **b.** $3 \cdot 3 \cdot 3$ **c.** $8 \cdot 8$

   d. $5 \cdot 5 \cdot 5 \cdot 5$ **e.** $9 \cdot 9$ **f.** $4 \cdot 4 \cdot 4$

   g. $6 \cdot 6 \cdot 6 \cdot 2$ **h.** $8 \cdot 3 \cdot 3$ **i.** $7 \cdot 2 \cdot 2 \cdot 2 \cdot 2$

8. Write each power in standard form.

   a. 7^2 **b.** 5^3 **c.** 2^5

   d. 12^2 **e.** 0^{12} **f.** 10^8

   g. 1436^1 **h.** 4^4 **i.** 1^{30}

9. Predict the 100th term of each sequence.

   a. $3^2, 6^2, 9^2, 12^2, \ldots$ **b.** $2^5, 4^5, 6^5, 8^5, \ldots$

10. Find the volume of a cube with edges of each length.

   a. 1 ft   **b.** 3 in.   **c.** 8 m

   d. 15 ft   **e.** 40 cm   **f.** 200 m

   g. 60 cm   **h.** 8 ft   **i.** 14 mm

   j. $\frac{1}{4}$ ft   **k.** 3.1 cm   **l.** $2\frac{1}{2}$ m

11. Copy and complete each table.

   a.

Side length (cm)	5	10	15	20
Area of a square (cm²)	?	?	?	?

   b.

Edge length (cm)	5	10	15	20
Volume of a cube (cm³)	?	?	?	?

12. The length of a side of a square room is 18 feet. How many square feet of carpet would be needed to cover the floor of the room?

Name _____   Date _____

For use with Exploration 1

1. Tell whether you think the probability of each event is 0, 1, or somewhere in between. If the probability is in between, do you think it is greater than or less than $\frac{1}{2}$? Give a reason for your answer.

   a. You will visit the zoo this year.

   b. You will go swimming this weekend.

   c. Someone in your household will go to the grocery store this week.

   d. You will hike to the top of a mountain today.

2. Jackie spun the spinner shown at the right 38 times. She got an odd number on 16 spins.

   a. Based on Jackie's results, what is the experimental probability of getting an odd number on a spin?

   b. Describe an event that has a probability of 1 and an event that has a probability of 0.

3. What are all the possible outcomes when you toss a number cube?

4. Toss a coin 30 times. Record your results in a frequency table. Then find the experimental probability of getting heads and the experimental probability of getting tails.

5. Suppose you spin the two spinners shown at the right. List at least 3 outcomes that will produce each event.

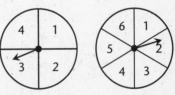

   a. a difference of 2

   b. a difference of 0

   c. a sum of 8

   d. an even sum

6. Suppose a bag contains 12 marbles, with 3 each of the colors red, yellow, blue, and green. An experiment involves picking a marble from the bag and putting it back in the bag. The table shows the results after the experiment has been repeated 100 times. Find each experimental probability.

Outcome	Frequency
red	24
yellow	30
blue	26
green	20

   a. *P* (red)

   b. *P* (yellow)

   c. *P* (blue)

   d. *P* (green)

   e. *P* (not green)

   f. *P* (green or yellow)

   g. *P* (not red)

   h. *P* (purple)

   i. *P* (not yellow)

(continued)

MODULE 1 SECTION 3

For use with Exploration 2

7. Suppose a number cube is rolled once. Find the theoretical probabilities $P(1)$, $P(2)$, and $P(5)$.

8. Suppose you spin the two spinners shown below. Copy and complete the table to show the sums (outcomes) that can occur.

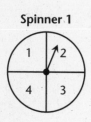 

Spinner 1   Spinner 2

Spinner 2	Spinner 1			
	1	2	3	4
1				
2				
3				
4				
5				
6				

Find the theoretical probability of each event.

a. $P(2)$ **b.** $P(6)$ **c.** $P(1)$

d. $P(8)$ **e.** $P(3)$ **f.** $P(7)$

g. $P(4 \text{ or } 5)$ **h.** $P(\text{even})$ **i.** $P(12)$

9. Suppose an experiment involves spinning the spinner once.

   a. What are all the possible outcomes of the experiment?

   b. Are spinning an A and spinning a B equally likely events? Why or why not?

   c. What fraction of the spins do you expect to land on A? on B? Give a reason for your answer.

   d. Suppose you repeat the experiment 30 times. What results do you expect? Do you think the results will always match your expectations? Why or why not?

10. Sketch a spinner for each situation.

   a. The possible outcomes are J and K. The probability of spinning a J is three times the probability of spinning a K.

   b. The possible outcomes are A, B, and C. The probability of spinning an A is $\frac{1}{2}$. The probability of spinning B is $\frac{1}{4}$.

MODULE 1 SECTION 4	PRACTICE AND APPLICATIONS

For use with Exploration 1

1. Assume a person bicycling 1 mi at a rate of 10 mi/h will burn 80 Cal.

   a. At this rate, how many minutes does it take to cycle 1 mi?

   b. At this rate, how many minutes per week must a person bicycle to burn 2000 Cal?

2. Denise earns $7.00 per hour plus $2.00 for every sale she makes. If Denise earned $239 for 25 hours of work last week, how many sales did she make?

For use with Exploration 2

3. Four equilateral triangles can be placed side by side as shown to form a parallelogram with a perimeter of 6 in. If another parallelogram is formed the same way using 30 triangles, what will its perimeter be?

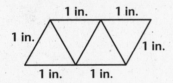

4. A farmer has 8 cows and horses. Each cow is fed 6 lb of hay per meal and each horse is fed 8 lb. It takes 52 lb of hay to feed all 8 animals one meal. How many horses are there?

5. Derrick's scores on his first three science tests are 88, 86, and 87. What score must he get on his fourth test to raise his average to 90?

6. Renzo needs $600 to buy some speakers. The table shows how much money he had in March, April, and May. If this pattern continues, in what month will he be able to buy the speakers?

Month	Amount of money
March	$90
April	$165
May	$240

7. Peter Pan Preschool has a phone relay to inform parents if the preschool is closed during bad weather. The director calls three parents who each call four other parents. These four parents then each call three other parents who each call two more parents. How many parents are called in all?

8. The chess club has enough money to buy 8 boards or 64 chess pieces. The members decide to buy 32 chess pieces. How many boards can they buy?

MODULE 1 SECTION 5   **PRACTICE AND APPLICATIONS**

For use with Exploration 1

1. Jared wanted to find the total number of squares in the diagram shown at the right.

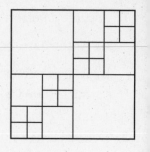

   a. Jared decided to solve the problem above by first counting the number of small squares. Then he planned on counting the larger squares. He counted 27 total squares and recorded 27 as his answer. How would you score Jared's work on the problem solving scale? Why?

   b. Solve the problem. Is your solution the same as Jared's?

   c. What score would you give your solution in part (b) on the problem solving scale?

2. **a.** Suppose you have quarters, dimes, and pennies with a total value of $1.08. How many of each coin can you have without being able to make change for a dollar?

   b. What score would you give your work in part (a) on the problem solving scale?

For use with Exploration 2

3. **a.** Suppose Julia has $15. She wants to buy at least one of each type of book at the book sale and she wants to use as much of $15 as possible to buy some gifts. How many of each type of book should Julia buy?

   b. What score would you give your solution in part (a) on the problem solving and connections scale?

Book Sale	
Mysteries	$1.95
Novel	$2.35
Science	$2.65
Fantasy	$1.45
Nature	$2.95

MODULE 1 SECTION 6   PRACTICE AND APPLICATIONS

For use with Exploration 1

1. Evaluate each expression using the order of operations.

a. $36 - 4 \cdot 5$

b. $8 \cdot (3 + 7) - 5$

c. $7 \cdot 6 - 40 \div 5$

d. $15 + 18 \div 3^2 - 6$

e. $36 \div (15 - 6) \cdot 4$

f. $(8 - 3)^2 \cdot (14 - 8)$

g. $\dfrac{(12 - 5) \cdot 6}{7 - 4}$

h. $\dfrac{80 \div (6 - 2)}{35 \div 7}$

i. $2^4 \div [5^2 - (13 + 7)]$

j. $40 - 2 \cdot 15$

k. $6 \cdot (8 - 4) + 5$

l. $9 \cdot 4 - 24 \div 4$

2. Write and evaluate an expression to represent the value (in cents) of 3 half dollars, 3 quarters, 8 nickels, 4 dimes, and 2 pennies.

3. Use grouping symbols to make each statement true.

a. $25 - 8 \cdot 3 = 51$

b. $9 + 4 \cdot 5 - 3 = 17$

c. $9 + 9 \div 3 \cdot 5 - 3 = 12$

d. $6 \cdot 5 - 5^2 + 2 = 3$

For use with Exploration 2

Use the line graph for Exercises 4 –6.

4. What was the approximate number of students playing baseball in 1992?

5. In what year was the number of students playing baseball about 2000?

6. Describe any trends in the data that the line graph helps you see.

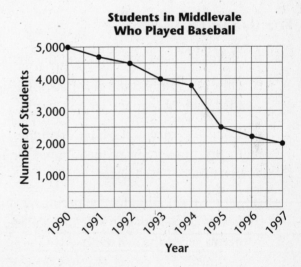

Students in Middlevale Who Played Baseball

7. A student was trying to choose the most accurate and appropriate diagram from the following to show that $\frac{3}{4}$ of 8 is 6. Which should the student choose and why?

a.

b.

c. ○ ○ ○ ○ ○ ○ ○ ○ ○

MODULE 1 SECTIONS 1–6   PRACTICE AND APPLICATIONS

For use with Section 1

Use the line graph for Exercises 1 and 2.

1. What is represented by each interval on the vertical scale?

2. a. In what year were the sales about $5000?

   b. Estimate the sales in 1997.

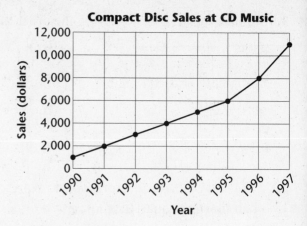

Compact Disc Sales at CD Music

3. For each group of people surveyed, tell whether 36% of the group *is more than*, *less than*, or *equal to* 36 people.

   a. 300 runners   b. 79 musicians

   c. 95 students   d. 450 skiers

4. Make a frequency table for the data.

   Scores on a ten-point quiz: 8, 6, 9, 9, 8, 8, 7, 10, 6, 8, 8, 6, 10, 7, 9

For use with Section 2

5. a. Sketch the next two shapes in the shape sequence.

   b. How can you find the perimeter of a square from the length of a side?

   c. If the sequence in the table continues, what are the next two terms of the number sequence for the perimeter of each shape?

   d. Write an equation for the perimeter of a square. Let s = the length of a side of a square. Let P = the perimeter of the square. Use your equation to find the perimeter of a square that has sides of length 20 cm.

   e. Make a table of values for the first 10 terms of the number sequence. Use it to make a graph of the sequence. Use your graph to predict the 15th term of the sequence.

Term number	Shape sequence	Number sequence
1	□	4
2	⊞	8
3	⊞	12

(continued)

MODULE 1   SECTIONS 1–6   PRACTICE AND APPLICATIONS

For use with Section 3

6. Suppose a bag contains 12 marbles, with 3 each of the colors red, yellow, blue, and green. An experiment involves picking a marble from the bag and putting it back in the bag. Find the theoretical probability of each event.

   a. P (red)   **b.** P (yellow)   **c.** P (not green)

   d. P (green or yellow)   **e.** P (not red)   **f.** P (purple)

   g. P (blue)   **h.** P (blue or green)   **i.** P (not yellow)

For use with Section 4

7. Katie earns $8.00 per hour plus $12.00 for every extra hour she works over 40 h per week. If Katie earned $392.00 last week, how many extra hours did she work?

For use with Section 5

8. a. A book states that an average teenager in the United States should spend at least 130 h a year exercising. Do you think this is a reasonable estimate? Explain.

   b. What score would you give your solution in part (a) on the problem solving and connections scale?

For use with Section 6

9. Evaluate each expression using the order of operations.

   a. $12 + 32 \div 4^2 \cdot 7$ **b.** $39 - (3^3 + 6) + 5^2$ **c.** $(3 + 4)^2 \cdot (25 - 15)^2$

   d. $\dfrac{18 \div (4 + 2)}{9 - 8}$ **e.** $\dfrac{14 + (8 - 6)}{20 \div 5}$ **f.** $\dfrac{(45 + 5) \div 5}{8 - 6}$

   g. $4 + [(6 + 9) \div 3] + 7 - 2$ **h.** $7 + [(3^2 - 2^2) - 3] \cdot 6$

10. Use grouping symbols to make each statement true.

   a. $28 - 10 \div 6 = 3$ **b.** $8 + 2 \cdot 7 = 70$

   c. $18 \div 2 + 4 = 3$ **d.** $4^2 + 2^2 \div 4 = 5$

MODULE 1 SECTION 1   **STUDY GUIDE**

Going for the Gold   Data Displays

GOAL   **LEARN HOW TO:** • interpret data in percent form
                                • interpret bar and line graphs
                                • make a frequency table

AS YOU: • explore data about the Olympics and education
            • gather and analyze data about time spent on homework

Exploration 1: Bar and Line Graphs

Analyzing Bar and Line Graphs

A **bar graph** displays data that fall into distinct
categories. A bar graph should always have a title and
should be clearly labeled. The categories for the bar
graph at the right appear along the **vertical axis**. The
horizontal axis is labeled with a scale of numbers.

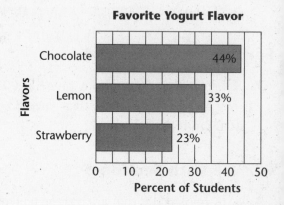

Percent

The symbol % on the bar graph above stands for
percent. **Percent** means "per hundred" or "out of 100."
Four different ways to express a percent are shown
at the right.

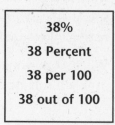

38%

38 Percent

38 per 100

38 out of 100

Interpreting Line Graphs

A **line graph** is often used to display data that change
over time. The double line graph at the right compares
two sets of data.

Each step between grid lines on a scale of a graph is
an *interval*. The interval used for the vertical scale on
the double line graph at the right is 75.

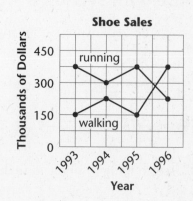

MODULE 1 SECTION 1   STUDY GUIDE

Exploration 2: Tallying Data

Using Frequency Tables

Frequency tables show how often each data item occurs. The frequency table at the right shows the number of students in two middle school classes who bought lunch in the cafeteria. The total number of tally marks in each category is the **frequency** for that category.

Students Buying Lunch

Class	Tally	Frequency
Mrs. Hall's	卌 卌 卌	15
Mr. Akee's	卌 卌 ‖	12

Example

Make a bar graph of the data given in the frequency table.

Number of Students Taking Work Home

Day	Tally	Frequency
Monday	卌 卌 卌 卌 卌	25
Tuesday	卌 卌 卌	15
Wednesday	卌 卌 卌 ‖‖	19
Thursday	卌 卌 卌 卌 卌 ‖‖	28
Friday	‖‖‖	4

Sample Response

First Give the bar graph a title.

Number of Students Taking Work Home

Next Label the axes, one to show the categories and the other to show a scale for the numerical values.

vertical axis: 0, 5, 10, 15, 20, 25, 30, 35

horizontal axis: Monday, Tuesday, Wednesday, Thursday, Friday

Then Draw the bars to model the data values in the table.

The completed graph is shown at the right.

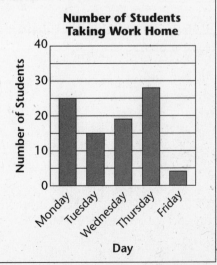

Math Thematics, Book 2 **25**

Name _____   Date _____

Exploration 1

Use the line graph at the right for Exercises 1–4.

1. What information is displayed in the graph?

2. What are the intervals of the horizontal and vertical axes?

3. What could you predict about the enrollment in the year 2000?

4. Did the enrollment between 1996 and 1997 increase by 20%? Explain.

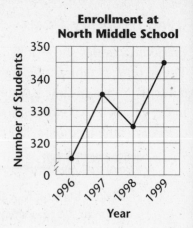

Exploration 2

Make a frequency table for each set of data.

5. Scores on an English grammar test: 88, 88, 76, 98, 100, 95, 76, 100, 85, 98, 88, 85, 76, 79, 75, 88, 91, 93, 71, 65, 88, 93, 65, 85

6. Favorite color of cross country team members: blue, red, yellow, yellow, red, green, green, orange, blue, blue, green, yellow, red

Spiral Review

Find the area of each rectangle. (Toolbox, p. 593)

7. length: 5 ft, width: 5 ft   8. length: 30 in., width: 18 in.

For Exercises 9–12, use mental math to find each value.
(Toolbox, p. 584)

9. $\frac{2}{3}$ of 18   10. $\frac{1}{2}$ of 24   11. $\frac{5}{8}$ of 16   12. $\frac{4}{5}$ of 55

13. How many squares of a 100-square grid would be shaded to show 45%?
(Toolbox, p. 588)

Name _____   Date _____

Patterns and Prediction   Sequences and Exponents

GOAL   **LEARN HOW TO:** • model sequences
                          • make predictions
                          • use exponents
                          • find the volume of a cube

   As you: • explore visual patterns
              • explore speeds of a skateboarder

Exploration 1: Modeling Sequences

Sequences

A **sequence** is an ordered list of numbers   2, 4, 6, 8, 10, … is a sequence.
or objects called **terms**.

The **term number** tells the position of   The *1st term* of the sequence above is 2.
each term in the sequence.   The *5th term* of the sequence above is 10.

You can use the pattern of a sequence to   Each term in the sequence is twice its
predict a specific term of the sequence.   term number. So, the 6th term is 12.

Equations and Variables

An **equation** is a mathematical sentence $5 = 2 + 3$ is an equation.
stating that two quantities are equal.

A **variable** is a letter used to represent a   Let $n =$ the term number and let
quantity that is unknown or that changes. $t =$ the term. Then,
You can use variables to write an
equation that shows how each term in a $t = 2 \cdot n$ or $t = 2n$
sequence is related to its term number.
                                                   models the sequence shown above.

Exploration 2: Exponents, Squares, and Cubes

Exponents

An **exponent** tells you how many times   base ⟍   exponent
a **base** is used as a factor. **Exponential**   ↓
form is a way of writing repeated $4^3 = 4 \cdot 4 \cdot 4 = 64$
multiplication of a number using   ↑   ↑
exponents. **Standard form** is a way of   exponential form   standard form
writing numbers using digits.

The **power** of a number in exponential 4^3 is read as "4 to the 3rd power"
form is its exponent.   or "4 cubed."

Math Thematics, Book 2 **27**

MODULE 1 SECTION 2   STUDY GUIDE

Squares and Cubes

A **cube** is a space figure with six square
surfaces, called **faces**. An **edge** is where
two faces are joined. A **vertex** is where
edges meet.

A cube has 6 faces, 12 edges, and 8 vertices.

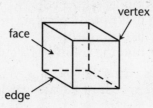

Area is the number of *unit squares* that
fill a figure. A unit square is 1 unit long
and 1 unit wide. The area formula for
a square can be written using exponents.

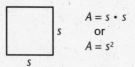

$A = s \cdot s$
or
$A = s^2$

Volume is the number of *unit cubes* that
fill a figure. A unit cube is 1 unit long,
1 unit wide, and 1 unit high. The volume
formula for a cube can be written
using exponents.

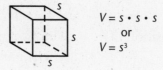

$V = s \cdot s \cdot s$
or
$V = s^3$

Example

Find the volume of a cube when the length of an edge is 6 cm.

■ **Sample Response** ■

$V = s^3$ ← volume formula for a cube
$\ = 6^3$ ← exponential form
$\ = 6 \cdot 6 \cdot 6$
$\ = 216$ ← standard form

The volume of the cube is 216 cm^3.

Name _____ Date _____

Exploration 1

For Exercises 1–3, write an equation for each word sentence. Use t for the term and n for the term number.

1. The term is four times the term number.

2. The term is two less than the term number.

3. The term is six more than twice the term number.

4. Make a table, draw a graph, and write an equation for the sequence 6, 12, 18, 24, … . Then predict the 100th term.

5. **Visual Thinking** Sketch the 6th shape in the sequence below.

 …

Exploration 2

Write each product in exponential form.

6. $7 \cdot 7 \cdot 7 \cdot 7 \cdot 7 \cdot 7$ 7. $12 \cdot 12 \cdot 12 \cdot 12 \cdot 12 \cdot 12 \cdot 12 \cdot 12$

Write each power in standard form.

8. 8^3 9. 9^2 10. 50^1 11. 0^4

For Exercises 12–15, find the volume of a cube with edges of each length.

12. 4 mm   13. 8 in.   14. 10 km   15. 30 ft

16. **Writing** Is the volume of a cube related to the area of one face of the cube? Explain.

Spiral Review

Use the bar graph at the right. (Module 1, pp. 2–3)

17. What percent of the blooms were yellow?

18. If there were 500 blooms in all, how many of them were white?

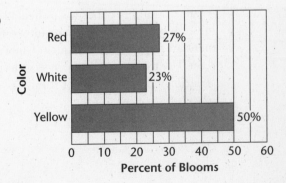

Write an equivalent fraction for each. (Toolbox, p. 585)

19. $\dfrac{4}{5}$ 20. $\dfrac{15}{25}$ 21. $\dfrac{1}{3}$ 22. $\dfrac{3}{45}$

MODULE 1 SECTION 3 | STUDY GUIDE

Likely or Unlikely Probability

GOAL **LEARN HOW TO:** • list the outcomes for an event
• find and compare experimental probabilities
• find theoretical probabilities

AS YOU: • analyze a game
• explore outcomes when rolling one or more number cubes

Exploration 1: What Are the Chances?

Probability and Experimental Probability

A **probability** is a number from 0 through 1 that tells how likely it is
that an event will happen. An **event** is any set of one or more outcomes.
An **impossible event** has a probability of 0. A **certain event** has a
probability of 1.

When you roll a number cube or spin a
spinner and record the outcome, you are
conducting an **experiment**. An **outcome**
is the result of an experiment.

When a probability is found by repeating
an experiment and recording the results,
the probability is called an **experimental
probability**. The experimental probability
is the ratio of the number of times an
event occurred to the number of times
the experiment was conducted.

Spinning the spinner below is an *experiment*.
There are two possible *outcomes*: A or B.

Suppose the spinner was spun 8 times and
"B" resulted 3 times. The experimental
probability would be $= \frac{3}{8}$.

Example

A pair of number cubes was rolled 32 times and
the sum was recorded. The results of this experiment are shown in the frequency table at the
right. Use the frequency table to determine the
experimental probability of rolling a sum of 5.

Sum	Frequency
2	1
3	3
4	3
5	**6**
6	4
7	5
8	4
9	4
10	2
11	1
12	0

MODULE 1 SECTION 3 STUDY GUIDE

Sample Response

Since a sum of 5 occurred in 6 of the 32 rolls, the experimental probability of a sum of 5 is $\frac{6}{32}$, or $\frac{3}{16}$. This can also be written as $P(\text{sum of } 5) = \frac{3}{16}$.

Exploration 2: Theoretical Probability

A **theoretical probability** is a probability that is determined without actually doing an experiment.

When two or more outcomes have the same chance of occurring, the outcomes are **equally likely**.

Example

Tell whether the outcomes W, X, Y, and Z on each spinner below are equally likely to occur. Then find the theoretical probability of spinning an X.

a.

b.

Sample Response

a. Since the spinner is divided into four equal-sized sectors, the four outcomes (W, X, Y, and Z) are equally likely to occur.

Since the four sectors of the spinner are the same size, the theoretical probability is

$$P(X) = \frac{1}{4}.$$

b. Since the spinner is not divided into four equal-sized sectors, the four outcomes (W, X, Y, and Z) are not equally likely to occur.

The sector labeled "X" appears to be approximately one-eighth of the whole spinner, so the theoretical probability of spinning X is

$$P(X) = \frac{1}{8}.$$

MODULE 1 SECTION 3 | PRACTICE & APPLICATION EXERCISES | STUDY GUIDE

Exploration 1

Trisha spun the spinner shown 25 times. She got an odd number 15 times. Use this information for Exercises 1 and 2.

1. Based on Trisha's results, what is the experimental probability of getting an odd number on a spin?

2. Describe an event that has a probability of 1 and an event that has a probability of 0.

3. What are the possible outcomes when you roll a number cube?

4. Toss a coin 30 times. Record your results in a frequency table. Then find the experimental probability of getting heads and the experimental probability of getting tails.

Exploration 2

Suppose you toss two coins. Find the theoretical probability of each event.

5. P (two heads)   **6.** P (two tails)   **7.** P (one heads)   **8.** P (one tails)

For Exercises 9–12, suppose an experiment involves spinning this spinner once.

9. What are all the possible outcomes of the experiment?

10. Are spinning an A, B, and C equally likely events? Why or why not?

11. What fractions of the spins do you expect to land on A? on B? on C?

12. Writing Suppose you repeat the experiment 20 times. What results do you expect? Do you think the results will always match your expectations? Why or why not?

13. Challenge Sketch a spinner for this situation: The possible outcomes are Red and Green. The probability of spinning Red is three times the probability of spinning Green.

Spiral Review

For each sequence, make a table, draw a graph, and write an equation. Then predict the 100th term. (Module 1, pp. 20–21)

14. 3, 4, 5, 6, …   **15.** 4, 7, 10, 13, …

For Exercises 16 –18, find each sum or difference. (Toolbox, p. 581)

16. 9 − 6.23   **17.** 37.18 + 47.25   **18.** 6 + 7.3 + 1.52

19. Find the mean of these running times, in seconds, at a track meet:
25.1, 23.2, 27.7, 26.0, 27.0, 25.0, 20.1, 22.5, 28.1, 23.7 (Toolbox, p. 595)

MODULE 1 SECTION 4   STUDY GUIDE

What Can You Expect?   Problem Solving

GOAL **LEARN HOW TO:** • recognize the steps of the 4-step approach to problem solving
• apply the 4-step approach to problem solving

AS YOU: • solve a problem
• predict outcomes

Exploration 1: Four Steps to Problem Solving

Step 1: Understand the Problem

• **Read** the **problem** carefully, probably several times.

• **Identify** what the **question** is.

• **Restate** the **problem** in your own words.

• **Identify** the **information needed** to solve the problem, and determine
if any of it is missing.

Step 2: Make a Plan

You may have to choose several problem solving strategies such as:

• try a simpler problem

• make an organized list

• act it out

• use logical reasoning

• make a picture or diagram

• make a table

• look for a pattern

• guess and check

• work backward

• use an equation

Step 3: Carry Out the Plan

• Solve the problem using the strategies you selected.

• You may need to change strategies.

Step 4: Look Back

• Check that you answered the question being asked.

• Check that your solution seems reasonable.

• Check that your work is accurate.

• Try to find another method to solve the problem and compare
the results.

• Study the solution to see if the method can be generalized or
extended to other situations or to solve other problems.

MODULE 1 SECTION 4 — STUDY GUIDE

Example

A phone call costs $.35 for the first minute and $.12 for each minute thereafter. Jordan's bill for calling her brother was $1.31. How many minutes did she talk?

■ Sample Response ■

Step 1:
- Read the problem carefully.
- Identify the question.
- Restate the problem in your own words.
- Identify the necessary information.

How many minutes did she talk?
first minute = $.35;
each additional minute = $.12;
Her bill was $1.31.

Step 2:
- Choose a strategy.

Since I know how much the bill was, I will *work backward* to solve.

Step 3:
- Solve the problem.

Subtract the charge for the first minute from the total. Divide by 12 to find the number of additional minutes.

$$
\begin{array}{ccc}
\$1.31 & 8 & 8 \\
-\,0.35 & 12\overline{)96} & +\,1 \\
\hline
\$\ .96 & \underline{96} & 9 \\
 & 0 &
\end{array}
$$

The phone call lasted 9 min.

Step 4:
- Check that you answered the question.
- Check that your answer seems reasonable.
- Check that your work is accurate.

Check:
$.35 + 8 \cdot \$.12 = \$.35 + \$.96$
$ = \$1.31 \checkmark$

Exploration 2: The Last Card Problem

Once you have solved a problem, you can use the pattern or model that you used to solve it to make predictions. For instance, in the Example above, you could predict the cost of a 30 min call by using the model $.35 + 29 \cdot \$.12 = \$3.83$.

Name _____ Date _____

MODULE 1 SECTION 4 | PRACTICE & APPLICATION EXERCISES | STUDY GUIDE

Exploration 1

Assume a person typing 360 words at the rate of 90 words per minute earns $2.

1. At this rate, how many minutes would it take to type 360 words?

2. At this rate, how many words would a person need to type to earn $30?

3. How many hours would a person need to type to earn $1000?

4. **Writing** Is getting paid $10 per 1800 words better pay? Explain.

Exploration 2

5. A restaurant has square tables that seat 2 people on each side. If two tables are placed end-to-end, then 12 people may be seated. If 10 tables are placed end-to-end, how many people may be seated?

6. Elizabeth's scores on her first three math tests were 89, 78, and 91. She reasons that if she scores high enough on her next test, then the mean of her scores will be an A. An A at her school is 93–100. Is her reasoning correct? Explain.

7. Inga and Dante work at a movie theater taking tickets. They are both working today, but they have different schedules. Inga works every third day and Dante works every other day. How many times will they both be working together on the same day during the next 27 days?

Spiral Review

The spinner shown is spun once and the number that the spinner lands on is recorded. (Module 1, p. 33)

8. What are all the possible outcomes of the experiment?

9. What is the theoretical probability of each outcome?

10. Suppose the spinner is spun 64 times. How many times would you expect to get an 8?

Use compatible numbers to estimate each quotient.
(Toolbox, p. 582)

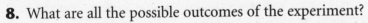

11. $21\overline{)599}$ 12. $63\overline{)127}$ 13. $309\overline{)883}$

MODULE 1 SECTION 5   **STUDY GUIDE**

Creative Solutions   Assessing Problem Solving

 GOAL **LEARN HOW TO:** • use the problem solving scale
                                 • use the connections scale

AS YOU: • evaluate solutions
            • find ways to extend a solution

Exploration 1: Evaluating Solutions

Problem Solving Scale

This problem solving scale is used to assess how well you apply the 4-step approach to problem solving.

?-! Problem Solving

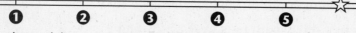

I did not understand the
problem well enough
to get started or I did
not show any work.

I understood the problem
well enough to make a
plan and to work toward
a solution.

I made a plan, I used
it to solve the problem,
and I verified my solution.

When you assess your work using the problem solving scale, think about whether you:

• understood the problem

• made a plan

• carried out the plan to solve the problem

• looked back to verify your solution

Example

Suppose you were asked to find the next number in the pattern 1, 4, 7, 10, ...

To solve the problem, you used a dot pattern to represent the numbers. You determined the answer was 13. What score would you rate on the problem solving scale?

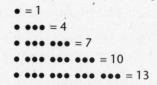

Sample Response

You would probably rate this solution a **4** on the problem solving scale because you made a plan, used it to solve the problem, but did not verify your solution.

Name _____   Date _____

Exploration 2: Making Connections

Connections Scale

You can use the connections scale to assess how well you make
connections to other problems, mathematical concepts, or applications.

 Connections

❶   **❷**   **❸**   **❹**   **❺**

I attempted or solved   I found patterns and used   I extended the ideas in the
the problem and   them to extend the   solution to the general case,
then stopped.   solution to other cases,   or I showed how this problem
                         or I recognized that this   relates to other problems,
                         problem relates to other   mathematical ideas, or
                         problems, mathematical   applications.
                         ideas, or applications.

You might score a **3** on the   You might score a **5** on the
connections scale if you: connections scale if you:

• recognize how the problem is   • show how the problem or
  related to other problems   mathematics can be applied
                                            elsewhere
• recognize connections to other
  mathematical topics   • extend the problem to the
                                            general case
• extend the solution

Example

Refer back to the problem in the previous Example.

Suppose you used a dot pattern to represent the numbers as shown below, indicating
the position of each number in the pattern. You then wrote a formula for finding any
number in the pattern, and used it to determine that the next number is 13. What
score would you rate on the connections scale?

1st ● = 1
2nd ● ●●● = 4
3rd ● ●●● ●●● = 7
4th ● ●●● ●●● ●●● = 10
5th ● ●●● ●●● ●●● ●●● = 13

Let t = the term number.
Then $1 + 3(t - 1)$ = the number in the t th position.

Find the number in the 5th position.

$1 + 3(t - 1) = 1 + 3(5 - 1) \leftarrow t = 5$
$= 1 + 3(4) = 1 + 12 = 13$

The next number in the pattern is 13.

■ Sample Response ■

You would probably rate this solution a **5** on the connections scale because you
extended the solution to the general case.

Math Thematics, Book 2 **37**

| **MODULE 1 SECTION 5** | **PRACTICE & APPLICATION EXERCISES** | **STUDY GUIDE** |

Exploration 1

1. Choose the letter of the pattern(s) that can be folded into a square pyramid. Then draw another pattern that will work.

A.   **B.** 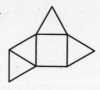   **C.**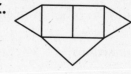

2. Suppose you did not answer Exercise 1. How would you rate your work on the problem solving scale? Why?

3. If you chose the correct letters in Exercise 1 but did not draw another pattern, how would you rate yourself on the problem solving scale? Why?

Exploration 2

4. Find the next number in the number pattern 3, 5, 7, 9, ... Extend your work to find the 200th number in the pattern. Assess your work using the connections scale.

Spiral Review

5. Matt threw three darts at the target shown at the right. All three darts hit the target, landing in two different scoring regions. Which of the following numbers could have been his score: 15, 25, 30, 45, or 70? Explain your reasoning.
(Module 1, p. 44)

Replace each   ?   with the correct measure. (Toolbox, p. 592)

6. 5 h = ___?___ min   **7.** 6 yd = ___?___ in.   **8.** 4 lb = ___?___ oz

9. 45 ft = ___?___ yd   **10.** 60 in. = ___?___ ft   **11.** 8 h = ___?___ s

Estimation Estimate the value of each expression. Explain how you made each estimate. (Toolbox, p. 582)

12. 327 · 38   **13.** 3572 ÷ 63   **14.** 145 + 796 + 62

15. 9017 − 893   **16.** 99 · 143   **17.** 201 + 75 + 123

Name _____   Date _____

The Clear Choice   Expressions and Representations

GOAL   **LEARN HOW TO:** • use the mathematical language scale
• evaluate expressions using the order of operations
• use the representations scale
• decide when a line graph is appropriate

AS YOU: • solve problems
• explore television viewing habits

Exploration 1: Order of Operations

Mathematical Language Scale

This mathematical language scale is used to assess how well you use
mathematical vocabulary and symbols.

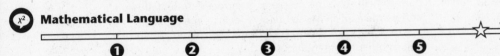

Mathematical Language

❶

I did not use any mathematical
vocabulary or symbols, or I did
not use them correctly, or my
use was not appropriate.

❷

❸

I used appropriate mathematical
language, but the way it was
used was not always correct
or other terms and symbols
were needed.

❹

❺

I used mathematical
language that was correct
and appropriate to make
my meaning clear.

An **expression** is a mathematical phrase that can be formed using
numbers, variables, and operation symbols.

The expression $3 \cdot 4 + y$ contains the numbers 3 and 4, the variable y, and
the operation symbols • and +.

Order of Operations

To **evaluate** an expression, you carry out the mathematical operations in
the correct order. This order is known as the **order of operations**. It is
important to use the correct order of operations when evaluating
expressions.

Step 1: Carry out the operations within
grouping symbols. Start with the
innermost grouping symbols first.

Step 2: Next evaluate all powers.

Step 3: Then do all multiplication and
division in order from left to right.

Step 4: Do all addition and subtraction in
order from left to right.

$2 + [2 \cdot (8 - 3)^2 \div 5] \div 2$ (*Step 1*)
$= 2 + [2 \cdot 5^2 \div 5] \div 2$ (*Steps 1, 2*)
$= 2 + [2 \cdot 25 \div 5] \div 2$ (*Steps 1, 3*)
$= 2 + [50 \div 5] \div 2$ (*Step 1*)
$= 2 + 10 \div 2$ (*Step 3*)
$= 2 + 5$ (*Step 4*)
$= 7$

MODULE 1 SECTION 6

When an expression contains a fraction bar, you carry out the operations in the numerator separately from those in the denominator. Then you divide the numerator by the denominator as the final step.

Exploration 2: Representations

Representations Scale

You can use the representations scale to assess how well you use equations, tables, graphs, and diagrams to help solve a problem or explain a solution.

 Representations

I did not use any representations such as equations, tables, graphs, or diagrams to help solve the problem or explain my solution.

I made appropriate representations to help solve the problem or help me explain my solution, but they were not always correct or other representations were needed.

I used appropriate and correct representations to solve the problem or explain my solution.

Example

Zack is buying paper towels. The brand he prefers comes in two different size rolls. One size has 75 sheets and sells for $0.79. The other sells for $1.29 and has 125 sheets. Which is the better buy? Explain how you made your decision. Use the representations scale to score your solution.

■ Sample Response ■

Think: $\dfrac{\$.79}{75}$ (>, <, or =) $\dfrac{\$1.29}{125}$

To find the unit cost of each roll, do the two divisions. Then compare the unit costs.

Since 0.01032 < 0.01053..., this means

$\dfrac{\$.79}{75} > \dfrac{\$1.29}{125}$.

Therefore, the $1.29 package is the better buy.

$$
\begin{array}{r}
0.01053 \\
75\overline{)0.79000} \\
75 \\
\hline
40 \\
0 \\
\hline
400 \\
375 \\
\hline
250 \\
225 \\
\hline
25
\end{array}
\qquad
\begin{array}{r}
0.01032 \\
125\overline{)1.29000} \\
1\,25 \\
\hline
40 \\
0 \\
\hline
400 \\
375 \\
\hline
250 \\
250 \\
\hline
0
\end{array}
$$

Since I wrote an equation, found the correct solution, and explained my solution I think I rate a **5** on the representations scale.

MODULE 1 SECTION 6 | PRACTICE & APPLICATION EXERCISES | STUDY GUIDE

Exploration 1

For Exercises 1– 9, evaluate each expression using the order of operations.

1. $36 - 5 \cdot 6$

2. $8 \cdot (5 + 7) - 4$

3. $4 \cdot 3 - 8 \div 2$

4. $10 + 25 \div 5 + 3^2$

5. $48 \div (13 - 7) \cdot 4$

6. $(12 - 9)^2 - (12 - 9)$

7. $\dfrac{(15 + 1) \cdot 2}{6 + 2}$

8. $\dfrac{90 \div (10 \div 5)}{9 - 4}$

9. $2^3 \div [3^2 - (5 + 3)]$

10. Write and evaluate an expression to represent the value (in cents) of 3 dollars, 2 half-dollars, 7 dimes, 4 nickels, and 8 pennies.

11. Challenge Use grouping symbols to make the statement
$2^3 + 6^2 - 4^2 \div 4 - 2 \cdot 3 = 7$ true.

Exploration 2

12. Jeremy's insect and spider collection consists of 5 bugs whose total number of legs are 34.

   a. If insects have 6 legs and spiders have 8 legs, how many insects and how many spiders does Jeremy have?

   b. Use the *Three Assessment Scales* shown on Labsheet 6A to assess your solution to part (a).

Spiral Review

For Exercises 13 –16, suppose a spinner has equal sectors lettered A, B, C, or D. The spinner was spun 50 times and the results were recorded in the table. Find each experimental probability. (Module 1, p. 33)

Outcome	Frequency
A	10
B	15
C	20
D	5

13. $P(A)$

14. $P(B)$

15. $P(C)$

16. $P(D)$

17. How many sectors do you think were labeled with each letter? Explain your thinking. (Module 1, p. 44 and 55)

Use a ruler to draw a segment of each length. (Toolbox, p. 591)

18. $1\frac{1}{4}$ in.

19. $4\frac{3}{8}$ in.

20. $6\frac{3}{4}$ in.

21. $2\frac{11}{16}$ in.

Types of Angles (Use with Question 10 on page 79.)

Directions Use a protractor to measure each angle.

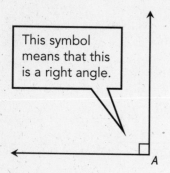

This symbol means that this is a right angle.

a. _____ degrees
a *right* angle

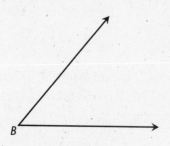

b. _____ degrees
an *acute* angle

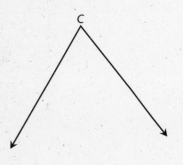

c. _____ degrees
an *acute* angle

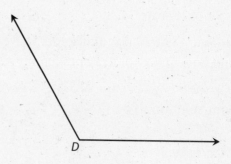

d. _____ degrees
an *obtuse* angle

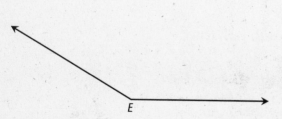

e. _____ degrees
an *obtuse* angle

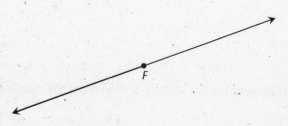

f. _____ degrees
a *straight* angle

MODULE 2

Heading Diagrams   (Use with Questions 13 and 20 on pages 81–82.)

Directions Draw rays on these diagrams to represent headings.

a. 20° heading

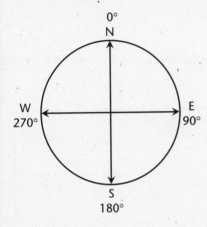

b. 120° heading

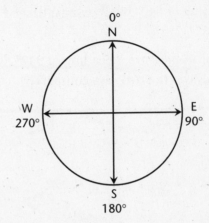

c. 225° heading

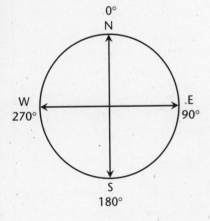

d. 345° heading

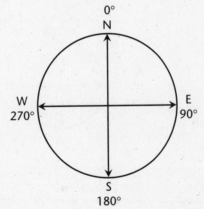

Math Thematics, Book 2 **43**

MODULE 2

Plotting a Heading (Use with Question 21 on page 82.)

Directions In the reading from *Hatchet* in your textbook, Brian guesses that the 342 on the display might be a compass heading. Suppose Brian's plane is at the center of the compass diagram on the map below.

a. Estimate a heading of 342° by drawing a dashed ray on the compass diagram.

b. Use a protractor to measure a heading of 342°. Use a solid ray to plot the heading. How do the two rays compare?

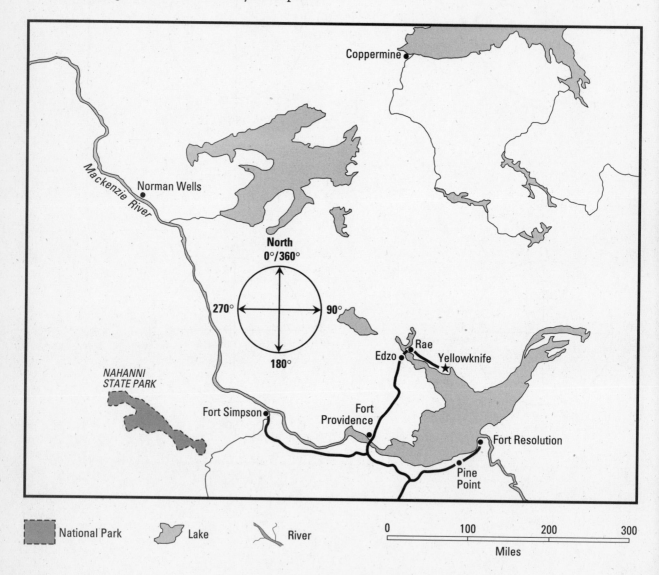

MODULE 2

Regional Map   (Use with Questions 1–4 on page 86.)

Directions Use headings to plan your initial search strategy.

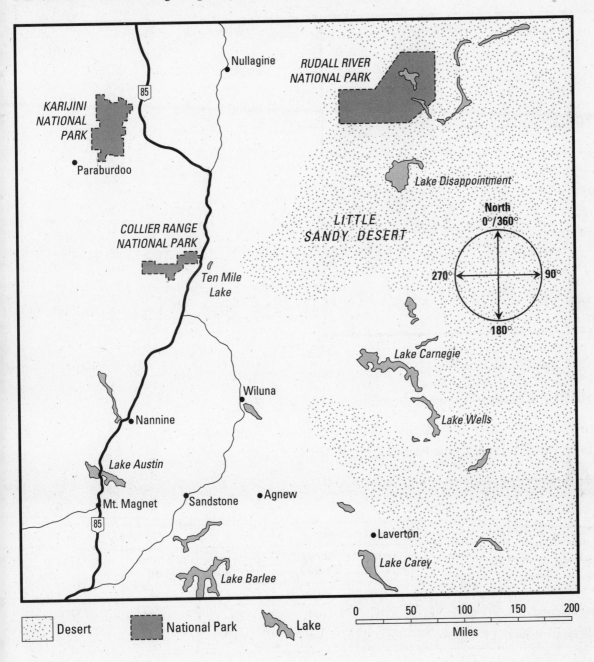

MODULE 2   **PROJECT LABSHEET** **B**

Map of Point Last Seen (Use with Questions 5, 7, and 8 on page 99.)

Directions Use the *Map of Point Last Seen* as you refine your search plan.

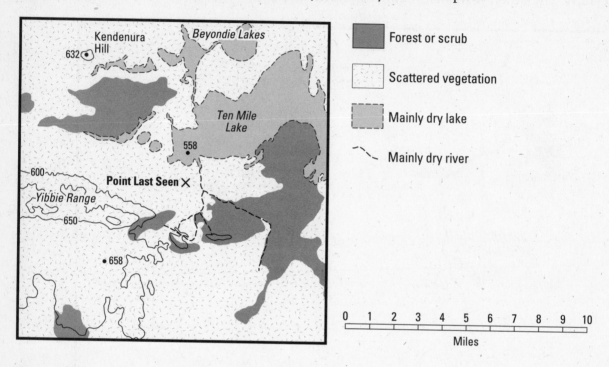

Probability Zones (Use with Questions 6–7 on page 99.)

Directions Use the chart of *Probability Zones* to help you predict where Gina will be found relative to the Point Last Seen (PLS).

9% of victims are found uphill from the PLS and within 1 mi of the PLS.

Probability Zones					
	Within 1 mi	Between 1 and 2 mi	Between 2 and 3 mi	Between 3 and 4 mi	Beyond 4 mi
Walk uphill	9%	10%	9%	0%	0%
Walk downhill	14%	18%	2%	2%	4%
Walk on same level	7%	16%	9%	0%	0%

Example: The probability that a victim will be found within 2 mi of the
PLS is as follows: 9% + 10% + 14% + 18% + 7% + 16% = 74%.

MODULE 2   LABSHEET **3A**

Number Line Markers   (Use with Question 3 on page 102.)

Directions Cut out these number line markers. Arrange the markers on
the floor from least to greatest to create a number line. Place them about
1 ft apart.

–6	**–5**	**–4**	**–3**
–2	**–1**	**0**	**1**
2	**3**	**4**	**5**
6	**POSITIVE DIRECTION**		
	NEGATIVE DIRECTION		

Math Thematics, Book 2 **47**

MODULE 2

Spinner for Hiking (Use with Question 3 on page 102.)

Directions

- Cut out each spinner along the rectangular border.

- Unfold three paper clips to use as pointers for the spinners.

- When you spin the pointer, hold it in place with the tip of a pen or a pencil at the center of the spinner.

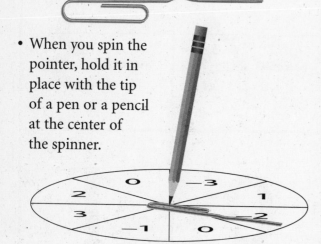

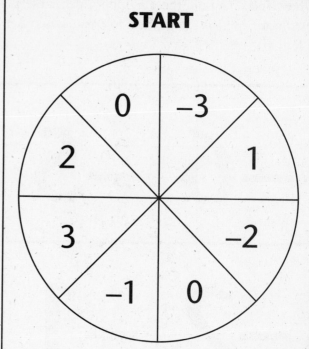

START

0 | −3
2 | 1
3 | −2
−1 | 0

DIRECTION

FACE THE − DIRECTION | FACE THE + DIRECTION

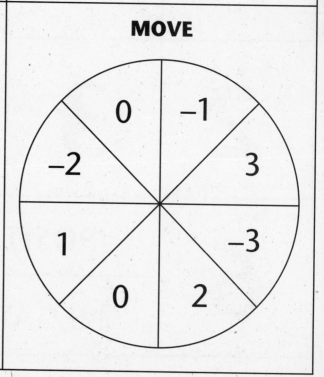

MOVE

0 | −1
−2 | 3
1 | −3
0 | 2

Name _____   Date _____

Table of Hikes (Use with Question 4 on page 103, and Question 6 on page 104.)

Directions Take turns hiking on your number line as described on page 102. Record each hike and the finishing position in the table. Continue until the table is full.

Hiker's name	Started at	Direction faced	Moved		Finishing position
Example	2 The starting position of the hike is 2.	– – tells the hiker to face the negative direction.	–3 –3 tells the hiker to move backward 3 units.	=	5
				=	
				=	
				=	
				=	
				=	
				=	
				=	
				=	
				=	
				=	
				=	

MODULE 2   PROJECT LABSHEET

Search Grid   (Use with Question 9 on page 114.)

Directions Use the grid to find how long it took searcher S4 to find footprints in the mud at point *F*.

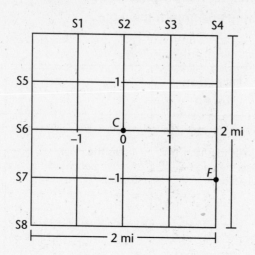

Revised Search Grid   (Use with Question 10 on page 114.)

Directions Plot point *F*, your starting point, at the origin in the center of the grid and draw the paths that you think the searchers should follow based on the information in Question 10.

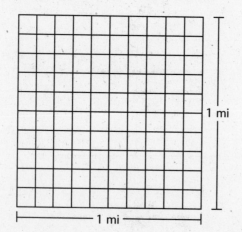

MODULE 2   LABSHEET **4A**

Location Table (Use with Question 13 on page 121.)

Directions Complete the table to show the ambulance's location (mile marker) at various times. Use the information in the diagram on page 121.

Ambulance Location								
Travel time (minutes)	0	4	8	12	16	20	24	*t*
Location (mile marker)	10	14						*m*

Location Grid (Use with Questions 15–18 on pages 121–122.)

Directions Plot the values from the table above on the grid below. Draw a line through the points to the edge of the grid.

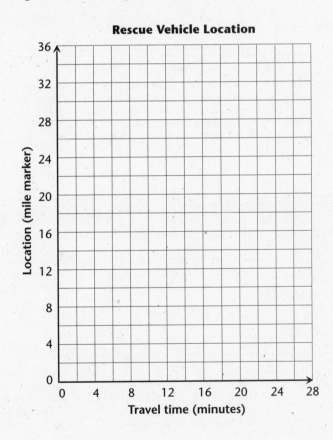

Rescue Vehicle Location

TEACHER   ASSESSMENT SCALES

☆ *The star indicates
that you excelled
in some way.*

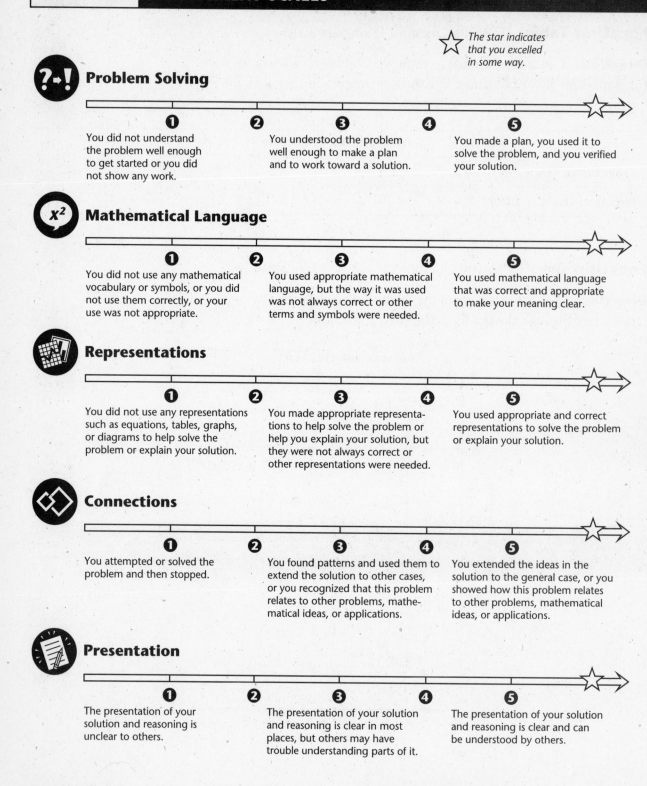

Problem Solving

❶ — **❷** — **❸** — **❹** — **❺**

❶ You did not understand the problem well enough to get started or you did not show any work.

❸ You understood the problem well enough to make a plan and to work toward a solution.

❺ You made a plan, you used it to solve the problem, and you verified your solution.

Mathematical Language

❶ — **❷** — **❸** — **❹** — **❺**

❶ You did not use any mathematical vocabulary or symbols, or you did not use them correctly, or your use was not appropriate.

❸ You used appropriate mathematical language, but the way it was used was not always correct or other terms and symbols were needed.

❺ You used mathematical language that was correct and appropriate to make your meaning clear.

Representations

❶ — **❷** — **❸** — **❹** — **❺**

❶ You did not use any representations such as equations, tables, graphs, or diagrams to help solve the problem or explain your solution.

❸ You made appropriate representations to help solve the problem or help you explain your solution, but they were not always correct or other representations were needed.

❺ You used appropriate and correct representations to solve the problem or explain your solution.

Connections

❶ — **❷** — **❸** — **❹** — **❺**

❶ You attempted or solved the problem and then stopped.

❸ You found patterns and used them to extend the solution to other cases, or you recognized that this problem relates to other problems, mathematical ideas, or applications.

❺ You extended the ideas in the solution to the general case, or you showed how this problem relates to other problems, mathematical ideas, or applications.

Presentation

❶ — **❷** — **❸** — **❹** — **❺**

❶ The presentation of your solution and reasoning is unclear to others.

❸ The presentation of your solution and reasoning is clear in most places, but others may have trouble understanding parts of it.

❺ The presentation of your solution and reasoning is clear and can be understood by others.

Content Used: _____   Computational Errors: Yes   No

Notes on Errors: _____

STUDENT | **SELF-ASSESSMENT SCALES**

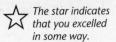 *If your score is in the shaded area, explain why on the back of this sheet and stop.*

 The star indicates that you excelled in some way.

Problem Solving

① I did not understand the problem well enough to get started or I did not show any work.

②

③ I understood the problem well enough to make a plan and to work toward a solution.

④

⑤ I made a plan, I used it to solve the problem, and I verified my solution.

Mathematical Language

① I did not use any mathematical vocabulary or symbols, or I did not use them correctly, or my use was not appropriate.

②

③ I used appropriate mathematical language, but the way it was used was not always correct or other terms and symbols were needed.

④

⑤ I used mathematical language that was correct and appropriate to make my meaning clear.

Representations

① I did not use any representations such as equations, tables, graphs, or diagrams to help solve the problem or explain my solution.

②

③ I made appropriate representations to help solve the problem or help me explain my solution, but they were not always correct or other representations were needed.

④

⑤ I used appropriate and correct representations to solve the problem or explain my solution.

Connections

① I attempted or solved the problem and then stopped.

②

③ I found patterns and used them to extend the solution to other cases, or I recognized that this problem relates to other problems, mathematical ideas, or applications.

④

⑤ I extended the ideas in the solution to the general case, or I showed how this problem relates to other problems, mathematical ideas, or applications.

Presentation

 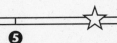

① The presentation of my solution and reasoning is unclear to others.

②

③ The presentation of my solution and reasoning is clear in most places, but others may have trouble understanding parts of it.

④

⑤ The presentation of my solution and reasoning is clear and can be understood by others.

MODULE 2 SECTION 1   **PRACTICE AND APPLICATIONS**

For use with Exploration 1

For Exercises 1– 6, use the diagram.

1. Name three angles that have point R as a vertex.

2. Name all the angles that have $\overrightarrow{SA}$ as a side.

3. Name two straight angles.

4. Name an acute angle that has S as its vertex and find its measure.

5. Name a right angle.

6. Name three obtuse angles and find their measures.

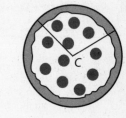

Draw an angle with each measure. Then classify each angle as *acute*, *right*, *obtuse*, or *straight*.

7. 155°   8. 25°   9. 180°   10. 90°

11. Two cuts have already been made in a pizza, as shown in the diagram at the right. Is it possible to make one more cut from the center C so that the three pieces of pizza will be the same size? Explain your thinking.

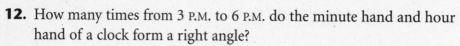

12. How many times from 3 P.M. to 6 P.M. do the minute hand and hour hand of a clock form a right angle?

13. Refer to the diagram at the right. If the gear on the right makes one full revolution, then the gear on the left makes two revolutions. Suppose the gear on the right is turned through an obtuse angle. Will the gear on the left make a full turn?

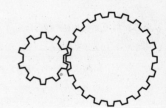

(continued)

MODULE 2 SECTION 1

For use with Exploration 2

14. Plane 1 is flying from point *A* at a heading of 50°. Plane 2 is flying from point *A* at a heading of 140°. What is the measure of the angle formed by the flight paths of the two planes?

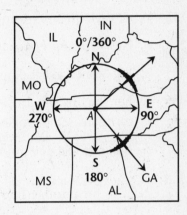

For each angle measure:
a. Find the measure of a supplementary angle.
b. Find the measure of a complementary angle, if possible.

15. 25°   **16.** 172°   **17.** 72°   **18.** 90°

19. 43°   **20.** 20°   **21.** 146°   **22.** 108°

For Exercises 23 and 24, refer to the map at the right.

23. A private plane and a jumbo jet both leave from Cary, but in opposite directions. The private plane is flying toward Jasper at a heading of 223°. What is the heading for the jumbo jet?

24. Morris is located due north of Jasper. Measure on the map with a protractor to find what heading should be used for a flight from Morris to Cary.

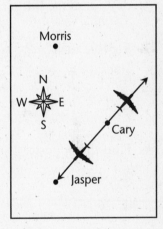

MODULE 2 SECTION 2   PRACTICE AND APPLICATIONS

For use with Exploration 1

1. Write each quantity using symbols instead of words.

  a. New Orleans, Louisiana is 8 ft below sea level.

  b. Big Stone Lake in South Dakota is 966 ft above sea level.

  c. For the first big drop on a roller coaster ride, the speed of Kim's car increased 60 miles per hour.

  d. Maurice lost 480 points on a quiz show.

2. Refer to the number line.

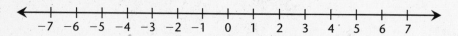

  a. Where on the number line are the integers less than –2?

  b. List all the negative integers that are greater than – 4.

  c. List all the positive integers that are less than 6.

  d. List all the integers that are less than 3 but greater than –7.

3. Replace each ___?___ with > or <.

  a. –8 ___?___ –5   **b.** 0 ___?___ –2   **c.** –9 ___?___ 9

  d. 12 ___?___ 7   **e.** –13 ___?___ –17   **f.** –25 ___?___ 14

4. Find the opposite of each integer.

  a. –12   **b.** 53   **c.** –42

  d. 26   **e.** 0   **f.** –84

5. Find each absolute value.

  a. $|-8|$ **b.** $|23|$ **c.** $|-95|$

  d. $|95|$ **e.** $|-16|$ **f.** $|44|$

6. Replace each ___?___ with > or <.

  a. 6 ___?___ $|-15|$ **b.** –8 ___?___ $|-8|$ **c.** $|-21|$ ___?___ $|-3|$

(continued)

MODULE 2 SECTION 2   **PRACTICE AND APPLICATIONS**

For use with Exploration 2

For Exercises 7–11, refer to the grid shown below.

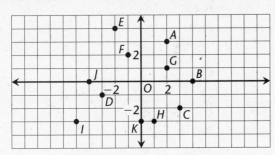

7. **a.** Name a point on the horizontal axis.

   b. Name a point on the vertical axis.

   c. Is the line through A and G horizontal or vertical?

   d. Is the line through H and I horizontal or vertical?

   e. How many horizontal lines go through point D?

   f. How many vertical lines go through point D?

8. Write the coordinates of each point.

   a. C **b.** E **c.** A

   d. I **e.** J **f.** K

9. Name two points that have the same first coordinate.

10. Name three points that have the same second coordinate.

11. Plot each point in a coordinate plane. Use the grid shown above.

   a. $M\,(6, -3)$ **b.** $N\,(-7, 0)$ **c.** $P\,(-8, 4)$

   d. $Q\,(7, 2)$ **e.** $R\,(-8, -4)$ **f.** $S\,(0, 1)$

12. How can you draw axes on a flat, rectangular table top so that the points on the table top can be located without using any negative coordinates? Can you do this for a mathematical plane? Explain your thinking.

MODULE 2 SECTION 3 **PRACTICE AND APPLICATIONS**

For use with Exploration 1

A hiker on a number line follows each set of directions. Determine where the hiker will finish. Record the moves as an addition problem with its sum or as a subtraction problem with its difference.

1. Start at –6. Face the negative direction. Move backward 2 units.

2. Start at 4. Face the positive direction. Move backward 6 units.

3. Start at 3. Face the negative direction. Move forward 7 units.

4. Start at –3. Face the positive direction. Move forward 5 units.

For use with Exploration 2

Use a number line to find each sum. Then write the addition problem with its sum.

5. –4 + 8

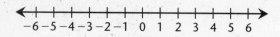

6. 3 + (–5)

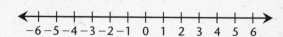

7. –2 + (–3)

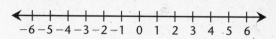

8. 0 + (–2)

Find each sum.

9. 3 + (–9)

10. –7 + 2

11. –5 + (– 4)

12. –8 + 8

13. 12 + (–6)

14. –11 + 7

15. 16 + (–10)

16. –9 + (–5)

17. –13 + 4

For Exercises 18–20, write and evaluate an addition expression to model each situation.

18. The temperature at 2 P.M. was –3°F. By 5 P.M., the temperature had risen 12°F.

19. In the first round of a game, Gabriela lost 500 points. In the second round, she gained 900 points.

20. A weather balloon was released from the top of a hill 250 ft above sea level. The balloon rose 830 ft and was later found floating in the ocean a few miles away.

(continued)

Name _____ Date _____

For use with Exploration 3

Use a number line to find each difference. Then write the subtraction problem with its difference.

21. $-1 - (-6)$

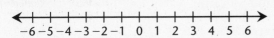

22. $5 - 8$

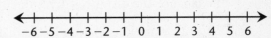

23. $-3 - 3$

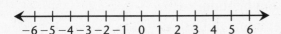

24. $2 - (-4)$

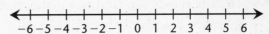

Write the related addition problem that has the same result.

25. $-17 - 2$ **26.** $8 - (-4)$ **27.** $5 - 10$

28. $-15 - (-6)$ **29.** $30 - 42$ **30.** $-9 - (-25)$

Find each difference.

31. $7 - 11$ **32.** $-3 - 8$ **33.** $5 - (-4)$

34. $-20 - (-10)$ **35.** $-35 - 16$ **36.** $-29 - (-15)$

Evaluate each expression using a calculator.

37. $3 + (-7) - 12$ **38.** $-42 + 6 - 15$ **39.** $(8 - 14) - (-3)$

40. $-2 - (4 - 29)$ **41.** $(8 - 3) - (3 - 8)$ **42.** $-6 + (-9) - (-2)$

43. The greatest known depth in the Pacific Ocean is 36,198 ft. The greatest known depth in the Atlantic Ocean is 30,246 ft. What is the difference between the deepest point in the Atlantic Ocean and the deepest point in the Pacific Ocean?

44. A diver from a seaside cliff went a vertical distance of 67 ft before coming up to the surface of the water. If the elevation of the cliff is 49 ft, to what depth did he go in the sea?

45. A quiz show contestant starts her second day on the show with 500 points. On the first round, she loses 700 points. On the second round, she gains 850 points. How many points does she have after the second round?

MODULE 2 SECTION 4   PRACTICE AND APPLICATIONS

For use with Exploration 1

1. a. Nita started at her home and has driven at a steady speed for 2 hours. She has driven 110 miles. What is Nita's rate of speed?

b. Suppose Nita keeps the same speed for the whole trip. Complete the table of the distances driven in 1, 2, 3, 4, and 5 hours.

Hours driven	Miles traveled
1	
2	
3	
4	
5	

c. Write an equation relating Nita's distance driven to her travel time.

d. Nita is going to Destin, which is 550 miles from her home. How many hours does it take her to drive from her home to Destin?

e. What does the expression $550 - 55t$ model?

f. What values of t make sense for the expression in part (e)?

Choose the letter of the expression that models each situation.

2. An amusement park charges $3 to enter and $2 for each ride. What is the price of going to the park and riding on k rides?

   a. $2k$ **b.** $2k - 3$ **c.** $3 + 2k$

3. Mr. Anderson gets his brakes checked every 6 months. How many times does he get his brakes checked over a period of y years?

   a. $2y$ **b.** $6y$ **c.** $2y - 6$

Evaluate each expression when $x = 5$, $y = -3$, and $z = 6$.

4. $10x$ **5.** $2z + y$ **6.** $y - x$

7. $60 \div x$ **8.** $y + 7x$ **9.** $5z - y$

10. $y + xz$ **11.** $y - xz$ **12.** $2x - 4z$

13. a. Describe a situation that can be modeled by the expression $25q$.

b. Make a table that shows the values of the expression $25q$ for $q = 1$, $q = 2$, $q = 3$, and $q = 4$.

(continued)

MODULE 2 SECTION 4   **PRACTICE AND APPLICATIONS**

For use with Exploration 2

**Copy and complete the table of values for each equation.
Then graph each equation in a coordinate plane.**

14. $y = x - 6$

x	−2	−1	0	1	2
y					

15. $y = x + 4$

x	−2	−1	0	1	2
y					

16. $y = 7 - x$

x	−2	−1	0	1	2
y					

17. $y = x + 5$

x	−2	−1	0	1	2
y					

**Make a table of values for each equation. Then graph the
equation in a coordinate plane.**

18. $y = 3 - x$ **19.** $y = x + 9$ **20.** $y = 8 - x$

21. Linda borrowed some money to buy new software for her
computer. Mike borrowed money for a CD player. The graph
shows how they paid back their loans.

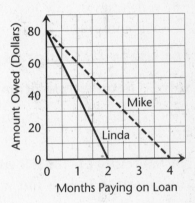

a. How much did each person borrow? How does the graph
show this information?

b. How much did Linda pay back each month? How does
the graph show this?

c. How much did Mike pay back each month?

d. Make tables to show how Linda and Mike paid back
their loans.

e. For each person, write an equation that describes how his
or her loan was repaid. Tell what each variable represents.

**Use each graph to make a table of values of x and y. Then
write an equation to model the relationship between x and y.**

22.

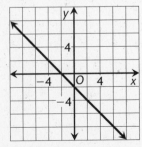

23.

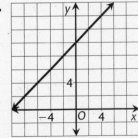

Name _____   Date _____

For use with Exploration 1

a. Write an equation that the model represents.

b. Solve the equation you wrote in part (a).

1. □ + □□/□□□ = □□□□□/□□□□□

2. □ + □□□□ = □□□□□□□

Write an addition equation to model each situation.

3. Sharlene has done 6 of her 10 homework problems.

4. Of the 23 mineral samples in Yoshi's collection, 4 are clear quartz.

Write a subtraction equation to model each situation.

5. The temperature dropped to –3°F after an afternoon high of 17°F.

6. A dentist sees only 36 patients, since 7 people cancelled appointments.

For use with Exploration 2

Solve. Check each solution.

7. $k - 19 = -80$ **8.** $a + 8 = 53$ **9.** $19 + m = 74$

10. $-15 + t = 24$ **11.** $n - 65 = 32$ **12.** $-17 = b + 50$

For Exercises 13–18, tell whether the number that follows the equation is or is not a solution of the equation.

13. $a - 14 = 30;\ 16$ **14.** $-9 + b = -4;\ 5$ **15.** $x - (-7) = 26;\ 19$

16. $w + 5 = -30;\ -35$ **17.** $k - 8 = -8;\ 16$ **18.** $51 + n = -61;\ 112$

Write an addition or subtraction equation to model each situation. Then solve and check the equation.

19. Two angles are supplementary. The larger has a measure of 139°.

20. After rising 55 m, a submarine was 63 m below sea level.

21. Andrew saved $85, but the CD player he plans to buy is $160.

Name _____   Date _____

MODULE 2 SECTIONS 1– 5

For use with Section 1

1. Draw an angle with each measure. Then classify each angle as acute, obtuse, right, or straight.

   a. 90° **b.** 25° **c.** 160°

2. For each angle measure:
   Find the measure of a supplementary angle.
   Find the measure of a complementary angle, if possible.

   a. 75° **b.** 98° **c.** 112°

For use with Section 2

3. Rewrite each elevation using symbols instead of words.

   a. Gannett Peak, Wyoming: 13,804 ft above sea level

   b. Bristol Bay, Alaska: at sea level

   c. New Orleans, Louisiana: 8 ft below sea level

   d. Death Valley, California: 282 ft below sea level

4. Find the opposite and the absolute value of each integer.

   a. 0 **b.** 49 **c.** −68

   d. −235 **e.** −99 **f.** 400

5. Replace each ___?___ with > or <.

   a. 12 ___?___ 0

   b. −6 ___?___ 6

   c. | −30| ___?___ | −50|

   d. | 14| ___?___ | −11|

   e. | −28| ___?___ | 45|

   f. −36 ___?___ −41

For use with Section 3

6. Find each sum or difference.

   a. 9 + (−16) **b.** −17 − 3 **c.** −5 + 25

   d. −10 − (−4) **e.** 5 + 28 **f.** 16 + (−5)

   g. 19 + (−19) **h.** −15 − 9 **i.** −26 − (−60)

(continued)

MODULE 2 SECTIONS 1–5   PRACTICE AND APPLICATIONS

For use with Section 4

7. Evaluate each expression when $x = 12$, $y = -4$, and $z = 6$.

  a. $3z + 6$ **b.** $2x - 21$ **c.** $11z - x$

  d. $y + 8z$ **e.** $y - 2x$ **f.** $xz - 20$

  g. $5x - y$ **h.** $xz + y$ **i.** $4z - y$

8. Copy and complete the table of values for each equation. Then graph each equation in the coordinate plane.

  a. $y = x - 5$

x	−10	−5	0	5	10
y	?	?	?	?	?

  b. $y = 2x + 1$

x	−2	−1	0	1	2
y	?	?	?	?	?

9. A bus travels at an average rate of 50 mi/h.

  a. Make a table showing the distance traveled for travel times of 0, 1, 2, 3, 4, 5, and 6 h.

  b. Write an equation to model the distance traveled d in relation to travel time t.

For use with Section 5

10. Write an addition equation and a subtraction equation to model each situation. Use one variable and tell what it represents.

  a. Diana has 38 marbles. She and her brother together have 75 marbles.

  b. Ramon needs 5 points in the last quarter of the game to tie his high score of 23 points.

  c. Spring spent $8 and has $9 remaining.

11. Solve. Check each solution.

  a. $a + 19 = 7$ **b.** $15 + w = 32$ **c.** $r - 17 = -11$

  d. $82 = v - 61$ **e.** $b + 26 = -49$ **f.** $k - 51 = -9$

  g. $-14 = n + 22$ **h.** $-43 + d = 39$ **i.** $y - 8 = -62$

Name _____   Date _____

MODULE 2 SECTION 1   **STUDY GUIDE**

Heading Out   Looking at Angles

GOAL   **LEARN HOW TO:** • name and measure angles
                           • classify angles
                           • use supplementary and complementary angles

   As you: • learn a skill SAR team members need
              • find compass headings

Exploration 1: Measuring Angles

Rays and Angles

A **ray** is a part of a line. It starts at an endpoint and goes on forever in
one direction. Ray BC is written $\overrightarrow{BC}$. Always write the endpoint first.

An **angle** is formed by two rays with a common endpoint called the
vertex of the angle. The angle at the right, formed by $\overrightarrow{BA}$ and $\overrightarrow{BC}$, can be
called $\angle ABC$, $\angle CBA$, or $\angle B$. Always write the vertex as the middle letter.

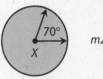

Measuring and Classifying Angles

The measure of an angle is the amount of rotation between its two
rays. An angle is measured in units called *degrees*. There are 360° in
a complete rotation, so one **degree** is $\frac{1}{360}$ of a complete rotation.

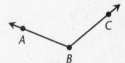

An angle can be classified by its measure.

The measure of an **acute angle** is between 0° and 90°.	The measure of a **right angle** is exactly 90°.	The measure of an **obtuse angle** is between 90° and 180°.	The measure of a **straight angle** is exactly 180°.

$m \angle Q = 50°$ $m \angle R = 90°$ $m \angle S = 105°$ $m \angle T = 180°$

MODULE 2 SECTION 1 STUDY GUIDE

Exploration 2: Angle Relationships

Supplementary and Complementary

Two angles are **supplementary angles** if the sum of the measures of the angles is 180°. $\angle P$ and $\angle Q$ at the right are supplementary angles.

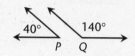

Two angles are **complementary angles** if the sum of the measures of the angles is 90°. $\angle X$ and $\angle Y$ at the right are complementary angles.

Example

Refer to the diagram.

a. Name two angles that are complementary.

b. Name two angles that are supplementary.

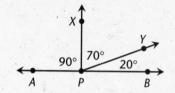

■ Sample Response ■

a. To identify two complementary angles, look for a *sum* of 90°.

Since $m\angle XPY = 70°$ and $m\angle YPB = 20°$, and $70° + 20° = 90°$, $\angle XPY$ and $\angle YPB$ are complementary angles.

b. To identify two supplementary angles, look for a *sum* of 180° or look for two angles that form a straight angle.

$\angle APB$ is a straight angle. One pair of angles that form $\angle APB$ is $\angle APY$ and $\angle YPB$.

Notice that $m\angle APY = 90° + 70°$, or 160°, $m\angle YPB = 20°$, and $160° + 20° = 180°$.

So, $\angle APY$ and $\angle YPB$ are one pair of supplementary angles.

Two other angles that are supplementary are $\angle APX$ and $\angle BPX$, whose measures are 90° and 70° + 20°, or 90°, respectively.

Name _____ Date _____

Exploration 1

For Exercises 1– 4, use the diagram.

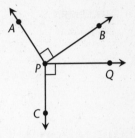

1. Name the ray that passes through point Q.

2. Name an acute angle and find its measure.

3. Name three angles that have $\overrightarrow{PB}$ as a side.

4. **Visual Thinking** Name all the angles that have vertex P.

5. What is the measure of an angle that is one quarter of a full rotation? By what special name is an angle of that measure called?

Exploration 2

For Exercises 6 – 8, use the diagram.

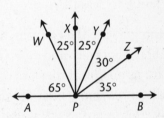

6. Name four pairs of supplementary angles.

7. Name five pairs of complementary angles.

8. **Writing** Are $\angle XPY$, $\angle YPZ$, and $\angle ZPB$ complementary angles? Explain.

9. Draw a pair of supplementary angles that are of equal measure. Classify these angles.

10. **Challenge** Find the measure of the angle whose complementary angle measures $\frac{1}{3}$ of its supplementary angle.

Spiral Review

11. **Patterning** Here are geometric models for the first four *triangular numbers.*

    Draw a geometric model for the fifth triangular number. What is the value of this number? **(Module 1, page 14)**

    1   3   6   10

12. **Probability** There are 6 boys and 4 girls on a school committee. One of the members is chosen at random to serve as secretary. What is the probability that the member selected is a boy? **(Module 1, page 30)**

MODULE 2 SECTION 2   STUDY GUIDE

Searching for Integers   Integers and Coordinates

GOAL **LEARN HOW TO:** • compare integers
                              • find opposites and absolute values of integers
                              • identify and plot points in a coordinate plane

AS YOU: • learn about elevation
             • work with parallel and perpendicular lines

Exploration 1: Comparing Integers

Integers

Numbers greater than zero are **positive**.

Numbers less than zero are **negative**.

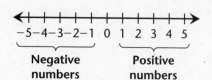

Negative numbers   Positive numbers

Integers are the counting numbers, their opposites, and zero. Two numbers are **opposites** if they are the same distance from 0 on a number line but on opposite sides of 0.

The opposite of 5 is –5.
The opposite of –8 is 8.
The opposite of 0 is 0.

The integers are the numbers …, –4, –3, –2, –1, 0, 1, 2, 3, 4, … .

An **inequality** is a mathematical sentence stating that one quantity is greater than or less than another. You can write inequalities to compare integers.

   –3 is greater than –6   or   –6 is less than –3
         –3 > –6   –6 < –3

Example

Write two inequalities to compare –9 and 7.

■ Sample Response ■

Graph the numbers on a number line. The integers increase as you go from left to right.

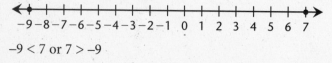

–9 < 7 or 7 > –9

MODULE 2 SECTION 2   **STUDY GUIDE**

The **absolute value** of a number is the distance from the number to 0 on a number line. You read $|-3|$ as "the absolute value of negative three."

Example

Find the absolute value of –5 and 5.

Sample Response ■

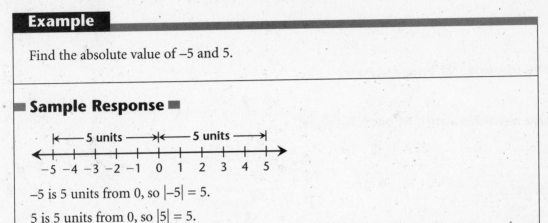

–5 is 5 units from 0, so $|-5| = 5$.

5 is 5 units from 0, so $|5| = 5$.

Exploration 2: Coordinate Graphing

Line Relationships

A **plane** can be thought of as a flat surface that goes on forever.

Two lines **intersect** if they meet or cross each other.
Lines a and b intersect.

Two lines in a plane are **parallel** if they do not intersect.
Lines c and d are parallel.

Two lines are **perpendicular** if they intersect at 90° angles.
Lines e and f are perpendicular.

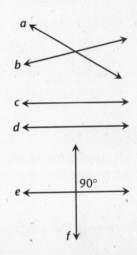

Graphing in a Coordinate Plane

The **coordinate plane** is a grid with a **horizontal axis** and a **vertical axis** that intersect at the **origin**.

An **ordered pair** of numbers, called **coordinates,** can be used to identify and plot points in a coordinate plane.

The *first coordinate* in an ordered pair gives a point's location to the left or right of zero on the horizontal axis. The *second coordinate* gives the point's location up or down from zero on the vertical axis.

The ordered pair for the **origin** is (0, 0).

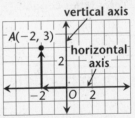

Point *A* has coordinates (–2, 3).

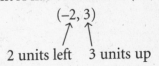

2 units left   3 units up

MODULE 2 SECTION 2 | PRACTICE & APPLICATION EXERCISES | STUDY GUIDE

Exploration 1

Replace each __?__ with > or <.

1. 9 __?__ 5

2. 0 __?__ −5

3. 43 __?__ −53

4. −16 __?__ −20

5. −3 __?__ −1

6. 8 __?__ 11

Find the opposite of each integer.

7. 5

8. −30

9. 588

10. −19

Find the absolute value of each integer.

11. $|{-10}|$

12. $|50|$

13. $|{-2}|$

14. $|312|$

Exploration 2

15. a. Identify the coordinates of the points *A* through *E* in the coordinate plane.

   b. Graph the ordered pairs (−3, 5) and (−3, −3) in a coordinate plane. Draw a segment to connect the points.

   c. Graph the ordered pairs (−1, 4) and (− 4, 1) in the coordinate plane for part (b). Draw a segment to connect the points.

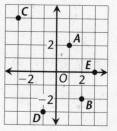

Spiral Review

For each angle measure in Exercises 16 –18, find the measure of a complementary angle. (Module 2, p. 83)

16. 37°

17. 16°

18. 69°

19. Displaying Data Make a bar graph of the data below. (Toolbox, p. 594)

Total Miles Logged This Week by Members of The Walkers Club			
Monday...15	Tuesday...25	Wednesday...40	Thursday...42
Friday...22	Saturday...50	Sunday...19	

Find each sum or difference. (Toolbox, p. 587)

20. $\frac{2}{7}+\frac{3}{7}$

21. $\frac{7}{9}-\frac{4}{9}$

22. $\frac{3}{4}-\frac{2}{4}$

23. $\frac{1}{8}+\frac{6}{8}$

Name _____ Date _____

A Call for Help   Integer Addition and Subtraction

GOAL **LEARN HOW TO:** • use a model to work with integers
• add integers
• use properties of addition
• subtract integers

AS YOU: • take and analyze hikes along a number line
• explore wind-chill temperatures

Exploration 1: Modeling Integer Operations

Number-Line Models

You can think of addition and subtraction as hikes on a number line.

Example
Find the sum $3 + (-5)$.
■ Sample Response ■
Start at 3, facing in the positive direction. Move backward 5 units. 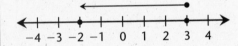 So, $3 + (-5) = -2$.

Exploration 2: Adding Integers

To add two integers with the *same sign*, add the absolute values of the integers. The sum has the same sign as the integers you are adding. For example, $9 + 3 = 12$ and $-5 + (-3) = -8$.

To add two integers that have *different signs*, subtract the lesser absolute value from the greater one. The sum has the same sign as the integer with the greater absolute value. For example, $2 + (-3) = -1$ and $-5 + 9 = 4$.

The sum of **0 and a number** is that number. For example, $0 + 6 = 6$ and $-3 + 0 = -3$.

The sum of **a number and its opposite** is 0. For example, $8 + (-8) = 0$.

Properties of Addition

The **commutative property of addition** says that you can change the order of numbers in an addition problem and still get the same sum.

> ### Example
>
> $8 + 3 = 11$ and $3 + 8 = 11$
>
> $-7 + 2 = -5$ and $2 + (-7) = -5$
>
> $-3 + (-4) = -7$ and $-4 + (-3) = -7$

The **associative property of addition** says that you can change the grouping when you add numbers and still get the same sum.

> ### Example
>
> $3 + (4 + 5) = 3 + 9 = 12$ and $(3 + 4) + 5 = 7 + 5 = 12$
>
> $-5 + [4 + (-3)] = -5 + 1 = -4$ and $[-5 + 4] + (-3) = -1 + (-3) = -4$

Exploration 3: Subtracting Integers

You can rewrite a subtraction problem as an addition problem. To subtract an integer, add its opposite.

> ### Example
>
> Find each difference.
>
> **a.** $4 - (-7)$ **b.** $3 - 9$
>
> ### ■ Sample Response ■
>
> **a.** Rewrite the subtraction as an addition and then add.
>
> $4 - (-7) = 4 + 7$ ← Add the opposite of –7.
>
> $\qquad\quad = 11$
>
> **b.** Rewrite the subtraction as an addition and then add.
>
> $3 - 9 = 3 + (-9)$ ← Add the opposite of 9.
>
> $\qquad\ = -6$

MODULE 2 SECTION 3 | PRACTICE & APPLICATION EXERCISES | STUDY GUIDE

Exploration 1

A hiker on a number line follows each set of directions. Determine where the hiker will finish. Record the moves as an addition problem with its sum or as a subtraction problem with its difference.

1. Start at –5. Face the positive direction. Move backward 2 units.

2. Start at 3. Face the negative direction. Move forward 4 units.

3. Start at –1. Face the negative direction. Move backward 2 units.

Exploration 2

Find each sum.

4. $-4 + (-2)$

5. $-5 + 0$

6. $7 + 5$

7. $-13 + (-18)$

8. $-9 + 5 + (-3)$

9. $5 + 0 + (-5)$

Mental Math Find each sum mentally. Use properties of addition.

10. $-7 + 0 + (-5) + 7$

11. $9 + (-4) + (-3) + 4 + (-6)$

12. $-8 + 5 + 13 + 0 + (-2)$

13. $3 + (-14) + (-8) + 5$

Exploration 3

For Exercises 14–17, rewrite each subtraction problem as the related addition problem that has the same answer. Then solve.

14. $9 - 5$

15. $-5 - (-8)$

16. $0 - (-3)$

17. $8 - (-2)$

18. Find the difference $-6 - (-5)$.

Spiral Review

19. Graph these ordered pairs in a coordinate plane:

$S(-2, 5)$, $T(3, 6)$, $U(2, -1)$, $V(-3, -5)$, $W(4, 0)$, and $X(0, 3)$
(Module 2, p. 95)

Mental Math Find each sum or difference mentally. (Toolbox, p. 581)

20. $1.46 + 0.95$

21. $36.55 - 20.99$

22. $12.18 - 9.2$

Find the next three terms of each sequence. (Module 1, p. 20)

23. $22, 27, 32, 37, \ldots$

24. $100, 89, 78, 67, \ldots$

Urban Rescue   Function Models

GOAL **LEARN HOW TO:** • model a function with a table or an equation
• evaluate expressions with variables
• model a function with a graph

AS YOU: • explore distance, rate, and time
• choose between emergency vehicles

Exploration 1: Modeling a Function

Evaluating Expressions

To **evaluate** an expression that has a variable, substitute a value for the
variable and perform the operations. When two expressions are equal, you
can write an **equation** to express the relationship.

> ### Example
>
> A hiker on a 50 mi journey has traveled for t hours at r miles per hour. Find the
> distance left to hike after 12 h at an average rate of 2 mi/h.
>
> ### ■ Sample Response ■
>
> Distance, rate, and time are related by the formula *distance traveled = rate × time*. So,
> the distance traveled in t hours at r miles per hour is the product rt.
>
> Therefore, an expression for the distance left to hike is $50 - rt$. Evaluate this expression
> for $r = 2$ and $t = 12$.
>
> $$50 - rt = 50 - 2 \cdot 12 \qquad \leftarrow \text{Substitute 2 for } r \text{ and 12 for } t.$$
> $$= 50 - 24$$
> $$= 26$$
>
> The hiker has 26 mi left to travel.

Modeling Functions

A **function** is a relationship between input and output. For each input,
there is exactly one output. You can model a function in many ways.
Making a table and writing an equation are two ways to model a function.

> ### Example
>
> A number y is 3 more than twice another number x. Model this function in two ways.
>
> Table:
>
> | Input x | 0 | 1 | 2 | 3 | 4 |
> |-----------|---|---|---|---|----|
> | Output y | 3 | 5 | 7 | 9 | 11 |
>
> **Equation:** $y = 2x + 3$

MODULE 2 SECTION 4   STUDY GUIDE

Exploration 2: Graphing a Function

A function can also be modeled using a graph.

Example

A festival sold tickets for a concert at $2.00 each. A local company has agreed to donate an additional $1.00 for each ticket sold. Model the relationship between the number of tickets sold and the amount of money collected using a table, an equation, and a graph. Then find out how much money is collected if 450 tickets are sold.

■ Sample Response ■

Make a table to show the relationship between the number of tickets sold (n) and the amount of money collected (c) for these values: 1, 2, 3, and n.

Tickets sold	Amount collected ($)
1	3
2	6
3	9
n	c

Write an equation to model the relationship between the number of tickets sold and the amount collected.

$c = 3n$

Make a graph of the equation using the values in the table.

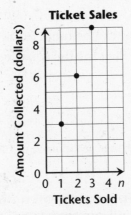

Ticket Sales

Use the equation to determine how much money is collected if 450 tickets are sold.

$c = 3n$
$ = 3(450)$ ← Replace n with 450.
$ = 1350$

For 450 tickets, $1350 is collected.

| MODULE 2 SECTION 4 | PRACTICE & APPLICATION EXERCISES | STUDY GUIDE |

Exploration 1

1. Choose the letter of the expression that models this situation. The price of a book is m dollars. What is the price after a $1.50 decrease?

   A. $m + \$1.50$ **B.** $m - \$1.50$ **C.** $\$1.50 \div m$

2. Write an expression that models this situation.
   Larry is 2 years older than Fran. Fran is t years old. How old is Larry?

Evaluate each expression when $a = 2$, $b = -2$, and $c = 3$.

3. $30a$ 4. $6b$ 5. $45 \div c$

6. $4b + 5$ 7. $-3a - 11$ 8. $b + 3c + a$

Exploration 2

For Exercises 9 and 10, copy and complete the table of values for each equation. Then graph each equation in a coordinate plane.

9. $y = x + (-2)$

x	−2	−1	0	1	2
y	?	?	?	?	?

10. $y = 2x - 1$

x	−10	−5	0	5	10
y	?	?	?	?	?

11. Describe a situation that can be modeled by the equation $y = x - 4$. Then make a table of values for the equation and graph the equation in a coordinate plane.

Spiral Review

Find each sum or difference. (Module 2, p. 109)

12. $-12 + (-31)$ 13. $-7 - (-5)$ 14. $-11 - 17$

For Exercises 15–17, suppose you roll a nine-sided die with faces labeled 1 to 9 and all outcomes are equally likely. Find the theoretical probability of each event. (Module 1, p. 33)

15. $P(8)$ 16. $P(13)$ 17. $P(\text{even number})$

18. Make a table, draw a graph, and write an equation for the sequence 11, 12, 13, 14, ... Then predict the 100th term. (Module 1, p. 20)

Name _____ Date _____

Searching for a Solution   Addition and Subtraction Equations

GOAL **LEARN HOW TO:** • write addition and subtraction equations
• solve addition equations using models
• use inverse operations to solve addition and subtraction equations
• check solutions

AS YOU: • examine the contents of a backpack
• explore weight limits for a backpack

Exploration 1: Write and Model Equations

Modeling Equations

A value of a variable that makes an equation true is a **solution of the equation**. The process of finding solutions is called **solving an equation**.

Balance models can help you visualize an equation and remember that both sides represent the same amount. *Algebra tile models* can help you solve (find a solution of) an equation.

Example

Model this situation: Derrick has 5 more colors of model paint than Sherry. Sherry has 11 colors. How many colors does Derrick have?

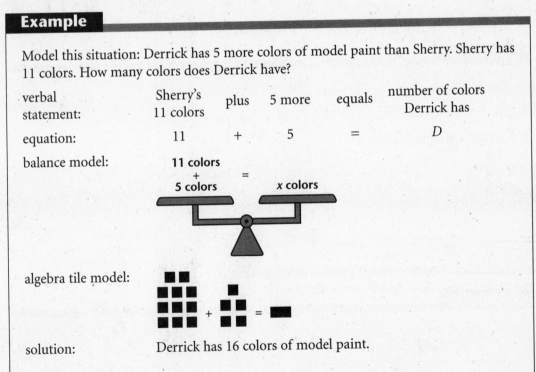

| verbal statement: | Sherry's 11 colors | plus | 5 more | equals | number of colors Derrick has |

| equation: | 11 | + | 5 | = | D |

balance model:

algebra tile model:

solution: Derrick has 16 colors of model paint.

MODULE 2 SECTION 5 — STUDY GUIDE

Exploration 2: Using Inverse Operations

Using Inverse Operations to Solve

Addition and subtraction are **inverse operations**. They "undo" each other.

When you use symbols and variables to solve an equation, you are solving the equation *algebraically*.

To solve an equation, remember these ideas:

- The goal is to get the variable alone on one side of the equation.

- Use inverse operations to "undo" one another.

- Any operation done on one side of an equation must also be done on the other side to keep the equation balanced.

- Check that your solution is correct by substituting the value for the variable into the equation.

- If necessary, use tiles to model the equation.

Subtraction "undoes" addition when you solve an equation.

Example

Solve $n + 5 = 8$.

Sample Response

$$n + 5 = 8$$
$$\underline{-5 = -5} \quad \leftarrow \text{Subtract 5 from both sides.}$$
$$n + 0 = 3$$
$$n = 3$$

Check:
$$n + 5 = 8 \quad \leftarrow \text{Substitute 3 for } n.$$
$$3 + 5 \overset{?}{=} 8$$
$$8 = 8 \checkmark$$

Addition "undoes" subtraction when you solve an equation.

Example

Solve $n - 5 = 8$.

Sample Response

$$n - 5 = 8$$
$$\underline{+5 = +5} \quad \leftarrow \text{Add 5 to both sides.}$$
$$n + 0 = 13$$
$$n = 13$$

Check:
$$n - 5 = 8 \quad \leftarrow \text{Substitute 13 for } n.$$
$$13 - 5 \overset{?}{=} 8$$
$$8 = 8 \checkmark$$

| MODULE 2 SECTION 5 | PRACTICE & APPLICATION EXERCISES | STUDY GUIDE |

Exploration 1

1. Write the equation represented by the model at the right.

2. **Open-ended** Describe a situation that can be modeled by the equation $x - 4 = 7$. Be sure to tell what the variable represents.

3. Make an algebra tile model that represents $x - 2 = 5$. Then use the model to help you find the solution.

4. Write an addition equation to model this situation: Dorothy enrolled 36 new newspaper customers raising her total subscriptions to 78. Use one variable and tell what it represents.

5. Write a subtraction equation to model this situation: After distributing 143 flyers, David had 7 left. Use one variable and tell what it represents.

Exploration 2

For Exercises 6–14, solve each equation. Check each solution.

6. $x - (-8) = -6$ 7. $45 = 34 + t$ 8. $y - 25 = -16$

9. $n + (-5) = 18$ 10. $k - 19 = 13$ 11. $49 = -5 + g$

12. $8 = 9 + c$ 13. $0 = y - (-4)$ 14. $w + 6 = 27$

15. Is 5 a solution of the equation $-9 + n = 4$? Explain.

Spiral Review

Evaluate each expression when $x = 5$, $y = 3$, and $z = -12$.
(Module 2, p. 124)

16. $x - 9$ 17. $-3 + 2y$ 18. $z - 6x$

For Exercises 19–22, tell whether each number is divisible by 2, 5, and 10. (Toolbox, p. 582)

19. 30   20. 130   21. 465   22. 123

23. James and Andy earned a total of $112. James worked 6 h and Andy worked 8 h. How much did each earn if they make the same amount per hour? Tell what problem solving strategy you used. (Module 2, p. 44)

MODULE 3

Dot Jumping Table (Use with Questions 3 and 4 on pages 149–150.)

Directions

- Start with the 12-dot clock face and use equal-sized jumps to move from dot to dot.

- Fill in the table with the jump sizes and the numbers of jumps that will let you land on START after one time around the 12-dot clock face.

- Do the same with the other clock faces.

Number of dots	Jump size	Number of jumps
12	1	12
12	3	4

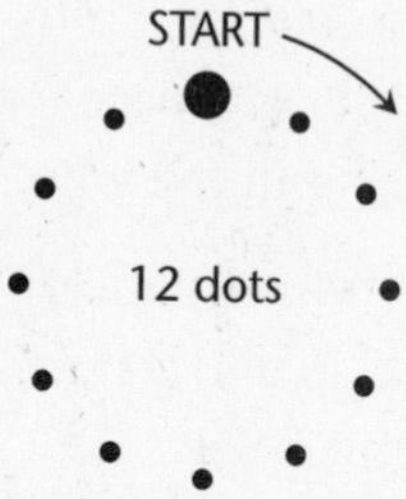

START

12 dots

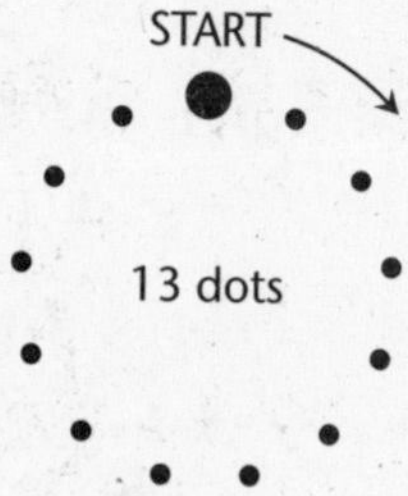

START

13 dots

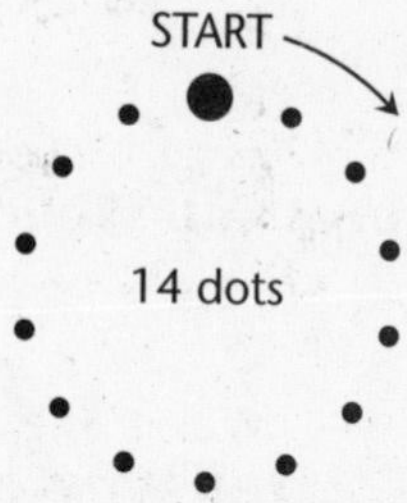

START

14 dots

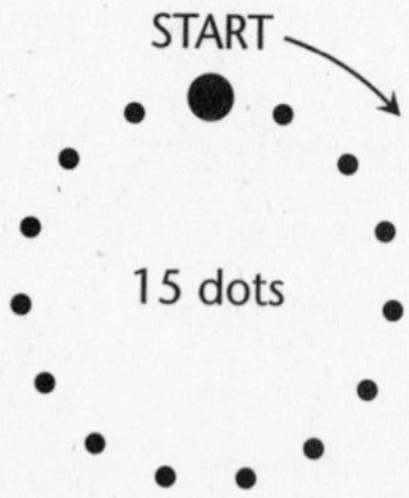

START

15 dots

MODULE 3   LABSHEET **1B**

Divisibility-by-Nine Table (Use with Question 14 on page 153.)

Directions Complete the table and look for a pattern involving the sum of the digits.

Number divisible by 9	Digits in the number	Sum of the digits
18	1, 8	
27	2, 7	2 + 7 = 9
54	5, 4	5 + 4 = 9
918	9, 1, 8	
2,457	2, 4, 5, 7	2 + 4 + 5 + 7 = 18
9,153		
71,127,207	7, 1, 1, 2, 7, 2, 0, 7	
943,280,307		

MODULE 3   LABSHEET **1C**

Calendar of Multiples (Use with Questions 22–25 on page 155.)

Directions

- First write a ① in the squares for the days of the month that are divisible by 1 (1, 2, 3, 4, …). These are the multiples of 1.

- Next write a ② in the squares for the days of the month that are multiples of 2.

- Then write a ③ in the squares for the days of the month that are multiples of 3.

1995 January 2006

S	M	T	W	T	F	S
1	2	3	4	5	6	7
8	9	10	11	12	13	14
15	16	17	18	19	20	21
22	23	24	25	26	27	28
29	30	31				

MODULE 3

Equivalent Fraction Models (Use with Question 18 on page 167.)

Directions For each equation, shade the equivalent amounts and complete the equivalent equation to find the sum or difference.

a. $\dfrac{1}{2}$ + $\dfrac{1}{5}$ =   _____

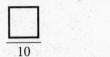

$\dfrac{\Box}{10}$ + $\dfrac{\Box}{10}$ = $\dfrac{\Box}{10}$

b. $\dfrac{2}{3}$ – $\dfrac{1}{4}$ = _____

 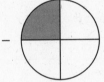 

$\dfrac{\Box}{12}$ – $\dfrac{\Box}{12}$ = $\dfrac{\Box}{12}$

c. $\dfrac{1}{3}$ + $\dfrac{1}{8}$ = _____

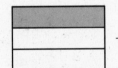  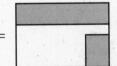

$\dfrac{\Box}{24}$ + $\dfrac{\Box}{24}$ = $\dfrac{\Box}{24}$

MODULE 3

Colonial Price List (Use with the *Setting the Stage* on page 177.)

Directions Use the price list below and your colonial money to "buy" items on your shopping list.

Food	Price
butter (2 lb)	1 bit
cheese (1 lb)	1 bit
coffee ($1\frac{1}{2}$ lb)	$\frac{1}{4}$ dollar
sugar (1 lb)	1 bit
brown sugar (3 lb)	1 bit
tea (1 oz)	1 bit
chocolate ($1\frac{1}{2}$ lb)	$\frac{5}{8}$ dollar
cinnamon ($1\frac{1}{2}$ oz)	$\frac{1}{2}$ dollar
corn (1 bushel)	3 bits
pepper (2 lb)	3 bits
salt (1 bushel)	$\frac{3}{8}$ dollar
apples (1 bushel)	3 bits
chickens (3)	2 bits
eggs (1 dozen)	$\frac{1}{8}$ dollar
oranges (1 dozen)	$\frac{1}{2}$ dollar
pineapples (each)	2 bits
turkeys (each)	$\frac{1}{4}$ dollar

Clothing	Price
shoes (pair)	1 dollar
breeches	1 dollar, 1 bit
cap	$\frac{5}{8}$ dollar
men's hat	3 dollars
women's hat	1 dollar, 5 bits
cotton shirt	1 dollar
spectacles	$\frac{1}{8}$ dollar
fine bob wig	$5\frac{3}{8}$ dollars
wool suit	10 dollars

Books and writing materials	Price
almanac	$\frac{1}{8}$ dollar
history book	1 bit
paper (24 sheets)	1 bit
pencils (3)	$\frac{1}{8}$ dollar
song book	$\frac{3}{8}$ dollar
arithmetic book	5 bits
Bailey's Dictionary	2 dollars
pen	2 bits
Gulliver's Travels	$\frac{7}{8}$ dollar
spelling book	2 bits

Household and other items	Price
candles ($2\frac{1}{2}$ lb)	$\frac{1}{8}$ dollar
playing cards	1 bit
fiddle	3 dollars, 2 bits
chair	$5\frac{7}{8}$ dollars
chest of drawers	8 dollars, 3 bits
dining table	5 dollars, 7 bits

Voyages	Price
round trip to England	$73\frac{3}{8}$ dollars

MODULE 3   **LABSHEET** (3B)

Shopping Lists and Coins (Use with the *Setting the Stage* on page 177.)

Directions Your group should have one shopping list and
$5–$8 made up of whole, $\frac{1}{2}$-, $\frac{1}{4}$-, and $\frac{1}{8}$-dollar pieces.

Shopping List #1

- 1 dozen oranges
- 1 turkey
- 2 lb sugar
- 2 lb cheese
- 3 lb coffee
- 1 fiddle
- paper (about 50 sheets)
- 6 pencils
- spelling book
- candles (2 lb or more)

Shopping List #2

- 2 bushels of corn
- 2 lb sugar
- 3 oz tea
- 6 lb coffee
- present for a teacher
- breeches
- cotton shirt
- cap
- pencils (at least 10)
- spectacles

Shopping List #3

- 3 chickens
- 1 pineapple
- 2 dozen oranges
- gift for a friend
- 3 lb chocolate
- 4 lb butter
- 2 lb cheese
- 2 lb sugar
- 3 oz cinnamon
- 1 pair of shoes

MODULE 3   LABSHEET **4A**

Positive Powers of 10 Table
(Use with Question 16 on page 194.)

Directions Use multiplication to complete the table.

Exponential form	Standard form
10^1	10
10^2	100
10^3	1000
10^4	
10^5	
10^6	

Integer Powers of 10 Table
(Use with Questions 17 and 18 on page 195.)

Directions Use division to complete the table.

Exponential form	Standard form using decimals	Standard form using fractions
10^3	1000	1000
10^2	100	100
10^1	10	10
10^0		
10^{-1}		$\frac{1}{10}$
10^{-2}	0.01	
10^{-3}		

Powers of 2 Table (Use with Question 19 on page 195.)

Directions

- Use patterns, your knowledge of exponents, and a calculator to complete the second and third rows of the table. Write all fractions in lowest terms.

- In the last row, rewrite each fraction so the denominator is written in exponential form with base 2.

Enter [**2**] [y^x] [**2**] [+⌐−] [**=**].
Remember, $0.25 = \frac{25}{100} = \frac{1}{4}$.

Power of 2	2^5	2^4	2^3	2^2	2^1	2^0	2^{-1}	2^{-2}	2^{-3}	2^{-4}	2^{-5}
Standard form using decimals			8					0.25			
using fractions			8					$\frac{1}{4}$			
Denominator in exponential form								$\frac{1}{2^2}$			

MODULE 3   LABSHEET **4B**

Product Table (Use with Questions 25 and 26 on pages 196–197.)

Directions

- Complete the table with the products that you know how to compute.

- Look for a pattern in the position of the decimal point and the digits in your answer. Use the pattern to complete the table.

Multiplication by Powers of 10		
$235 \cdot 10^3 =$		
$235 \cdot 10^2 =$	$235 \cdot 100 =$	23,500
$235 \cdot 10^1 =$		
$235 \cdot 10^0 =$		
$235 \cdot 10^{-1} =$		
$235 \cdot 10^{-2} =$		
$235 \cdot 10^{-3} =$	$235 \cdot 0.001 =$	

Quotient Table (Use with Questions 27 and 28 on page 197.)

Directions

- Complete the table with the quotients that you know how to compute.

- Look for a pattern in the position of the decimal point and the digits in your answer. Use the pattern to complete the table.

Division by Powers of 10		
$2300 \div 10^3 =$		
$2300 \div 10^2 =$	$2300 \div 100 =$	23
$2300 \div 10^1 =$		
$2300 \div 10^0 =$		
$2300 \div 10^{-1} =$	$2300 \div 0.1 =$	
$2300 \div 10^{-2} =$		
$2300 \div 10^{-3} =$		

MODULE 3   LABSHEET <u>6A</u>

Flags with Triangles (Use with Questions 3–5 on page 217.)

Directions

• Measure the lengths of the sides of one triangle on each flag to the nearest millimeter. Record the measurements next to each flag.

• Based on the lengths of the sides, separate the triangles you measured into 3 groups and complete the first two blank columns of the table.

• In the last column of the table, explain your method for grouping the triangles.

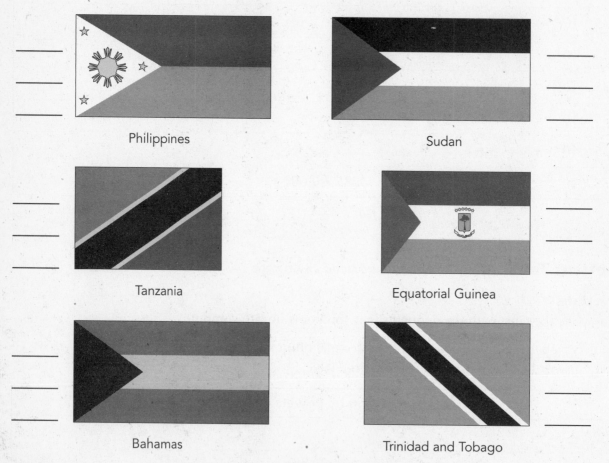

Philippines   Sudan

Tanzania   Equatorial Guinea

Bahamas   Trinidad and Tobago

Group	Countries	Lengths of sides of triangles (mm)	Reason for grouping
1			
2			
3			

Name _____   **Problem** _____

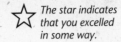
The star indicates that you excelled in some way.

 Problem Solving

❶   ❷   ❸   ❹   ❺

❶ You did not understand the problem well enough to get started or you did not show any work.

❸ You understood the problem well enough to make a plan and to work toward a solution.

❺ You made a plan, you used it to solve the problem, and you verified your solution.

 Mathematical Language

❶   ❷   ❸   ❹   ❺

❶ You did not use any mathematical vocabulary or symbols, or you did not use them correctly, or your use was not appropriate.

❸ You used appropriate mathematical language, but the way it was used was not always correct or other terms and symbols were needed.

❺ You used mathematical language that was correct and appropriate to make your meaning clear.

 Representations

❶   ❷   ❸   ❹   ❺

❶ You did not use any representations such as equations, tables, graphs, or diagrams to help solve the problem or explain your solution.

❸ You made appropriate representations to help solve the problem or help you explain your solution, but they were not always correct or other representations were needed.

❺ You used appropriate and correct representations to solve the problem or explain your solution.

 **Connections**

❶   ❷   ❸   ❹   ❺

❶ You attempted or solved the problem and then stopped.

❸ You found patterns and used them to extend the solution to other cases, or you recognized that this problem relates to other problems, mathematical ideas, or applications.

❺ You extended the ideas in the solution to the general case, or you showed how this problem relates to other problems, mathematical ideas, or applications.

 Presentation

❶   ❷   ❸   ❹   ❺

❶ The presentation of your solution and reasoning is unclear to others.

❸ The presentation of your solution and reasoning is clear in most places, but others may have trouble understanding parts of it.

❺ The presentation of your solution and reasoning is clear and can be understood by others.

Content Used: _____   **Computational Errors:**   Yes   No

Notes on Errors: _____

_____

STUDENT | SELF-ASSESSMENT SCALES

If your score is in the shaded area, explain why on the back of this sheet and stop.

☆ The star indicates that you excelled in some way.

 ### Problem Solving

① ② ③ ④ ⑤ ☆

① I did not understand the problem well enough to get started or I did not show any work.

③ I understood the problem well enough to make a plan and to work toward a solution.

⑤ I made a plan, I used it to solve the problem, and I verified my solution.

 ### Mathematical Language

① ② ③ ④ ⑤ ☆

① I did not use any mathematical vocabulary or symbols, or I did not use them correctly, or my use was not appropriate.

③ I used appropriate mathematical language, but the way it was used was not always correct or other terms and symbols were needed.

⑤ I used mathematical language that was correct and appropriate to make my meaning clear.

 ### Representations

① ② ③ ④ ⑤ ☆

① I did not use any representations such as equations, tables, graphs, or diagrams to help solve the problem or explain my solution.

③ I made appropriate representations to help solve the problem or help me explain my solution, but they were not always correct or other representations were needed.

⑤ I used appropriate and correct representations to solve the problem or explain my solution.

 ### Connections

① ② ③ ④ ⑤ ☆

① I attempted or solved the problem and then stopped.

③ I found patterns and used them to extend the solution to other cases, or I recognized that this problem relates to other problems, mathematical ideas, or applications.

⑤ I extended the ideas in the solution to the general case, or I showed how this problem relates to other problems, mathematical ideas, or applications.

 ### Presentation

① ② ③ ④ ⑤ ☆

① The presentation of my solution and reasoning is unclear to others.

③ The presentation of my solution and reasoning is clear in most places, but others may have trouble understanding parts of it.

⑤ The presentation of my solution and reasoning is clear and can be understood by others.

| MODULE 3 SECTION 1 | PRACTICE AND APPLICATIONS |

For use with Exploration 1

1. Find all the factors of each number.

    a. 10   **b.** 14   **c.** 18

    d. 62   **e.** 81   **f.** 98

    g. 125   **h.** 169   **i.** 230

2. Tell whether each number is *prime* or *composite*.

    a. 5   **b.** 14   **c.** 17

    d. 26   **e.** 27   **f.** 35

    g. 49   **h.** 61   **i.** 55

3. Find the prime factorization of each number.

    a. 18   **b.** 24   **c.** 27

    d. 35   **e.** 38   **f.** 40

    g. 125   **h.** 110   **i.** 150

4. Tour Bus A has 42 people and Tour Bus B has 36 people. The two buses are going to a historic mansion together. At the mansion the people will be divided into smaller groups to go on guided tours. Each group must contain people from both buses, and the people from each bus must be divided evenly among the groups.

    a. List all the possible ways the groups can be set up.

    b. The mansion limits the size of each tour group to a maximum of 15 people. Which groups will be allowed on the tours?

5. For each rectangle:
    Find the area and the perimeter.
    Find the length and width of a rectangle with the same area and a smaller perimeter.
    Find the length and width of a rectangle with the same area and a greater perimeter.

    a. [rectangle] 2 in. / 9 in.   **b.** [rectangle] 2 m / 16 m   **c.** [rectangle] 2 ft / 10 ft

(continued)

MODULE 3 SECTION 1   **PRACTICE AND APPLICATIONS**

For use with Exploration 2

6. Tell whether each number is divisible by each of the numbers 2, 3, 4, 5, 6, 9, and 10.

a. 35	**b.** 44	**c.** 118
d. 138	**e.** 141	**f.** 225
g. 279	**h.** 350	**i.** 371
j. 420	**k.** 608	**l.** 685

7. Find the greatest common factor of each group of numbers.

a. 12, 24	**b.** 16, 36	**c.** 20, 45
d. 15, 24	**e.** 12, 25	**f.** 14, 42
g. 54, 126	**h.** 50, 125	**i.** 16, 20, 30
j. 9, 18, 21	**k.** 18, 24, 32	**l.** 60, 84, 108
m. 72, 88, 136	**n.** 55, 121, 132	**o.** 28, 42, 84

8. Mr. Brown has $76.50. She wants to distribute the money evenly between her 2 nieces and 4 nephews. Can she do this? Explain.

9. Find the least common multiple of each group of numbers.

a. 4, 5	**b.** 12, 20	**c.** 18, 10
d. 15, 25	**e.** 64, 16	**f.** 3, 8, 12
g. 54, 126	**h.** 50, 125	**i.** 16, 20, 30
j. 9, 18, 21	**k.** 18, 24, 32	**l.** 60, 84, 108

10. The price for one type of balloon is $.16. Another type costs $.20 per balloon. Suppose the same amount of money is spent on each type.

a. What is the least total amount that can be spent?

b. How many of each type of balloon are there when you spend the least total amount?

MODULE 3 SECTION 2   PRACTICE AND APPLICATIONS

For use with Exploration 1

1. Write each fraction in lowest terms.

    a. $\dfrac{4}{16}$ **b.** $\dfrac{18}{27}$ **c.** $\dfrac{15}{35}$

    d. $\dfrac{6}{9}$ **e.** $\dfrac{12}{20}$ **f.** $\dfrac{25}{30}$

    g. $\dfrac{42}{77}$ **h.** $\dfrac{21}{36}$ **i.** $\dfrac{18}{81}$

2. Tell whether each fraction is *greater than* or *less than* $\dfrac{1}{2}$.

    a. $\dfrac{11}{19}$ **b.** $\dfrac{14}{30}$ **c.** $\dfrac{63}{130}$

3. Tell whether each fraction is closer to $0, \dfrac{1}{2},$ or 1.

    a. $\dfrac{1}{12}$ **b.** $\dfrac{5}{8}$ **c.** $\dfrac{8}{9}$

    d. $\dfrac{3}{7}$ **e.** $\dfrac{2}{15}$ **f.** $\dfrac{9}{10}$

4. Replace each ___?___ with >, <, or =.

    a. $\dfrac{4}{5}$ __?__ $\dfrac{4}{15}$ **b.** $\dfrac{7}{8}$ __?__ $\dfrac{8}{9}$ **c.** $\dfrac{2}{5}$ __?__ $\dfrac{2}{3}$

    d. $\dfrac{8}{15}$ __?__ $\dfrac{64}{120}$ **e.** $\dfrac{11}{12}$ __?__ $\dfrac{23}{27}$ **f.** $\dfrac{19}{37}$ __?__ $\dfrac{41}{95}$

For use with Exploration 2

5. Find each sum or difference. Write each answer in lowest terms.

    a. $\dfrac{1}{4} + \dfrac{3}{5}$ **b.** $\dfrac{5}{8} + \dfrac{1}{4}$ **c.** $\dfrac{5}{12} + \dfrac{3}{8}$

    d. $\dfrac{7}{10} - \dfrac{3}{5}$ **e.** $\dfrac{8}{9} - \dfrac{5}{12}$ **f.** $\dfrac{7}{8} - \dfrac{1}{2}$

6. Kim has $\dfrac{3}{4}$ c celery. He uses $\dfrac{3}{8}$ c celery to make a tuna salad. He uses

    $\dfrac{1}{6}$ c celery to make a sauce. How much celery does Kim have left?

(continued)

MODULE 3 SECTION 2   PRACTICE AND APPLICATIONS

For use with Exploration 3

7. A bag holds 4 items: a crayon, a ball, a cube, and a jack. Suppose you conduct an experiment by drawing one item at a time from the bag until all items have been drawn. Use the tree diagram to help you answer the questions.

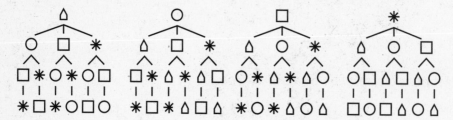

a. How many outcomes are possible for the experiment?

b. Does this experiment involve replacement?

8. Refer to the tree diagram for Exercise 7. Event A is taking a crayon out first and taking a cube out second. Event B is taking a ball out first and taking a crayon out second. Find the probability of each event.

a. $P(A)$ **b.** $P(B)$ **c.** $P(A \text{ or } B)$

9. Refer to the tree diagram for Exercise 7.

a. Event A is taking a crayon out first, taking a cube out second, and taking a ball out third. Find $P(A)$. If Event A occurs, what will be the last item you take out of the bag?

b. Event B is drawing a cube on the first draw. Find $P(B)$.

c. What is the probability of drawing a crayon or a ball on the first draw?

10. Three children decide to let their mother draw the numbers 1, 2, and 3 out of a hat to assign chores. The "1" corresponds to taking out the garbage. The "2" corresponds to setting the table. The "3" corresponds to washing the dishes.

a. Would it make sense to put each number back in the hat before taking out the next number? Why or why not?

b. Draw a tree diagram to show all the possible outcomes.

c. What is the probability that the first draw is 1? What is the probability that the first draw is a 2 and the second draw is a 3?

Name _____ Date _____

For use with Exploration 1

1. Write each fraction as a mixed number.

   a. $\dfrac{15}{4}$ **b.** $\dfrac{9}{5}$ **c.** $\dfrac{22}{6}$

   d. $\dfrac{13}{8}$ **e.** $\dfrac{11}{3}$ **f.** $\dfrac{35}{8}$

2. Write each mixed number or whole number as a fraction.

   a. $1\dfrac{7}{12}$ **b.** $2\dfrac{5}{6}$ **c.** 8

   d. $5\dfrac{1}{3}$ **e.** $9\dfrac{3}{8}$ **f.** $12\dfrac{4}{5}$

3. Replace each __?__ with >, <, or =.

   a. $2\dfrac{1}{2}$ __?__ $\dfrac{5}{3}$ **b.** $\dfrac{9}{8}$ __?__ $1\dfrac{1}{8}$ **c.** 8 __?__ $\dfrac{9}{2}$

   d. $\dfrac{17}{6}$ __?__ $3\dfrac{1}{6}$ **e.** $\dfrac{27}{5}$ __?__ $5\dfrac{5}{2}$ **f.** $3\dfrac{2}{3}$ __?__ $\dfrac{8}{3}$

For use with Exploration 2

4. Find each sum or difference. Write each answer in lowest terms.

   a. $1\dfrac{2}{3}+2\dfrac{1}{4}$ **b.** $3\dfrac{1}{5}+4\dfrac{2}{3}$ **c.** $6\dfrac{1}{4}+2\dfrac{5}{8}$

   d. $8\dfrac{2}{3}-3\dfrac{1}{4}$ **e.** $10\dfrac{5}{9}-4\dfrac{1}{6}$ **f.** $15\dfrac{1}{2}-8\dfrac{3}{4}$

   g. $2\dfrac{1}{6}+3\dfrac{2}{3}$ **h.** $3\dfrac{3}{8}+4\dfrac{3}{4}$ **i.** $5\dfrac{1}{6}+7\dfrac{1}{2}$

5. Annie ran $3\dfrac{1}{2}$ mi on Monday and $4\dfrac{3}{4}$ mi on Wednesday. How many more miles must Annie run if she wants to run 15 miles by Friday?

6. To make school banners, volunteers need $32\dfrac{5}{8}$ yd of fabric.

   a. They have $18\dfrac{1}{2}$ yd of fabric. How many more yards of fabric do they need?

   b. A parent donates $10\dfrac{2}{3}$ yd of fabric. How many more yards of fabric will the volunteers need now?

MODULE 3 SECTION 4   **PRACTICE AND APPLICATIONS**

For use with Exploration 1

1. Write each number in words.

  a. 3284.15   **b.** 0.835   **c.** 5.025

  d. 2.003   **e.** 0.0103   **f.** 10.061

  g. 0.00205   **h.** 5.0001   **i.** 31.502

2. Write each number as a fraction or a mixed number.

  a. 0.73   **b.** 41.9   **c.** 0.305

  d. 0.0063   **e.** 1.0071   **f.** 4.36005

  g. 6.0804   **h.** 12.01012   **i.** 18.00026

3. Write each number as a fraction or mixed number in lowest terms.

  a. 0.002   **b.** 0.18   **c.** 14.6

  d. 2.125   **e.** 3.05   **f.** 10.105

  g. 6.50   **h.** 9.4   **i.** 7.225

4. Replace each __?__ with >, <, or =.

  a. 0.36 __?__ 0.036   **b.** 1.895 __?__ 1.859   **c.** 0.209 __?__ 0.3

  d. 14.091 __?__ 14.101   **e.** 0.72 __?__ 0.720   **f.** 8.61 __?__ 8.612

  g. 42.7 __?__ 4.27   **h.** 0.008 __?__ 0.080   **i.** 0.518 __?__ 0.517

  j. 0.39 __?__ 0.391   **k.** 17.6 __?__ 17.59   **l.** 0.25 __?__ 0.205

  m. 0.032 __?__ 0.0320   **n.** 0.46 __?__ 0.416   **o.** 19.8 __?__ 20.12

5. To pass inspection, a bolt must be between 0.45 and 0.55 cm wide.

  a. Which of the following bolts will pass inspection: 0.445, 0.521, 0.457, 0.553, 0.551, 0.459, 0.5, 0.508, 0.52, 0.46, and 0.533?

  b. Order the bolts that will pass inspection in order of increasing width.

(continued)

Name _____   Date _____

For use with Exploration 2

6. Write each power of ten in standard form.

   a. 10^3 **b.** 10^5 **c.** 10^0

   d. 10^{-2} **e.** 10^4 **f.** 10^{-3}

   g. 10^6 **h.** 10^{-4} **i.** 10^{-1}

7. Write each power as a fraction with its denominator in standard form.

   a. 2^{-5} **b.** 4^{-3} **c.** 9^{-2}

   d. 6^{-3} **e.** 15^{-2} **f.** 30^{-3}

8. Write each number in exponential form with base 10.

   a. 10,000,000   **b.** 0.1   **c.** 1000

   d. 0.00001   **e.** 1   **f.** 0.001

For use with Exploration 3

9. Write each product or quotient in standard form.

   a. $4.6 \cdot 10^4$ **b.** $16.35 \cdot 10^{-4}$ **c.** $14.2413 \cdot 10^3$

   d. $3.47 \cdot 10^4$ **e.** $0.0351 \cdot 10^3$ **f.** $231,467 \cdot 10^{-6}$

   g. $6215 \div 10^2$ **h.** $572 \div 1000$ **i.** $42 \div 0.001$

10. Write each number in scientific notation.

   a. 16,302   **b.** 0.0047   **c.** 6325.7

   d. 0.2416   **e.** 624,100   **f.** 0.000058

11. The polar diameter of Earth is $7.8998 \cdot 10^3$ mi. The mean diameter of Earth is $7.91752 \cdot 10^3$ mi.

   a. Write each diameter in standard form.

   b. Which diameter is greater?

MODULE 3 SECTION 5   **PRACTICE AND APPLICATIONS**

For use with Exploration 1

1. Replace each ___?___ with the correct conversion.

   a. 400 cm = ___?___ m

   b. 36 km = ___?___ m

   c. 9.21 cm = ___?___ mm

   d. 900 m = ___?___ km

   e. 1.8 km = ___?___ cm

   f. 27.8 mm = ___?___ m

   g. 7.1 cm = ___?___ km

   h. 600 km = ___?___ mm

   i. 763 m = ___?___ cm

   j. 256 mm = ___?___ cm

2. Replace each ___?___ with >, <, or =.

   a. 0.056 km ___?___ 5.6 m

   b. 3120 mm ___?___ 3.12 m

   c. 9 cm ___?___ 12 mm

   d. 19.6 cm ___?___ 18.1 m

   e. 7.01 cm ___?___ 10 km

   f. 6.2 mm ___?___ 62 km

   g. 86 mm ___?___ 25 cm

   h. 5.6 km ___?___ 5600 mm

3. Todd jumped 0.0015 km in a long jump. How many meters did Todd jump? How many centimeters?

For use with Exploration 2

4. Use benchmarks to estimate and draw a segment with each length. Then check your estimates with a metric ruler.

   a. 5 cm

   b. 80 mm

   c. 0.3 m

5. Copy each measurement. Then place a decimal point in the number so that the measurement is reasonable.

   a. thickness of a ruler: 200 mm

   b. height of a desk: 60 m

   c. length of a pencil: 1370 cm

   d. length of a car: 85 m

MODULE 3   SECTION 6   **PRACTICE AND APPLICATIONS**

For use with Exploration 1

1. Use a compass and a ruler to construct each triangle. Label the sides with their lengths.

   a. an isosceles triangle with sides of length 5 in., 5 in., and 6 in.

   b. a scalene triangle with sides of length 2 in., 4 in., and 5 in.

   c. an equilateral triangle with sides of length $2\frac{1}{2}$ in.

2. Tell whether each set of side lengths *can* or *cannot* form a triangle. If they can, tell whether the triangle is *isosceles*, *equilateral*, or *scalene*.

   a. 7 cm, 9 cm, 12 cm   **b.** 18 in., 18 in., 23 in.

   c. 8 km, 15 km, 24 km   **d.** 31 in., 31 in., 22 in.

   e. 3.8 m, 3.8 m, 3.8 m   **f.** 6.5 in., 7.3 in., 15 in.

   g. 4.1 ft, 5.8 ft, 6.2 ft   **h.** $2\frac{1}{2}$ ft, $4\frac{1}{4}$ ft, 8 ft

3. An artist is etching an isosceles triangle in a metal plate. The lengths of two of the sides of the triangle are 4 cm long. Which length *cannot* be the length of the third side of the triangle: 4 cm, 6.9 cm or 11 cm?

For use with Exploration 2

4. Solve. Check each answer.

   a. $\frac{x}{3} = 8$ **b.** $4q = 28$ **c.** $8 = \frac{y}{4}$

   d. $380 = 10k$ **e.** $12 = \frac{y}{6}$ **f.** $\frac{x}{5} = 30$

   g. $6x = 126$ **h.** $15y = 90$ **i.** $\frac{z}{32} = 4$

   j. $8h = 208$ **k.** $85 = 5y$ **l.** $1 = \frac{x}{18}$

5. Write a multiplication or division equation to model each situation. Then solve each equation.

   a. Jeremy has 4 times as many baseball cards as football cards. He has 116 baseball cards.

   b. A fruit stand has twice as many bushels of apples as pears. The fruit stand has 18 bushels of pears.

MODULE 3 SECTIONS 1–6   PRACTICE AND APPLICATIONS

For use with Section 1

1. Find all the factors of each number.

    a. 23   **b.** 36   **c.** 45

2. Tell whether each number is *prime* or *composite*.

    a. 37   **b.** 39   **c.** 42

    d. 63   **e.** 83   **f.** 95

3. Find the prime factorization of each number.

    a. 42   **b.** 56   **c.** 65

For use with Section 2

4. Replace each __?__ with >, <, or =.

    a. $\dfrac{5}{9}$ __?__ $\dfrac{5}{11}$ **b.** $\dfrac{47}{48}$ __?__ $\dfrac{48}{49}$ **c.** $\dfrac{12}{25}$ __?__ $\dfrac{10}{12}$

    d. $\dfrac{24}{25}$ __?__ $\dfrac{8}{9}$ **e.** $\dfrac{14}{25}$ __?__ $\dfrac{14}{27}$ **f.** $\dfrac{9}{16}$ __?__ $\dfrac{13}{18}$

5. Find each sum or difference. Write each answer in lowest terms.

    a. $\dfrac{2}{3} - \dfrac{4}{9}$ **b.** $\dfrac{11}{12} - \dfrac{5}{8}$ **c.** $\dfrac{4}{15} + \dfrac{2}{3}$

    d. $\dfrac{3}{8} + \dfrac{1}{6}$ **e.** $\dfrac{2}{3} - \dfrac{5}{11}$ **f.** $\dfrac{5}{12} + \dfrac{2}{9}$

6. Carl has a rock collection. Of the rocks, $\dfrac{3}{8}$ are quartz and $\dfrac{1}{3}$ are granite. What fraction of Carl's rocks are quartz or granite?

For use with Section 3

7. Find each sum or difference. Write each answer in lowest terms.

    a. $3\dfrac{2}{3} + 1\dfrac{5}{9}$ **b.** $6\dfrac{2}{3} - 4\dfrac{2}{5}$ **c.** $48\dfrac{1}{3} - 26\dfrac{1}{2}$

    d. $6\dfrac{3}{4} + 9\dfrac{5}{6}$ **e.** $6\dfrac{3}{4} - 2\dfrac{1}{2}$ **f.** $15 - 4\dfrac{7}{12}$

    g. $78\dfrac{1}{2} - 24\dfrac{3}{4}$ **h.** $12\dfrac{1}{2} + 8\dfrac{7}{10}$ **i.** $18\dfrac{5}{6} - 4\dfrac{3}{5}$

(continued)

MODULE 3 SECTIONS 1–6   **PRACTICE AND APPLICATIONS**

For use with Section 4

8. Write each power of ten in standard form.

   a. 10^1 **b.** 10^2 **c.** 10^{-5}

9. Write each power as a fraction with its denominator in standard form.

   a. 3^{-4} **b.** 5^{-3} **c.** 4^{-4}

10. The mean distance from Earth to the sun is 93,020,000 mi. What is this distance in scientific notation?

For use with Section 5

11. Replace each __?__ with the correct conversion.

   a. 3 km = __?__ mm   **b.** 850 m = __?__ km

   c. 55 mm = __?__ m   **d.** 6.3 cm = __?__ m

12. Replace each __?__ with >, <, or =.

   a. 27,000 m __?__ 27 km   **b.** 12 cm __?__ 6 km

   c. 90 cm __?__ 0.5 m   **d.** 48 mm __?__ 4800 m

13. Leonie is 2.1 m tall and Kyle is 201 cm tall. Who is taller? Explain.

14. Copy each measurement. Then place a decimal point in the number so that the measurement is reasonable.

   a. width of a window: 600 cm

   b. length of a calculator: 1200 cm

For use with Section 6

15. Solve. Check each answer.

   a. $\dfrac{x}{4} = 9$ **b.** $7q = 49$ **c.** $6 = \dfrac{y}{5}$

   d. $360 = 20k$ **e.** $23 = \dfrac{y}{4}$ **f.** $\dfrac{x}{9} = 12$

   g. $3x = 135$ **h.** $21y = 84$ **i.** $\dfrac{z}{25} = 5$

MODULE 3 SECTION 1

It's Universal   Factors, Divisibility, and Multiples

GOAL **LEARN HOW TO:** • find factors
• find the prime factorization of a number
• use divisibility rules to find factors
• find the greatest common factor of two or more numbers
• find the least common multiple of two or more numbers

AS YOU: • explore different clock faces
• explore the Chinese calendar
• work with a January calendar

Exploration 1: Prime Factorization

A **factor** is a number that divides another number with no remainder. A number is **divisible** by another number when it can be divided by that number without leaving a remainder.

The *factors* of 12 are 1, 2, 3, 4, 6, and 12.

12 is *divisible* by 1, 2, 3, 4, 6, and 12.

A **prime** number has only two factors, 1 and itself. A **composite** number has more than two factors. 0 and 1 are neither prime nor composite.

5 is *prime* because its only factors are 1 and 5.

12 is a *composite* number.

The **prime factorization** of a number is the product of its prime factors.

Example

a. Find all the factors of 20.

b. Tell if 20 is prime or composite.

c. Write the prime factorization of 20.

■ Sample Response ■

a. Start a list with 1 and the number 20. Then think of all the other pairs of factors.

$1 \cdot 20 = 20, 2 \cdot 10 = 20,$ and $4 \cdot 5 = 20$

The factors of 20 are 1, 2, 4, 5, 10, and 20.

b. Since there are more than two factors, 20 is a *composite* number.

c. Use a factor tree to find the prime factors of 20.

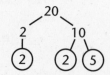

The prime factorization of 20 is $2 \cdot 2 \cdot 5,$ or $2^2 \cdot 5.$

Exploration 2: Common Factors

Divisibility and Common Factors

To find some factors of a number, you can use **divisibility rules**.

A number is divisible by:

- 2, if the number is an even number.
- 3, if the sum of the digits is divisible by 3.
- 4, if the number formed by the tens and ones digits is divisible by 4.
- 5, if the number ends in a 5 or a 0.
- 6, if the ones digit is even and the sum of the digits is divisible by 3.
- 9, if the sum of the digits is divisible by 9.
- 10, if the number ends in a 0.

The **greatest common factor (GCF)** of two or more numbers is the greatest factor that is common to those numbers.

Example

Find the GCF of 12 and 20.

■ Sample Response ■

Make separate lists of the factors. Identify the greatest factors in *both* lists.

factors of 12: **1, 2,** 3, **4,** 6, 12 ⎫
factors of 20: **1, 2, 4,** 5, 20   ⎬ common factors: 1, 2, 4
                                         ⎭

The GCF of 12 and 20 is 4.

Exploration 3: Common Multiples

Multiples

A **multiple** of a whole number is the product of that number and any nonzero whole number.

The **least common multiple (LCM)** of two or more numbers is the least number that is a multiple of each number. For example, to find the LCM of 12 and 20, make partial lists of the multiples until the first common multiple appears.

multiples of 12: 12, 24, 36, 48, **60,** 72, …
multiples of 20: 20, 40, **60,** 80, 100, …

The LCM of 12 and 20 is 60.

| MODULE 3 SECTION 1 | PRACTICE & APPLICATION EXERCISES | STUDY GUIDE |

Exploration 1

Find all the factors of each number.

1. 15   **2.** 63   **3.** 140   **4.** 216

Tell whether each number is *prime* or *composite*. If a number is composite, write its prime factorization.

5. 17   **6.** 47   **7.** 34   **8.** 343

Exploration 2

Tell whether each number is divisible by each of the numbers 2, 3, 4, 5, 6, 9, and 10.

9. 88   **10.** 405   **11.** 540   **12.** 435

Find the greatest common factor of each group of numbers.

13. 45, 150   **14.** 60, 70, 80   **15.** 23, 53

Exploration 3

Find the least common multiple of each group of numbers.

16. 3, 9   **17.** 24, 30   **18.** 5, 15, 45

Spiral Review

Solve. Check each answer. (Module 2, p. 137)

19. $x - 43 = 70$ **20.** $-53 + y = 19$ **21.** $z - 16 = -5$

Find the measure of each angle. Then classify each angle as *acute, obtuse, right,* or *straight*. (Module 2, p. 83)

22.

23.

24.

Find each sum or difference. (Toolbox, p. 587)

25. $\frac{4}{5} + \frac{1}{5}$ **26.** $\frac{8}{9} - \frac{5}{9}$ **27.** $\frac{13}{57} + \frac{25}{57}$ **28.** $\frac{12}{49} - \frac{3}{49}$

Mathematically Speaking   Fractions and Tree Diagrams

GOAL   **LEARN HOW TO:** • write fractions in lowest terms
   • compare fractions using least common denominators
   • add and subtract fractions with unlike denominators
   • use a tree diagram to find outcomes and probabilities

   As you: • read a flow chart
   • explore fraction models
   • think about choosing marbles from a jar

Exploration 1: Comparing Fractions

Equivalent Fractions

Fractions that represent the same amount are **equivalent fractions**. To find an equivalent fraction, you multiply or divide the numerator and denominator by the same number.

A fraction is written in **lowest terms** when the greatest common factor of the numerator and denominator is 1. For example, to write $\frac{36}{81}$ in lowest terms, divide the numerator and denominator by their GCF, 9.

$$\frac{36}{81} = \frac{36 \div 9}{81 \div 9} = \frac{4}{9}$$

Comparing Fractions

The **least common denominator** of two fractions is the least common multiple of the denominators. Fractions can be compared by renaming them as equivalent fractions using the least common denominator.

Example

Compare $\frac{3}{4}$ and $\frac{5}{7}$.

■ Sample Response ■

The LCM of 4 and 7 is 28. So the least common denominator of $\frac{3}{4}$ and $\frac{5}{7}$ is 28.

Rename each fraction as an equivalent fraction with the common denominator.

$$\frac{3}{4} = \frac{3 \cdot 7}{4 \cdot 7} = \frac{21}{28} \quad \text{and} \quad \frac{5}{7} = \frac{5 \cdot 4}{7 \cdot 4} = \frac{20}{28}$$

Compare the fractions that have the same denominator.

$$\frac{21}{28} > \frac{20}{28}, \text{ so } \frac{3}{4} > \frac{5}{7}$$

MODULE 3 SECTION 2	STUDY GUIDE

Exploration 2: Adding and Subtracting Fractions

Adding and Subtracting Fractions

You can add or subtract fractions by using a common denominator.

Example

Find $\frac{2}{5} + \frac{3}{8}$.

■ **Sample Response** ■

The LCM of 5 and 8 is 40. So, the least common denominator of $\frac{2}{5}$ and $\frac{3}{8}$ is 40.

Rename each fraction as an equivalent fraction with the common denominator.

$\frac{2}{5} = \frac{2 \cdot 8}{5 \cdot 8} = \frac{16}{40}$ and $\frac{3}{8} = \frac{3 \cdot 5}{8 \cdot 5} = \frac{15}{40}$

Add the equivalent fractions and simplify if possible.

$\frac{16}{40} + \frac{15}{40} = \frac{31}{40}$, so $\frac{2}{5} + \frac{3}{8} = \frac{31}{40}$

Exploration 3: Tree Diagrams and Probability

Tree Diagrams

A **tree diagram** is a display whose branches show all the possible outcomes of an experiment.

Example

There are three balls in a bag. One is labeled X, one Y, and one Z. You choose two balls, one after the other, from the bag without looking. If event A is choosing a ball labeled X first and choosing a ball labeled Y second, find $P(A)$ when:

a. the first ball chosen is replaced.   **b.** the first ball chosen is not replaced.

■ **Sample Response** ■

a.

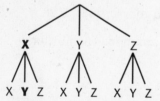

There are 9 possible outcomes, only one of which is X first, then Y.

So, $P(A) = \frac{1}{9}$.

b.

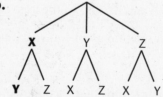

There are just 6 possible outcomes, with one being X first, then Y.

So, $P(A) = \frac{1}{6}$.

| MODULE 3 SECTION 2 | PRACTICE & APPLICATION EXERCISES | STUDY GUIDE |

Exploration 1

Write each fraction in lowest terms.

1. $\dfrac{6}{18}$

2. $\dfrac{21}{27}$

3. $\dfrac{240}{360}$

4. $\dfrac{35}{55}$

Choosing a Method Tell whether you would use *mental math*, *estimation*, or *paper-and-pencil* to compare each pair of fractions. Then replace each ___?___ with >, <, or =.

5. $\dfrac{3}{11}$ __?__ $\dfrac{3}{8}$

6. $\dfrac{4}{13}$ __?__ $\dfrac{9}{13}$

7. $\dfrac{6}{35}$ __?__ $\dfrac{3}{7}$

Exploration 2

Find each sum or difference. Write each answer in lowest terms.

8. $\dfrac{8}{12} - \dfrac{2}{3}$

9. $\dfrac{4}{5} + \dfrac{2}{45}$

10. $\dfrac{11}{18} - \dfrac{3}{15}$

Exploration 3

11. A teacher uses a bag containing 4 cubes—one red, one green, one yellow, and one black—to assign his 24 students to one of four cooperative learning groups. To do this, he has groups of 4 students come to his desk, where each student selects one of the cubes from the bag without looking.

  a. If the teacher wants the same number of students in each group, would it make sense for students to put their cube back in the bag before the next student chooses a cube? Why or why not?

  b. Draw a tree diagram to show all the possible outcomes for a set of four drawings.

  c. What is the probability that the first draw puts a student on the green team and the second draw puts a student on the red team?

Spiral Review

Find the GCF of each pair of numbers. (Module 3, p. 156)

12. 15, 50

13. 45, 36

14. 8, 44

Write each power in standard form. (Module 1, p. 20)

15. 3^5

16. 45^0

17. 10^8

Find each sum or difference. (Toolbox, p. 587)

18. $8\dfrac{2}{5} + 5\dfrac{1}{5}$

19. $6\dfrac{7}{9} - 1\dfrac{5}{9}$

20. $\dfrac{1}{4} + 6\dfrac{3}{4}$

Two Bits for Your Thoughts Fractions and Mixed Numbers

GOAL **LEARN HOW TO:** • write fractions as mixed numbers
• write mixed numbers as fractions
• add and subtract mixed numbers

AS YOU: • exchange colonial money
• think about buying and selling using Spanish dollars and bits

Exploration 1: Renaming Fractions and Mixed Numbers

A **mixed number** is the sum of a nonzero whole number and a fraction between 0 and 1. You can write a fraction as a mixed number.

Example

Write $\frac{13}{4}$ as a mixed number.

■ Sample Response ■

$\frac{13}{4} = \frac{4}{4} + \frac{4}{4} + \frac{4}{4} + \frac{1}{4}$

$= 1 + 1 + 1 + \frac{1}{4}$ ← *Think*: 4 fourths make 1 whole.

$= 3\frac{1}{4}$

You can write a mixed number as a fraction by reversing the process shown in the Example above.

Example

Write $2\frac{1}{8}$ as a fraction.

■ Sample Response ■

$2\frac{1}{8} = 1 + 1 + \frac{1}{8}$ ← *Think*: 1 whole makes 8 eighths.

$= \frac{8}{8} + \frac{8}{8} + \frac{1}{8}$

$= \frac{17}{8}$

Name _____   Date _____

Exploration 2: Adding and Subtracting Mixed Numbers

You can add and subtract mixed numbers.

Example

a. Find $5\frac{2}{3} - 4\frac{1}{3}$.

b. Find $4\frac{3}{4} + 5\frac{1}{2}$.

■ **Sample Response** ■

a.
$$
\begin{array}{r}
5\frac{2}{3} \\
-4\frac{1}{3} \\
\hline
1\frac{1}{3}
\end{array}
$$

b.
$$
\begin{array}{r}
4\frac{3}{4} = \quad 4\frac{3}{4} \\
+5\frac{1}{2} = +5\frac{2}{4} \\
\hline
9\frac{5}{4} = 10\frac{1}{4}
\end{array}
$$
← The common denominator is 4.

Mixed number subtraction problems may require regrouping, where one whole is written as a fraction whose denominator matches the denominator of the fractional part of the mixed number.

Example

Find $7\frac{1}{4} - 2\frac{5}{8}$.

■ **Sample Response** ■

Rewrite each fractional part using a common denominator. Then subtract, regrouping as necessary. The difference should be simplified, if possible.

$$
\begin{array}{r}
7\frac{1}{4} = \quad 7\frac{2}{8} = \quad 6\frac{10}{8} \\
-2\frac{5}{8} = -2\frac{5}{8} = -2\frac{5}{8} \\
\hline
4\frac{5}{8}
\end{array}
$$
← $7\frac{2}{8} = 6 + \frac{8}{8} + \frac{2}{8} = 6\frac{10}{8}$

| MODULE 3 SECTION 3 | PRACTICE & APPLICATION EXERCISES | STUDY GUIDE |

Exploration 1

Write each fraction as a mixed number.

1. $\dfrac{37}{4}$ **2.** $\dfrac{41}{6}$ **3.** $\dfrac{29}{3}$ **4.** $\dfrac{125}{12}$

Write each mixed number or whole number as a fraction.

5. $2\dfrac{3}{4}$ **6.** $11\dfrac{6}{7}$ **7.** $7\dfrac{2}{3}$ **8.** 6

Exploration 2

Find each sum or difference.

9. $2\dfrac{1}{3} + 3\dfrac{5}{6}$ **10.** $12 + 1\dfrac{3}{4}$ **11.** $4\dfrac{1}{9} + 3\dfrac{5}{18}$

12. $14\dfrac{1}{2} - 9\dfrac{1}{3}$ **13.** $4\dfrac{4}{9} - 2\dfrac{1}{3}$ **14.** $9\dfrac{9}{11} - 3\dfrac{5}{7}$

15. $2\dfrac{4}{7} + 3\dfrac{5}{28}$ **16.** $5\dfrac{7}{12} - 3\dfrac{4}{15}$ **17.** $11\dfrac{5}{18} + 1\dfrac{3}{10}$

18. $7\dfrac{1}{3} - 3\dfrac{1}{2}$ **19.** $9\dfrac{3}{22} - 2\dfrac{5}{11}$ **20.** $\dfrac{3}{4} + 5\dfrac{7}{12}$

21. $22 - \dfrac{5}{18}$ **22.** $25 + \dfrac{3}{16}$ **23.** $4\dfrac{1}{10} - 2\dfrac{9}{25}$

24. $15\dfrac{1}{3} - 12\dfrac{3}{16}$ **25.** $4\dfrac{3}{8} + 9\dfrac{5}{24}$ **26.** $10\dfrac{1}{5} - 4\dfrac{2}{3}$

27. **Algebra Connection** Write an equation relating the perimeter and the lengths of the sides of the triangle. Then solve for x.

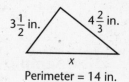

$3\dfrac{1}{2}$ in. $4\dfrac{2}{3}$ in.

x

Perimeter = 14 in.

Spiral Review

Find each sum or difference. (Module 3, p. 170)

28. $\dfrac{1}{2} - \dfrac{2}{5}$ **29.** $\dfrac{2}{3} - \dfrac{2}{15}$ **30.** $\dfrac{7}{9} + \dfrac{2}{5}$

For Exercises 31–33, find each sum or difference.
(Toolbox, p. 581)

31. $0.368 + 2.571$ **32.** $8.25 - 1.099$ **33.** $7.19 + 6.89$

34. What is the measure of each angle formed by the hands on a clock at 3:00? at 6:00? at 2:00? (Module 2, p. 83)

MODULE 3 SECTION 4   **STUDY GUIDE**

Bright Ideas   Decimals and Exponents

GOAL   **LEARN HOW TO:** • compare numbers using the decimal place value system
• write a decimal as a fraction
• use integer exponents to read and write numbers
• multiply and divide decimals by powers of 10
• write numbers in scientific notation

As you: • play a game with square numbers
• explore powers of 10
• look at calculator displays

Exploration 1: Decimal Place Values

In the **decimal place** value system, the position of the digit in
a number determines its value.

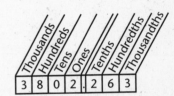

The digits to the left of the decimal point form the whole number
part of the decimal number, while the digits to the right of the
decimal point form the fractional part.

You can compare and order decimals by comparing digits with
the same place value, beginning at the left.

Example

Compare 3.507 and 3.52.

◾ Sample Response ◾

The ones and tenths digits are equal, so compare the hundredths digits.

Since 0 < 2, therefore 3.507 < 3.52.

You can write decimal numbers as fractions or mixed numbers.

Example

Write 3.24 as a fraction or mixed number in lowest terms.

◾ Sample Response ◾

$3.24 = 3\frac{24}{100}$ ← $\frac{24}{100}$ can be simplified; there is a common factor of 4.

$= 3\frac{6}{25}$

MODULE 3 SECTION 4

Exploration 2: Integer Exponents

Positive and negative integers and zero can be used as exponents. A number that can be written in exponential form is a **power** of the base. The 0th power of any nonzero number is 1.

Example

a. Write 6^3 in standard form.   **b.** Write 5^{-4} as a fraction.

Sample Response

a. $6^3 = 6 \cdot 6 \cdot 6 = 216$ ← Read: "6 to the 3rd power (or 6 cubed) equals 216."

b. $5^{-4} = \dfrac{1}{5^4} = \dfrac{1}{5 \cdot 5 \cdot 5 \cdot 5} = \dfrac{1}{625}$ ← Read: "5 to the negative 4th power equals $\dfrac{1}{625}$."

Exploration 3: Scientific Notation

Multiplying and Dividing by Powers of Ten

When multiplying and dividing by powers of ten, the exponent can help you decide where to place the decimal point.

Example

Write each product or quotient in standard form.

a. $16.234 \cdot 10^2$ **b.** $16.234 \cdot 10^{-2}$ **c.** $16.234 \div 10^2$ **d.** $16.234 \div 10^{-2}$

Sample Response

a. $16.234 \cdot 10^2 = 1623.4$ ← Move the decimal point **right** 2 places.

b. $16.234 \cdot 10^{-2} = 0.16234$ ← Move the decimal point **left** 2 places.

c. $16.234 \div 10^2 = 0.16234$ ← Move the decimal point **left** 2 places.

d. $16.234 \div 10^{-2} = 1623.4$ ← Move the decimal point **right** 2 places.

Scientific notation is a way to write numbers as the product of a decimal and a power of 10. The decimal must be greater than or equal to 1 and less than 10. For example, in scientific notation:

$425 = 4.25 \cdot 100 = 4.25 \cdot 10^2$

$0.0015 = 1.5 \cdot 0.001 = 1.5 \cdot 10^{-3}$.

Name _____   Date _____

Exploration 1

Write each number in words and as a fraction or a mixed number.

1. 0.025   **2.** 15.555   **3.** 23.1099   **4.** 18.5

Replace each __?__ with >, <, or =.

5. 0.91 __?__ 0.95   **6.** 3.2 __?__ 3.02   **7.** 15.988 __?__ 13.999

8. 0.901 __?__ 0.0913   **9.** 14.9 __?__ 1.49   **10.** 7.812 __?__ 7.8120

Exploration 2

Write each power of ten in standard form.

11. 10^{-5} **12.** 10^0 **13.** 10^4 **14.** 10^{-2} **15.** 10^{10}

Write each power as a fraction with its denominator in standard form.

16. 5^{-3} **17.** 7^{-1} **18.** 2^{-6} **19.** 3^{-5} **20.** 4^{-2}

Exploration 3

Write each product or quotient in standard form.

21. $2.7 \cdot 10^5$ **22.** $25.19 \cdot 10^{-4}$ **23.** $0.0099 \div 0.0001$

24. $3610 \div 10^2$ **25.** $4.5 \cdot 0.00001$ **26.** $12.768 \div 10^{-3}$

Write each number in scientific notation.

27. 4512   **28.** 0.0305   **29.** 56,983   **30.** 56.9

Spiral Review

Find each sum or difference. (Module 3, p. 170)

31. $9\frac{1}{2} + 2\frac{2}{5}$ **32.** $5\frac{2}{3} - 1\frac{1}{4}$ **33.** $4\frac{7}{9} + 6\frac{1}{18}$ **34.** $3\frac{6}{7} - 2\frac{2}{3}$

Find the volume of a cube with each side length. (Module 1, p. 21)

35. 8 in.   **36.** 4.1 cm   **37.** 2 mm   **38.** 100 ft

MODULE 3 SECTION 5   **STUDY GUIDE**

A Winning Measure   Metric Units of Length

GOAL   **LEARN HOW TO:** • convert from one metric unit to another
• recognize metric benchmarks
• use benchmarks to estimate lengths in metric units

AS YOU: • look at long jump results
• estimate and measure lengths in your classroom

Exploration 1: Metric Conversions

Metric System

Metric measures of length are based on the **meter (m)**. The most
commonly used metric units of length are related as follows:

1 **meter (m)** = 0.001 km = 100 cm = 1000 mm
1 **centimeter (cm)** = 0.01 m = 10 mm
1 **millimeter (mm)** = 0.001 m = 0.1 cm
1 **kilometer (km)** = 1000 m   ← A kilometer is used to measure long distances.

This conversion chart shows the relationship between metric units of length.

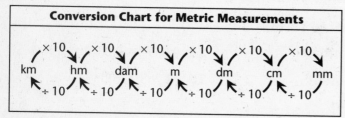

Conversion Chart for Metric Measurements

You change from one metric unit of length to another by multiplying or
dividing by a power of 10.

Example

Replace each ___?___ with the correct measure.

a. 5.3 m = ___?___ mm   **b.** 2.6 cm = ___?___ m

■ **Sample Response** ■

a. Using the conversion chart above, you must multiply by 10 three times to convert
from meters (m) to millimeters (mm).

$5.3 \times 10 \times 10 \times 10 = 5300$, so 5.3 m = 5300 mm

b. Using the conversion chart again, you must divide by 10 twice to convert from
centimeters (cm) to meters (m).

$2.6 \div 10 \div 10 = 0.026$, so 2.6 cm = 0.026 m

MODULE 3 SECTION 5   STUDY GUIDE

Exploration 2: Metric Length Benchmarks

Benchmarks

A **benchmark** is a number or an object that can be used as a reference.
The best benchmarks are ones that can be easily and conveniently used in
a variety of situations.

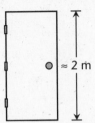

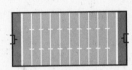

The thickness of
a dime is about
1 mm.

The diameter of
a penny is about
2 cm.

The height of a
door is about
2 m.

Three laps around
a football field is a
distance of about 1 km.

You can use something whose measure you know as a benchmark to
estimate lengths.

Example

Use a benchmark measure to estimate the length of this line segment in centimeters.

■ Sample Response ■

The length of the line segment is about the same as the combined diameters of
4 pennies aligned in a row.

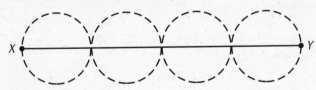

So, the length of the line segment is about 8 cm.

| MODULE 3 SECTION 5 | PRACTICE & APPLICATION EXERCISES | STUDY GUIDE |

Exploration 1

Replace each ___?___ with the correct measure.

1. 315 m = ___?___ cm

2. 2.3 km = ___?___ m

3. 8.112 cm = ___?___ mm

4. 0.07 m = ___?___ km

5. 1256 mm = ___?___ km

6. 7.01 mm = ___?___ cm

Replace each ___?___ with >, <, or =.

7. 7.7 m ___?___ 77 cm

8. 0.17 km ___?___ 170,000 cm

9. 3.1 m ___?___ 310 km

10. 5.4 cm ___?___ 54 mm

Exploration 2

11. Choose the most reasonable measurement for the height of a house.

   A. 6 mm   **B.** 6 cm   **C.** 6 m   **D.** 6 km

12. Choose the most reasonable measurement for the length of a table.

   A. 150 cm   **B.** 150 mm   **C.** 150 m

Spiral Review

Write each number in exponential form with base 10.
(Module 3, p. 198)

13. 100,000

14. 0.01

15. 100

16. 0.000001

Interpreting Data **Doctors say children need to eat and drink foods that have lots of calcium. Milk is one drink that provides calcium. Use the graph for Exercises 17 and 18.** (Module 1, p. 7)

17. About how many glasses of milk do children of age 9 need to drink each day?

18. During what ages do children need to drink about $1\frac{2}{3}$ glasses of milk?

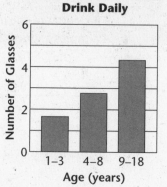

Recommended Amount of Milk Children Should Drink Daily

Solve each equation. Then check each solution. (Module 2, p. 137)

19. $40 = n - 8$

20. $n + 21 = 66$

21. $n - (-4) = 7$

22. $-6 + n = 34$

23. $9 + n = -28$

24. $75 = n - 200$

MODULE 3 SECTION 6   **STUDY GUIDE**

Symbols of the People   Triangles and Equations

GOAL **LEARN HOW TO:** • classify triangles by side length
• construct triangles and circles
• determine which side lengths will form a triangle
• write and solve multiplication and division equations

As you: • examine flags
• explore size relationships in flag design

Exploration 1: Constructing Triangles

Classifying and Constructing Triangles

Two segments equal in length are **congruent**. In the figure, segments AB and CD are congruent. This is written $\overline{AB} \cong \overline{CD}$.

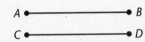

Triangles can be classified by their sides. Triangles with at least two sides congruent are **isosceles** triangles. Triangles with three congruent sides are **equilateral** triangles. Triangles with no congruent sides are **scalene** triangles.

   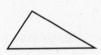

Isosceles Triangle
(at least two congruent sides)

Equilateral Triangle
(three congruent sides)

Scalene Triangle
(no congruent sides)

You can draw a triangle using a compass and a straightedge. These drawings are **constructions**. A triangle can be constructed only if the sum of the lengths of any two sides is greater than the length of the third side.

Example

a. Can a 2 in. segment, a 3 in. segment, and a 7 in. segment form a triangle?

b. Can a 3 cm segment, a 4 cm segment, and a 5 cm segment form a triangle?

■ Sample Response ■

a. Since $2 + 3 < 7$, a triangle cannot be formed.

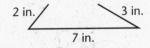

b. Since $3 + 4 > 5$, $4 + 5 > 3$, and $3 + 5 > 4$, a triangle can be formed.

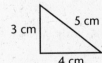

MODULE 3 SECTION 6   STUDY GUIDE

A circle can be constructed using a compass. A **circle** is the set of all points in a plane that are the same distance from a given point called the **center**. A segment drawn from the center of a circle to any point on the circle is called a **radius**. The length of such a segment is also called a radius. A **chord** is a segment that has both endpoints on a circle. Any chord that passes through the center of its circle is a **diameter** of that circle. The length of such a chord is also called a diameter.

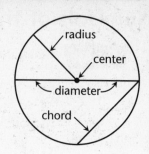

Exploration 2: Multiplication and Division Equations

Multiplication and division are *inverse operations*. They "undo" each other. You can use multiplication and division to solve equations.

In the Example below, the equation is solved by using multiplication to "undo" division.

Example

Solve the equation $\frac{a}{3} = 17$.

■ Sample Response ■

$\frac{a}{3} = 17$ $\leftarrow$ *a* is *divided* by 3.

$3 \cdot \frac{a}{3} = 3 \cdot 17$ $\leftarrow$ *Multiply* both sides by 3.

$a = 51$

Division "undoes" multiplication when solving the equation in the following Example.

Example

Solve the equation $4x = 68$.

■ Sample Response ■

$4x = 68$ $\leftarrow$ *x* is *multiplied* by 4.

$\frac{4x}{4} = \frac{68}{4}$ $\leftarrow$ *Divide* both sides by 4.

$x = 17$

MODULE 3 SECTION 6 | PRACTICE & APPLICATION EXERCISES | STUDY GUIDE

Exploration 1

For Exercises 1–6, tell whether each set of side lengths *can* or *cannot* form a triangle. If they can, tell whether the triangle is *isosceles*, *equilateral*, or *scalene*.

1. 3.1 m, 4.5 m, 3.1 m

2. 8 km, 11 km, 2 km

3. 5 ft, 5 ft, 5 ft

4. $5\frac{1}{2}$ in., $3\frac{2}{3}$ in., $7\frac{1}{8}$ in.

5. 22 mm, 33 mm, 44 mm

6. 5.16 cm, 2.4 cm, 2.4 cm

7. Use a compass and a ruler to construct a triangle whose sides are 4.5 cm, 5.5 cm, and 6.6 cm long. Label the sides with their lengths. Classify the triangle as *isosceles*, *equilateral*, or *scalene*.

Exploration 2

Solve. Check each answer.

8. $8m = 96$

9. $7 = \frac{t}{8}$

10. $610 = 10h$

11. $48 = \frac{y}{4}$

12. $\frac{n}{6} = 17$

13. $9b = 180$

14. $4 = \frac{d}{311}$

15. $\frac{x}{5} = 11$

Spiral Review

For Exercises 16–19, replace each __?__ with the correct measure. (Module 3, p. 210)

16. 30 km = __?__ m

17. 3.5 cm = __?__ mm

18. 8.07 m = __?__ km

19. 0.6 m = __?__ cm

20. The temperature is 15°F at 11 P.M. It falls 20°F by noon the next day, then rises x°F to a temperature of 18°F by 5 P.M. that afternoon. (Module 2, p. 109)

a. Write an equation involving x to describe the situation.

b. Solve the equation to find the value of x.

Find the perimeter of a rectangle with each length *l* and width *w*. (Toolbox, p. 593)

21. $l = 8$ cm, $w = 6$ cm

22. $l = 4\frac{1}{2}$ ft, $w = 1\frac{3}{4}$ ft

23. $l = 35$ m, $w = 25$ m

24. $l = 10.2$ mm, $w = 7.12$ mm

MODULE 4　　　　　　　　　　　　　　　　　　　　　　**LABSHEET** **1A**

Zoetrope Side Strips　(Use with Question 8 on page 234.)

MODULE 4   LABSHEET **1B**

Animation Strip (Use with Question 10 on page 235.)

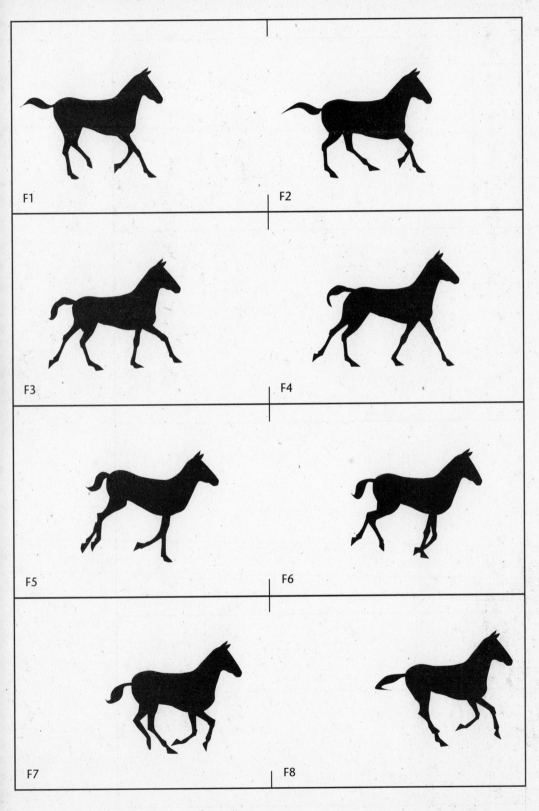

F1

F2

F3

F4

F5

F6

F7

F8

Name Date

MODULE 4 LABSHEET 1C

Animated Rectangle (Use with Questions 13 and 15 on page 236, and Questions 30–31 on page 240.)

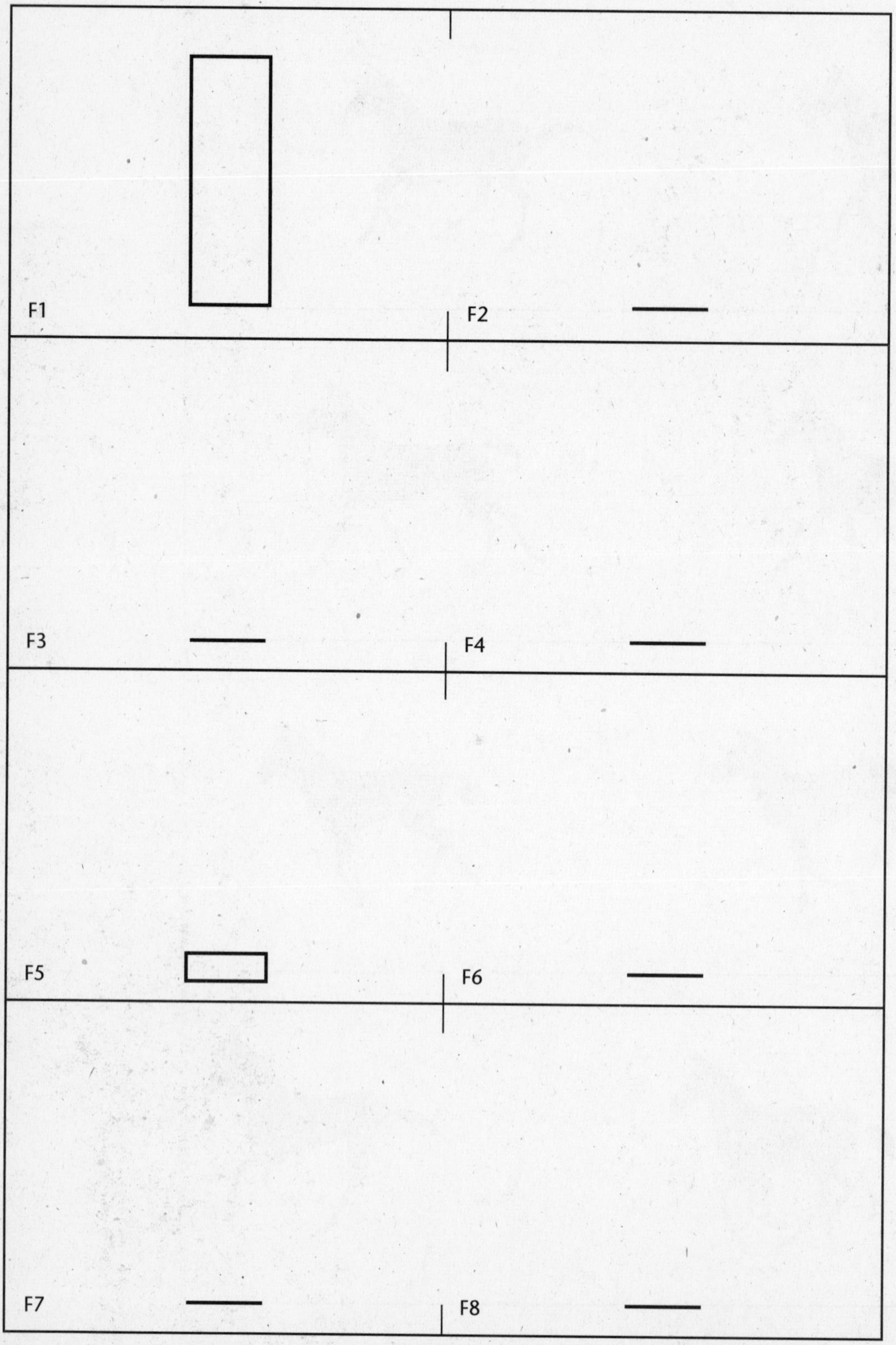
F1
F2
F3
F4
F5
F6
F7
F8

MODULE 4 PROJECT LABSHEET

Blank Zoetrope Strip A

(Use with Project Questions 2 and 3 on pages 260 and 275.)

F1	F2
F3	F4
F5	F6
F7	F8

Name Date

MODULE 4 **LABSHEET 3A**

Jewelry Design Zoetrope Strip (Use with Question 3 on page 263.)

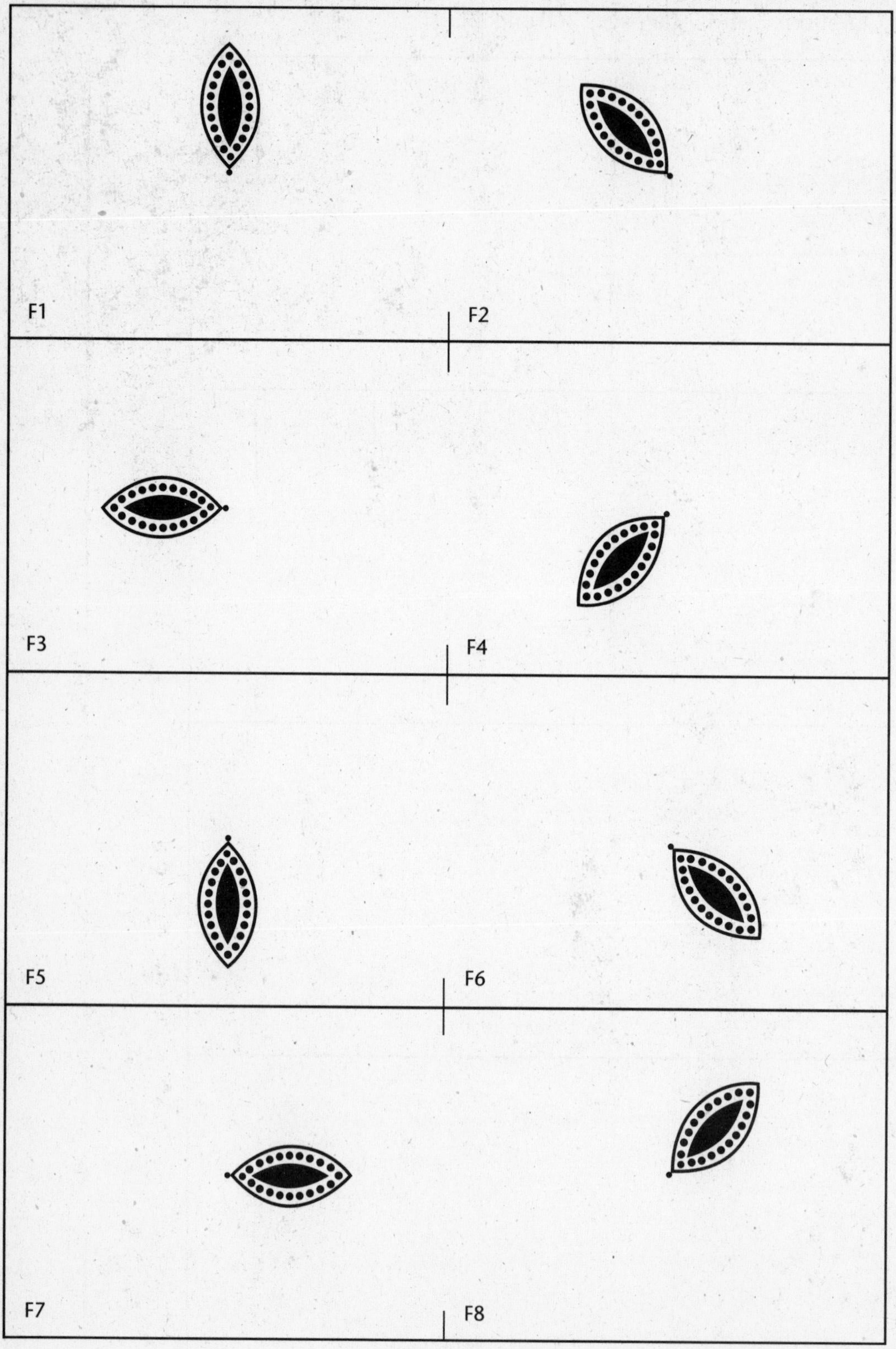
F1
F2
F3
F4
F5
F6
F7
F8

MODULE 4   LABSHEET **3B**

Stick Figure   (Use with Question 4 on page 263.)

Directions

a. Draw a segment from point Y on Stick Figure 1 to point P. Draw another segment from point Z on Stick Figure 2 to point P.

b. Trace Stick Figure 1 and point P on tracing paper.

c. Place your tracing of Stick Figure 1 and point P so it fits exactly on the original.

d. Place the tip of your pencil on point P to keep it from moving. Then rotate your tracing paper clockwise until Stick Figure 1 fits exactly on Stick Figure 2.

e. How many degrees did you have to rotate Stick Figure 1 to match with Stick Figure 2? Explain how you found out.

f. Repeat parts (c)–(e), but this time rotate counterclockwise.

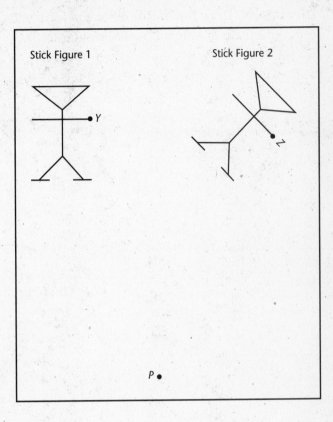

Six-Pointed Star   (Use with Questions 8–9 on page 265.)

Directions

a. Trace the star and point P on tracing paper. Be sure to include the labels.

b. Place your tracing of the star so that it fits exactly on the original star. Then place the tip of your pencil on point P and slowly rotate the tracing clockwise until point A on the tracing reaches point B on the original star.

c. Does the rotated star fit exactly on itself?

d. Continue rotating the tracing of the star clockwise around point P until point A on the tracing reaches points C, D, E, F, and, finally, A on the original star.

e. How many times does the star fit exactly on itself before returning to its original position?

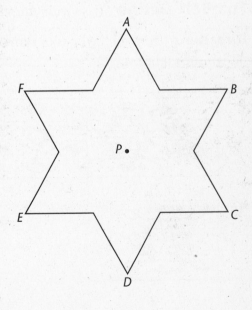

MODULE 4   LABSHEET **3C**

Congruent Butterflies (Use with Question 20 on page 268.)

Directions Draw the line of reflection for a reflection that makes the top butterfly fit exactly on the bottom butterfly.

Fox Belt Design (Use with Question 21 on page 268.)

Directions Draw all the lines of symmetry on each part of the belt design shown below.

a.

b.

c.

MODULE 4   **LABSHEET 3D**

Rotated Stick Figure (Use with Exercises 45 and 46 on page 275.)

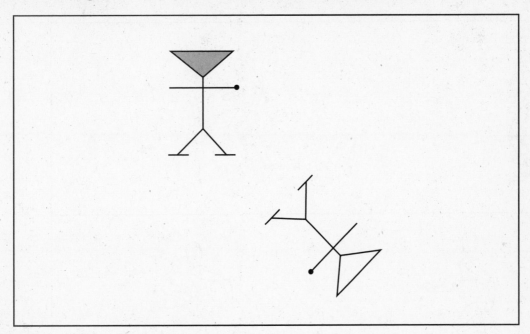

Directions

a. Trace the shaded Stick Figure. Experiment with rotating the shaded figure using different centers of rotation. Then estimate the location of the center of rotation and the amount of rotation that will describe the movement of the shaded figure to its image.

b. Draw a segment connecting any point on the shaded figure with its image.

c. Fold your paper so that the endpoints of the segment you drew in part (b) meet. Mark the fold line with a pencil.

d. Look at the four angles formed where the fold line intersects the segment in part (b). What do you notice?

e. Measure the distance between the point and the fold line, and the distance between the image of the point and the fold line. How do the two distances compare?

f. Mark another point on the shaded figure. Then repeat parts (b)–(e).

g. The center of rotation is the point where the two fold lines intersect. Find the center of rotation and label it point *P*. How does its location compare with your estimate in part (a)?

h. Use a protractor to measure the amount of rotation. How does it compare with your estimate in part (a)?

MODULE 4

A Person Walking Forward (Use with Question 2 on page 279.)

F1

F2

F3

F4

F5

F6

F7

F8

MODULE 4

A Person Walking Backward (Use with Question 3 on page 279.)

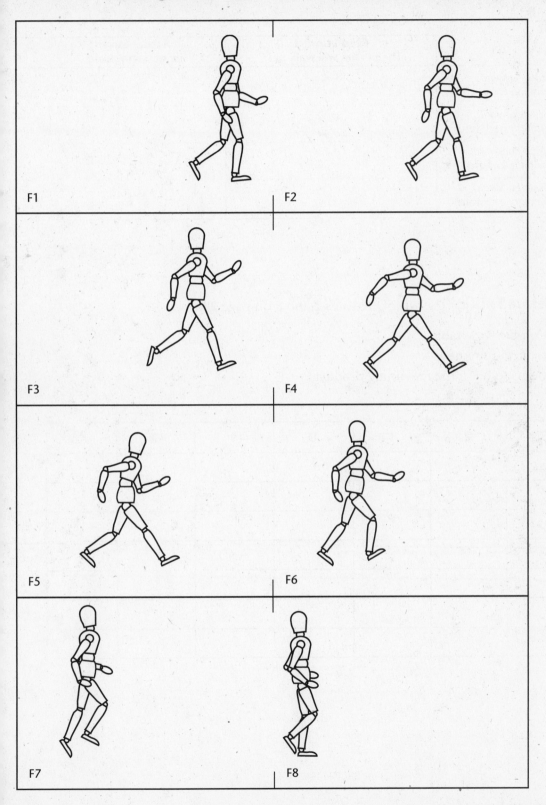

F1

F2

F3

F4

F5

F6

F7

F8

MODULE 4   **LABSHEET 4C**

Walking Person Table (Use with Questions 2–4 on page 279.)

	Prediction: The person will walk . . .	Actual Result: The person walked . . .
A Person Walking Forward (Zoetrope spinning forward)		
A Person Walking Forward (Zoetrope spinning backward)		
A Person Walking Backward (Zoetrope spinning forward)		
A Person Walking Backward (Zoetrope spinning backward)		

Multiplication Table (Use with Questions 7 and 8 on page 280.)

Directions Complete the table.
• Fill in the products you know.
• Look for patterns to fill in the remaining products.

×	3	2	1	0	−1	−2	−3
3							
2							
1							
0							
−1							
−2							
−3							

Translating a Figure   (Use with Question 9 on page 293.)

Directions

a. Suppose figure *WXYZ* shown below is translated using the transformation $(x + 1, y - 2)$. Use the directions *up* or *down* and *left* or *right* to describe the location of the image.

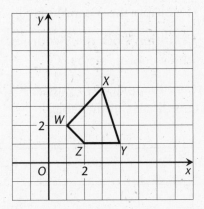

b. Complete the table. Identify the coordinates of the vertices of figure *WXYZ*. Then find the coordinates of the vertices of the image of figure *WXYZ* after the translation $(x + 1, y - 2)$.

	Coordinates of vertices			
Original figure (figure *WXYZ*)	W(__, __)	X(__, __)	Y(__, __)	Z(__, __)
Image (figure *W′X′Y′Z′*)	W′(__, __)	X′(__, __)	Y′(__, __)	Z′(__, __)

c. Use your results from part (b) to draw the image of figure *WXYZ* on the coordinate plane.

d. How does the actual location of the image compare with your prediction in part (a)?

Stretching and Squashing a Figure (Use with Questions 15–17 on pages 294–295.)

Directions

a. Each member of your group should choose a different transformation from the list below.

       Transformation 1: $(3x, y)$ (Multiply the x-coordinate by 3.)

       Transformation 2: $(x, 3y)$ (Multiply the y-coordinate by 3.)

       Transformation 3: $(3x, 3y)$ (Multiply both the x-coordinate and the y-coordinate by 3.)

b. Find the coordinates of the vertices of the image of figure *ABCDE* for your transformation. Record the coordinates in the table.

Original (x, y)	$A(-2, 0)$	$B(-2, 1)$	$C(0, 2)$	$D(2, 1)$	$E(2, 0)$
Transformation (___ , ___)	$A'($ ___ , ___ $)$	$B'($ ___ , ___ $)$	$C'($ ___ , ___ $)$	$D'($ ___ , ___ $)$	$E'($ ___ , ___ $)$

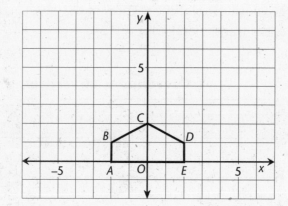

c. Use your results from part (b) to draw the image of figure *ABCDE* on the coordinate plane.

d. Use your group's results from part (c). For each transformation, explain how the image of figure *ABCDE* is different from the original figure. How are the image and the original figure alike?

MODULE 4   LABSHEET **5C**

Flag (Use with Questions 22 and 24 on pages 296 and 297.)

Directions

a. Find the coordinates of the vertices of the image of the flag after the transformation $(2x + 3, 3y - 4)$. Record the coordinates in the table below.

b. Use the coordinates you found to draw the image of the flag on the coordinate plane.

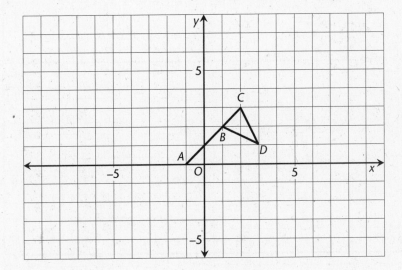

	Image Points		
	x-coordinate (2x + 3)	y-coordinate (3y – 4)	(x, y)
A(–1, 0)	2(–1) + 3 = ___	3(0) – 4 = ____	A'(___ , ___)
B(1, 2)			B'(___ , ___)
C(2, 3)			C'(___ , ___)
D(3, 1)			D'(___ , ___)

MODULE 4   PROJECT LABSHEET

Blank Zoetrope Strip B   (Use with Project Question 6 on page 305.)

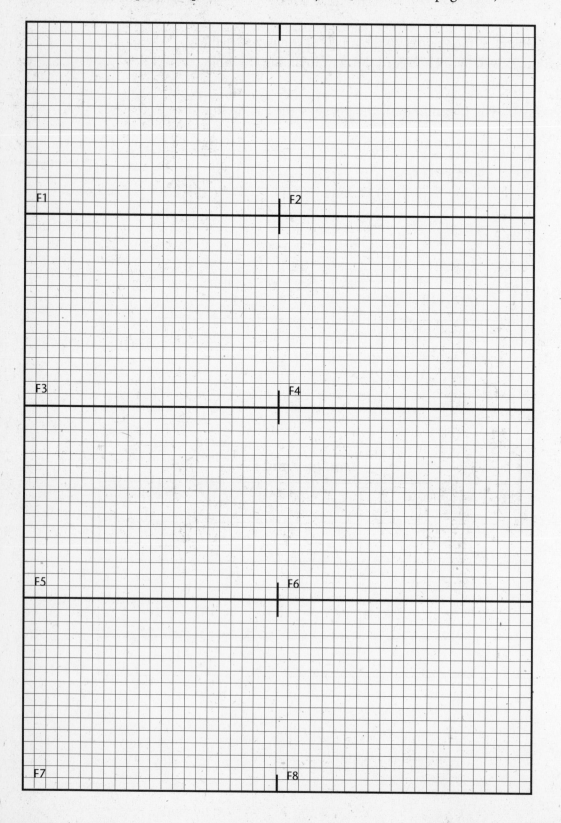

TEACHER **ASSESSMENT SCALES**

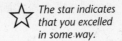
The star indicates that you excelled in some way.

 Problem Solving

1   **2**   **3**   **4**   **5**

You did not understand the problem well enough to get started or you did not show any work.

You understood the problem well enough to make a plan and to work toward a solution.

You made a plan, you used it to solve the problem, and you verified your solution.

 Mathematical Language

1   **2**   **3**   **4**   **5**

You did not use any mathematical vocabulary or symbols, or you did not use them correctly, or your use was not appropriate.

You used appropriate mathematical language, but the way it was used was not always correct or other terms and symbols were needed.

You used mathematical language that was correct and appropriate to make your meaning clear.

 Representations

1   **2**   **3**   **4**   **5**

You did not use any representations such as equations, tables, graphs, or diagrams to help solve the problem or explain your solution.

You made appropriate representations to help solve the problem or help you explain your solution, but they were not always correct or other representations were needed.

You used appropriate and correct representations to solve the problem or explain your solution.

 Connections

1   **2**   **3**   **4**   **5**

You attempted or solved the problem and then stopped.

You found patterns and used them to extend the solution to other cases, or you recognized that this problem relates to other problems, mathematical ideas, or applications.

You extended the ideas in the solution to the general case, or you showed how this problem relates to other problems, mathematical ideas, or applications.

 Presentation

1   **2**   **3**   **4**   **5**

The presentation of your solution and reasoning is unclear to others.

The presentation of your solution and reasoning is clear in most places, but others may have trouble understanding parts of it.

The presentation of your solution and reasoning is clear and can be understood by others.

Content Used: _____   Computational Errors: Yes   No

Notes on Errors: _____

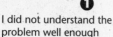

STUDENT   **SELF-ASSESSMENT SCALES**

▬ If your score is in the shaded area, explain why on the back of this sheet and stop.

☆ The star indicates that you excelled in some way.

Problem Solving

①   **②**   **③**   **④**   **⑤**   ☆→

I did not understand the problem well enough to get started or I did not show any work.

I understood the problem well enough to make a plan and to work toward a solution.

I made a plan, I used it to solve the problem, and I verified my solution.

Mathematical Language

①   **②**   **③**   **④**   **⑤**   ☆→

I did not use any mathematical vocabulary or symbols, or I did not use them correctly, or my use was not appropriate.

I used appropriate mathematical language, but the way it was used was not always correct or other terms and symbols were needed.

I used mathematical language that was correct and appropriate to make my meaning clear.

Representations

①   **②**   **③**   **④**   **⑤**   ☆→

I did not use any representations such as equations, tables, graphs, or diagrams to help solve the problem or explain my solution.

I made appropriate representations to help solve the problem or help me explain my solution, but they were not always correct or other representations were needed.

I used appropriate and correct representations to solve the problem or explain my solution.

Connections

①   **②**   **③**   **④**   **⑤**   ☆→

I attempted or solved the problem and then stopped.

I found patterns and used them to extend the solution to other cases, or I recognized that this problem relates to other problems, mathematical ideas, or applications.

I extended the ideas in the solution to the general case, or I showed how this problem relates to other problems, mathematical ideas, or applications.

Presentation

①   **②**   **③**   **④**   **⑤**   ☆→

The presentation of my solution and reasoning is unclear to others.

The presentation of my solution and reasoning is clear in most places, but others may have trouble understanding parts of it.

The presentation of my solution and reasoning is clear and can be understood by others.

MODULE 4 SECTION 1   **PRACTICE AND APPLICATIONS**

For use with Exploration 1

1. Find the circumference of each circle with the given diameter. Use 3.14 or the $\boxed{\pi}$ key on a calculator. Round each answer to the nearest hundredth.

   a. 6 m   **b.** 28 cm   **c.** 34 ft

   d. 18 in.   **e.** 6.3 cm   **f.** 8.2 m

   g. 1.5 ft   **h.** 42 in.   **i.** 17.1 m

2. A circular painting has a radius of $5\frac{1}{2}$ in. What is the circumference of the painting? Use 3.14 or the $\boxed{\pi}$ key on a calculator. Round the answer to the nearest hundredth.

For use with Exploration 2

3. Find each product. Write each answer in lowest terms.

   a. $\frac{2}{5} \cdot \frac{1}{4}$

   b. $\frac{4}{5} \cdot \frac{5}{12}$

   c. $\frac{2}{3} \cdot \frac{9}{10}$

   d. $\frac{3}{4} \cdot \frac{5}{6}$

   e. $\frac{1}{2} \cdot \frac{8}{9}$

   f. $\frac{1}{8} \cdot \frac{1}{5}$

   g. $2\frac{1}{3} \cdot 4\frac{1}{2}$

   h. $3\frac{1}{4} \cdot 2\frac{2}{5}$

   i. $3\frac{1}{4} \cdot 4\frac{3}{8}$

   j. $\frac{3}{8} \cdot \frac{4}{5}$

   k. $\frac{10}{20} \cdot \frac{6}{8}$

   l. $\frac{1}{10} \cdot \frac{2}{3}$

   m. $\frac{16}{25} \cdot \frac{5}{12}$

   n. $\frac{7}{8} \cdot \frac{16}{21}$

   o. $\frac{2}{3} \cdot \frac{4}{9} \cdot \frac{3}{8}$

4. Calvin has $2\frac{5}{6}$ yd of fabric. He uses $\frac{3}{8}$ of the fabric to make a kite. How much of the fabric does Calvin use to make the kite?

5. Find the reciprocal of each number.

   a. $\frac{1}{5}$

   b. $2\frac{1}{6}$

   c. 27

   d. $\frac{6}{7}$

   e. $3\frac{3}{5}$

   f. $\frac{5}{6}$

   g. $\frac{17}{6}$

   h. $4\frac{2}{3}$

   i. 8

(continued)

MODULE 4 SECTION 1   **PRACTICE AND APPLICATIONS**

For use with Exploration 3

6. Find each quotient. Write each answer in lowest terms.

a. $\dfrac{3}{4} \div \dfrac{3}{8}$

b. $\dfrac{18}{5} \div \dfrac{3}{8}$

c. $\dfrac{5}{12} \div \dfrac{3}{4}$

d. $2\dfrac{1}{5} \div \dfrac{1}{5}$

e. $2\dfrac{3}{4} \div \dfrac{1}{3}$

f. $5\dfrac{2}{3} \div 1\dfrac{3}{5}$

g. $4\dfrac{2}{7} \div 2$

h. $3\dfrac{1}{4} \div 1\dfrac{1}{2}$

i. $8 \div \dfrac{4}{5}$

j. $6\dfrac{1}{2} \div 1\dfrac{3}{4}$

k. $16 \div \dfrac{8}{9}$

l. $4\dfrac{2}{3} \div 2\dfrac{1}{3}$

m. $4 \div \dfrac{7}{4}$

n. $8 \div \dfrac{3}{2}$

o. $2 \div \dfrac{3}{4}$

p. $8\dfrac{1}{2} \div \dfrac{5}{8}$

q. $6 \div 3\dfrac{3}{4}$

r. $2\dfrac{1}{3} \div 1\dfrac{1}{2}$

s. $3\dfrac{1}{5} \div 2\dfrac{1}{4}$

t. $4 \div \dfrac{2}{5}$

u. $4 \div \dfrac{3}{4}$

7. Paul has a 15 ft long piece of rope. He wants to cut the rope into sections that are $3\dfrac{3}{4}$ ft long.

    a. How many $3\dfrac{3}{4}$ ft long pieces of rope can Paul make?

    b. Will there be any rope left over? If so, how much?

8. A sculptor has $15\dfrac{3}{8}$ lb of clay. She divides the clay into $1\dfrac{1}{2}$ lb pieces to use for models.

    a. How many pieces of clay does the sculptor have?

    b. Is there any clay left over? If so, how much?

9. A baker at the Delicious Breadbasket Bakery uses $3\dfrac{2}{3}$ c flour for each small loaf of French bread that he makes. He uses $4\dfrac{3}{4}$ c flour for every large loaf of French bread he makes. He always makes the same number of small and large loaves of French bread.

    a. How much flour does he use for one small loaf and one large loaf?

    b. How much flour will he need to make a total of 12 loaves of French bread?

| **MODULE 4 SECTION 2** | **PRACTICE AND APPLICATIONS** |

For use with Exploration 1

1. Copy each problem. Use estimation to place the decimal point in each product.

a. $(0.18)(6.1) = 1098$

b. $(318.7)(0.09) = 28683$

c. $(5.91)(0.328) = 193848$

d. $(612.3)(2.85) = 1745055$

2. Find each product. Show your work.

a. $(26.3)(5.32)$

b. $(0.07)(2.7)$

c. $(108.6)(0.6)$

d. $(218.5)(0.73)$

e. $(42.15)(0.029)$

f. $(0.34)(0.47)$

g. $(8.6)(1.93)$

h. $(1.03)(0.05)$

i. $(4.62)(0.73)$

3. Predict whether each product will be *greater than*, *less than*, or *equal to* the boldface number. Explain how you know.

a. $(\mathbf{29.7})(0.46)$

b. $(1.59)(\mathbf{359.4})$

c. $(\mathbf{463.8})(1)$

4. Fresh asparagus costs \$3.49 per pound and fresh snow peas cost \$1.89 per pound at the vegetable market. Caitlin buys 1.8 lb of asparagus and 2.45 lb of snow peas. How much do the asparagus and snow peas cost altogether?

For use with Exploration 2

5. Copy each problem. Use estimation with powers of 10 to place the decimal point in each quotient.

a. $28.5 \div 0.04 = 7125$

b. $92.8 \div 6.4 = 145$

c. $136 \div 3.2 = 425$

d. $61.2 \div 2.4 = 255$

6. Find each quotient. Show your work.

a. $28 \div 3.5$

b. $0.45 \div 0.06$

c. $21\overline{)9.03}$

d. $4.32 \div 0.6$

e. $0.003\overline{)42}$

f. $5.04 \div 1.4$

g. $2.16 \div 0.4$

h. $0.34 \div 0.05$

i. $7.15 \div 2.2$

7. A circular track has a circumference of 188.4 m. What is the diameter of the track? Use 3.14 for π.

(continued)

MODULE 4 SECTION 2 — PRACTICE AND APPLICATIONS

For use with Exploration 3

8. Write each decimal carried out to 6 decimal places.

a. $0.2\overline{69}$ **b.** $4.\overline{71}$ **c.** $0.04\overline{3}$

d. $21.5\overline{3}$ **e.** $1.0\overline{4}$ **f.** $6.18\overline{}$

g. $3.\overline{102}$ **h.** $123.\overline{65}$ **i.** $4.12\overline{7}$

j. $19.\overline{2}$ **k.** $1.7\overline{62}$ **l.** $1.\overline{809}$

9. Find each quotient. Show your work.

a. $0.58 \div 0.6$ **b.** $0.45\overline{)14.8}$ **c.** $1.6 \div 2.7$

d. $\dfrac{1.4}{9}$ **e.** $62.73 \div 0$ **f.** $0.11\overline{)83.5}$

g. $0 \div 0.384$ **h.** $4.3 \div 0.9$ **i.** $25.4 \div 0.22$

10. Write each fraction as a decimal rounded to the nearest hundredth.

a. $\dfrac{3}{8}$ **b.** $\dfrac{1}{6}$ **c.** $\dfrac{7}{9}$

d. $\dfrac{4}{7}$ **e.** $\dfrac{2}{9}$ **f.** $\dfrac{5}{12}$

g. $\dfrac{1}{3}$ **h.** $\dfrac{3}{11}$ **i.** $\dfrac{5}{6}$

j. $\dfrac{6}{11}$ **k.** $\dfrac{5}{7}$ **l.** $\dfrac{7}{8}$

m. $\dfrac{11}{12}$ **n.** $\dfrac{4}{9}$ **o.** $\dfrac{8}{11}$

11. Predict whether each quotient *will be greater than, less than*, or *equal to* the boldface number. Explain how you know.

a. $32.56 \div \mathbf{0.29}$ **b.** $174\overline{)\mathbf{69.28}}$ **c.** $418.2 \div \mathbf{1}$

d. $82.17 \div \mathbf{0.92}$ **e.** $436 \div \mathbf{2163}$ **f.** $53 \div \mathbf{53.4}$

g. $289 \div \mathbf{0.5}$ **h.** $0.428 \div \mathbf{6}$ **i.** $327 \div \mathbf{1.9}$

12. Photographs taken for the student yearbook are 4.5 cm high. The photographs must be 1.2 cm high to fit in their spaces in the yearbook. What reduction is needed to make the photographs fit perfectly into the spaces in the yearbook?

MODULE 4 SECTION 3   PRACTICE AND APPLICATIONS

For use with Exploration 1

1. Determine whether each shape has rotational symmetry. For each shape that has rotational symmetry, find all its rotational symmetries.

a.

b.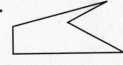

c.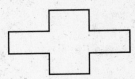

d.

e.

f.

For use with Exploration 2

2. Tell whether each diagram shows a reflection of the original figure across the line.

a.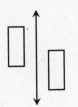

b.

c.

d.

e.

f.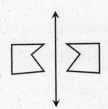

3. Tell whether the figures in each pair are congruent.

a.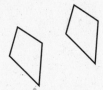

b.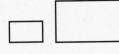

c.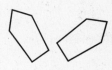

d.

e.

f.

MODULE 4 SECTION 4   **PRACTICE AND APPLICATIONS**

For use with Exploration 1

1. Find each product.

a. $(-3)(7)$ b. $12(-5)$ c. $6(-9)$

d. $(-5)(-4)$ e. $(14)(-9)$ f. $(-2)(53)$

g. $40(-6)$ h. $(-12)(12)$ i. $(-25)(-5)$

j. $(-15)(7)$ k. $(-16)(-8)$ l. $(-18)(20)$

2. Write and solve the related multiplication equation to find each quotient.

a. $45 \div (-9) = x$ b. $-18 \div 3 = x$ c. $-8 \div (-2) = x$

d. $-25 \div 25 = x$ e. $48 \div (-12) = x$ f. $-42 \div 7 = x$

3. Find each quotient.

a. $36 \div (-6)$ b. $\dfrac{54}{-9}$ c. $-63 \div (-9)$

d. $\dfrac{-42}{6}$ e. $\dfrac{-96}{-4}$ f. $\dfrac{120}{-5}$

g. $45 \div (-3)$ h. $\dfrac{99}{-9}$ i. $-168 \div (-6)$

j. $-160 \div 4$ k. $\dfrac{-300}{6}$ l. $-75 \div 3$

4. Find each product.

a. $(-4)(-3)(-5)$ b. $(2)(-26)(-1)$ c. $4(5)(-3)(6)$

d. $(-3)(-5)(-7)(-2)$ e. $(-8)(-5)(9)$ f. $2(-25)(-8)(-5)(-4)$

5. Find each product or quotient.

a. $56 \div (-8)$ b. $(-15)(6)$ c. $\dfrac{270}{-9}$

d. $(41)(-18)$ e. $\dfrac{-64}{-4}$ f. $(-5)(-9)(-2)$

6. On January 1, the temperature reading was –5°C. One month later on February 1, the temperature reading was 3 times that of January 1. What was the temperature reading on February 1?

(continued)

MODULE 4 SECTION 4 | **PRACTICE AND APPLICATIONS**

For use with Exploration 2

7. Evaluate each expression.

  a. $-12 + 4^2 (-8)$

  b. $\left(\dfrac{1}{4} + \dfrac{3}{8}\right) \div \dfrac{1}{2}$

  c. $(2.6)(4) - 5.6$

  d. $2\dfrac{2}{3} \cdot \dfrac{5}{6} + 15$

  e. $-118 \div (-8 + 4)$

  f. $6^2 \cdot (28.6 - 5.28)$

  g. $4.9 \cdot 6 - 26$

  h. $-98 \div (-8 - 6)$

  i. $-16 + 5^2 (-2)$

8. Evaluate each expression when $a = \dfrac{2}{3}$, $b = 8$, and $c = 1\dfrac{1}{4}$.

  a. $6 \div c$

  b. ab

  c. $3a + c$

  d. $6 - ac$

  e. $12 \div a$

  f. $bc - a$

  g. $8 \div c$

  h. $4c - b$

  i. $3b + 2a$

9. Evaluate each expression when $q = 3.2$, $r = 0.4$, and $s = 6$.

  a. $4q$

  b. $q \div r$

  c. $(q - r) \cdot s$

  d. $s \div r$

  e. $5r + q$

  f. $(q + r) \div s$

  g. $4q \div r$

  h. $(s + r) \div q$

  i. $(s - q) \cdot r$

10. Evaluate each expression when $x = -4$, $y = 7$, and $z = -6$.

  a. $32 - z$

  b. $15x \div z$

  c. $y + z \cdot x$

  d. $(45 - y) \div x$

  e. $x \cdot z - 10$

  f. $z - 3y$

  g. $y \cdot x + 8$

  h. $y \cdot z \div x$

  i. $z - x \cdot y$

  j. $\dfrac{66}{z}$

  k. $\dfrac{x}{-2}$

  l. $5z + 5$

11. A phone company charges $.50 for the first minute of a long distance telephone call and $.15 for each additional minute. Each call is rounded up to the nearest minute.

  a. Let $x =$ the number of additional minutes after the first minute. Write an expression that represents the total cost of the call for any number of minutes.

  b. How much will a 16 minute call cost?

MODULE 4 SECTION 5   PRACTICE AND APPLICATIONS

For use with Exploration 1

1. Tell whether each diagram shows a translation of the original figure. If not, explain why not.

a.   **b.** 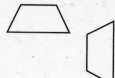   **c.**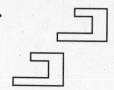

2. Describe each translation using coordinates.

a. 5 units to the left

b. 8 units down

c. 6 units up

d. 4 units to the right

e. 2 units to the right and 6 units up

f. 3 units to the left and 5 units down

g. 5 units to the left and 1 unit up

h. 7 units to the right and 4 units down

3. Draw a rectangle on a coordinate plane. Then draw its image after each translation.

a. $(x + 2, y - 1)$

b. $(x - 3, y - 2)$

For use with Exploration 2

4. Tell whether each transformation will result in an image that is similar to the original figure. Explain your reasoning.

a. $\left(\dfrac{1}{3} x, 3y\right)$

b. $(6x, y)$

c. $\left(\dfrac{1}{4} x, \dfrac{1}{4} y\right)$

d. $\left(\dfrac{1}{3} x, \dfrac{1}{6} y\right)$

e. $(5x, 5y)$

f. $(x, 4y)$

g. $\left(2x, \dfrac{1}{2} y\right)$

h. $(4x, 2y)$

i. $(3x, 3y)$

5. Suppose a computer animator wants to use the transformation $(x, 2y)$ to stretch the figure shown. Make a sketch of how the figure will look after the transformation.

(continued)

MODULE 4 SECTION 5   **PRACTICE AND APPLICATIONS**

For use with Exploration 5

6. Solve each equation. Check each solution.

a. $3t + 8 = 23$ **b.** $\frac{n}{4} - 5 = 3$ **c.** $14 + 6y = -22$

d. $4m - 6.2 = 1$ **e.** $8 + \frac{x}{9} = 8$ **f.** $-6b + 5 = 12$

g. $\frac{p}{7} - 15 = 13$ **h.** $15h + 29 = 68$ **i.** $\frac{k}{8} + 0.7 = 6.8$

j. $6x + 9 = 51$ **k.** $2y + 18 = -54$ **l.** $\frac{m}{9} - 0.2 = 0.5$

m. $16t - 11 = 17$ **n.** $9 + \frac{k}{8} = 54$ **o.** $86 + 5r = 46$

7. Write an equation to represent each statement. Then solve the equation and check your solution.

  a. Five more than three times a number is thirty-two.

  b. A number divided by four and then decreased by six is six.

  c. Eight increased by the product of a number and seven is forty-three.

  d. Nine more than six times a number is eighty-one.

  e. A number divided by five and then decreased by four is three.

  f. Twelve increased by twice a number is twenty-eight.

8. A sports store charges a flat fee of $35 plus $8 per day to rent a canoe.

  a. Let x = the number of days a canoe is rented. Write an equation to show the cost c of renting a canoe.

  b. Suppose a person was charged $67 for renting a canoe. For how many days did the person rent the canoe?

9. Kent has a coupon for $5 off any shirt purchase from a department store. He buys three shirts and spends a total of $43 after using the coupon. Each shirt cost the same amount of money.

  a. Let x = the cost of one shirt. Write an equation to model the situation.

  b. What is the cost of one shirt?

MODULE 4 SECTIONS 1–5   PRACTICE AND APPLICATIONS

For use with Section 1

1. Find each product. Write each answer in lowest terms.

a. $4 \cdot 2\frac{1}{6}$ **b.** $5 \cdot 2\frac{1}{4}$ **c.** $\frac{3}{4} \cdot \frac{8}{9}$

d. $\frac{5}{8} \cdot \frac{2}{5}$ **e.** $2\frac{3}{5} \cdot 1\frac{3}{8}$ **f.** $1\frac{3}{4} \cdot \frac{2}{3}$

2. Find each quotient. Write each answer in lowest terms.

a. $6 \div \frac{5}{6}$ **b.** $3\frac{1}{4} \div 1\frac{3}{4}$ **c.** $3 \div 1\frac{2}{7}$

d. $9 \div \frac{3}{8}$ **e.** $2\frac{5}{6} \div \frac{1}{3}$ **f.** $2\frac{4}{9} \div \frac{2}{3}$

3. Sonya has 9 yd of wrapping paper. She cuts the paper into pieces that are $\frac{2}{3}$ yd long. How many pieces does she have?

4. A recipe for rice pudding calls for $3\frac{3}{4}$ c milk. How much milk would you need to triple the original recipe?

For use with Section 2

5. Find each product. Show your work.

a. $0.4 \cdot 0.17$ **b.** $3.7 \cdot 6.2$ **c.** $1.8 \cdot 3.02$

d. $412 \cdot 1.18$ **e.** $32.1 \cdot 0.25$ **f.** $1.92 \cdot 0.53$

6. Predict whether each product will be *greater than*, *less than*, or *equal to* the number in boldface. Explain how you know.

a. $3.7 \cdot 1.2$ **b.** $0.26 \cdot 0.95$ **c.** $0.048 \cdot 1$

7. Write each fraction as a decimal rounded to the nearest hundredth.

a. $\frac{3}{14}$ **b.** $\frac{5}{9}$ **c.** $\frac{7}{12}$

d. $\frac{7}{8}$ **e.** $\frac{3}{16}$ **f.** $\frac{9}{11}$

8. Predict whether each quotient will be *greater than*, *less than*, or *equal to* the number in boldface. Explain how you know.

a. $41.85 \div 0.32$ **b.** $118\overline{)71.04}$ **c.** $612.9 \div 1$

(continued)

MODULE 4 SECTIONS 1–5   **PRACTICE AND APPLICATIONS**

For use with Section 3

9. Tell whether the figures in each pair are congruent.

a.   **b.**   **c.**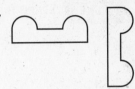

For use with Section 4

10. Find each product or quotient.

    a. $48 \div (-4)$ **b.** $(-14)(3)$ **c.** $\dfrac{350}{-5}$

    d. $(38)(-16)$ **e.** $\dfrac{-72}{-3} \cdot$ **f.** $(-6)(-4)(-3)$

11. A low temperature reading of –2°C was recorded last week. This week the low temperature reading is 8 times that of last week. What is this week's low temperature reading?

12. Evaluate each expression when $x = -5$, $y = 3$, and $z = -4$.

    a. $32 - z$ **b.** $15x \div y$ **c.** $\dfrac{z}{-2}$

    d. $(48 - y) \div x$ **e.** $x \cdot z - 10$ **f.** $y \cdot z \div 6$

For use with Section 5

13. Describe each translation using coordinates.

    a. 7 units to the right and 1 unit up   **b.** 2 units to the left and 8 units down

14. Tell whether each transformation will result in an image that is similar to the original figure. Explain your reasoning.

    a. $\left(\dfrac{1}{5}x, 5y\right)$ **b.** $(7x, y)$ **c.** $(6x, 6y)$

15. Solve each equation. Check each solution.

    a. $6t + 9 = 57$ **b.** $\dfrac{n}{5} - 8 = 3$ **c.** $19 + 4y = -13$

16. Eight more than six times a number is fifty. Write an equation to represent the statement. Then solve the equation.

MODULE 4 SECTION 1   STUDY GUIDE

The Wheel of Life   Circumference, and Multiplication and Division of Fractions

GOAL   **LEARN HOW TO:** • find the circumference of a circle
• multiply fractions and mixed numbers
• use the distributive property
• find reciprocals
• divide fractions and mixed numbers

As you: • build a zoetrope
• create a zoetrope strip

Exploration 1: Circumference of a Zoetrope

Circumference

Circumference is the distance around a circle. The relationship between the circumference, C, of a circle and its diameter, d, is given by

$$\pi = \frac{C}{d} \text{ or } C = \pi d.$$

The value of the constant π (read "pi") is about 3.14.

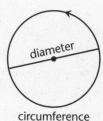

circumference

Rounding Decimals

You round decimals the same way you round whole numbers.

> **Example**
>
> Rounded to the nearest hundredth, 3.1415297 is 3.14.
>
> Rounded to the nearest thousandth, 18.849556 is 18.850.

Exploration 2: Multiplying Fractions

To multiply fractions, you first multiply the numerators. Then you multiply the denominators.

> **Example**
>
> Find $\frac{1}{8} \cdot \frac{3}{5}$ in lowest terms.
>
> **■ Sample Response ■**
>
> $\frac{1}{8} \cdot \frac{3}{5} = \frac{1 \cdot 3}{5 \cdot 8} = \frac{3}{40}$

MODULE 4 SECTION 1   **STUDY GUIDE**

Sometimes it is easier to divide by the common factors before multiplying.

Example

Find $\dfrac{3}{25} \cdot \dfrac{20}{33}$ in lowest terms.

■ Sample Response ■

$$\dfrac{3}{25} \cdot \dfrac{20}{33} = \dfrac{\overset{1}{\cancel{3}}}{\underset{5}{\cancel{25}}} \cdot \dfrac{\overset{4}{\cancel{20}}}{\underset{11}{\cancel{33}}} \qquad \leftarrow \text{There are common factors of 3 and 5.}$$

$$= \dfrac{1 \cdot 4}{5 \cdot 11} = \dfrac{4}{55}$$

You can use the **distributive property** to multiply a fraction and a mixed number.

Example

Find $\dfrac{3}{7} \cdot 2\dfrac{1}{4}$ in lowest terms.

■ Sample Response ■

$$\dfrac{3}{7} \cdot 2\dfrac{1}{4} = \dfrac{3}{7}\left(2 + \dfrac{1}{4}\right) = \left(\dfrac{3}{7} \cdot 2\right) + \left(\dfrac{3}{7} \cdot \dfrac{1}{4}\right) \qquad \leftarrow \text{Use the distributive property.}$$

$$= \dfrac{6}{7} + \dfrac{3}{28} = \dfrac{24}{28} + \dfrac{3}{28} = \dfrac{27}{28}$$

Reciprocals

Two numbers whose product is 1, such as $\dfrac{3}{4}$ and $\dfrac{4}{3}$, are **reciprocals**.

Exploration 3: Dividing Fractions

To divide by a fraction, you multiply by the reciprocal.

Example

Find $1\dfrac{2}{3} \div \dfrac{5}{7}$ in lowest terms.

■ Sample Response ■

$$1\dfrac{2}{3} \div \dfrac{5}{7} = \dfrac{5}{3} \div \dfrac{5}{7} = \dfrac{5}{3} \cdot \dfrac{7}{5} = \dfrac{\overset{1}{\cancel{5}}}{3} \cdot \dfrac{7}{\underset{1}{\cancel{5}}} = \dfrac{1 \cdot 7}{3 \cdot 1} = \dfrac{7}{3}, \text{ or } 2\dfrac{1}{3}$$

MODULE 4 SECTION 1 | PRACTICE & APPLICATION EXERCISES | STUDY GUIDE

Exploration 1

Find the circumference of each circle with the given diameter. If necessary, round each answer to the nearest hundredth. Use 3.14 or the π key on a calculator.

1. 12 cm $\qquad$ **2.** 1.4 mm $\qquad$ **3.** 15 ft $\qquad$ **4.** 1 km $\qquad$ **5.** 2.3 m

Exploration 2

Find each product. Write each answer in lowest terms.

6. $\frac{4}{7} \cdot \frac{1}{9}$ $\qquad$ **7.** $\frac{5}{6} \cdot 3$ $\qquad$ **8.** $\frac{6}{14} \cdot \frac{7}{48}$

9. $7 \cdot 3\frac{2}{7}$ $\qquad$ **10.** $2\frac{4}{5} \cdot \frac{10}{28}$ $\qquad$ **11.** $1\frac{1}{2} \cdot 3\frac{4}{6}$

Find the reciprocal of each number.

12. 8 $\qquad$ **13.** $\frac{2}{3}$ $\qquad$ **14.** $\frac{5}{8}$ $\qquad$ **15.** $\frac{23}{5}$ $\qquad$ **16.** $5\frac{4}{9}$

Exploration 3

Find each quotient. Write each answer in lowest terms.

17. $\frac{4}{9} \div \frac{2}{3}$ $\qquad$ **18.** $3 \div \frac{1}{5}$ $\qquad$ **19.** $\frac{3}{7} \div \frac{3}{7}$ $\qquad$ **20.** $\frac{1}{2} \div 1\frac{1}{2}$

21. $\frac{7}{9} \div \frac{14}{27}$ $\qquad$ **22.** $3\frac{2}{3} \div \frac{6}{7}$ $\qquad$ **23.** $1\frac{1}{2} \div 1\frac{4}{5}$ $\qquad$ **24.** $3\frac{1}{9} \div 32$

Spiral Review

Tell whether each combination of side lengths can form a triangle. (Module 3, p. 223)

25. 11 mm, 5 mm, 8 mm $\qquad$ **26.** 15 ft, 2 ft, 7 ft

Evaluate each expression. (Module 1, p. 65)

27. $26 - 7 \cdot 3$ $\qquad$ **28.** $3^3 + (23 - 6)$ $\qquad$ **29.** $81 \div 3 - 2$

Replace each __?__ with the power of 10 that makes the equation true. (Module 3, p. 199)

30. $3.5 \cdot \underline{\ ?\ } = 3500$ $\qquad$ **31.** $0.00052 \cdot \underline{\ ?\ } = 5.2$

32. $0.0281 \div \underline{\ ?\ } = 2.81$ $\qquad$ **33.** $19 \div \underline{\ ?\ } = 19{,}000$

MODULE 4 SECTION 2 | **STUDY GUIDE**

Through the Camera's Eye

Decimal Multiplication and Division

GOAL **LEARN HOW TO:** • estimate decimal products and quotients
• multiply and divide decimals
• find quotients that repeat
• write a fraction as a decimal
• interpret division with zero

AS YOU: • examine a photo
• investigate the flight of a golf ball

Exploration 1: Multiplying Decimals

To multiply decimal numbers, you first multiply them as whole numbers.
Then the number of decimal places in the product is the sum of the
number of decimal places in the factors.

Example

Find the product $(23.1)(0.34)$.

■ Sample Response ■

$$
\begin{array}{r}
23.1 \quad \leftarrow \quad 1 \text{ decimal place} \\
\times\, 0.34 \quad \leftarrow \quad +\,2 \text{ decimal places} \\
\hline
924 \qquad\qquad 3 \text{ decimal places} \\
6\,930 \\
\hline
7.854 \\
\end{array}
$$

Exploration 2: Dividing Decimals

To divide decimal numbers, you first multiply the divisor and the dividend
by a power of 10 that will make the divisor a whole number. Write zeros at
the end of the dividend as needed. Then you divide.

Example

Find the quotient $4.2 \div 0.56$.

■ Sample Response ■

$$
\begin{array}{r}
7.5 \\
56\,)\overline{420.0} \\
\underline{392} \\
28\,0 \\
\underline{28\,0} \\
0 \\
\end{array}
$$

← Insert two zeros to continue the division.

MODULE 4 SECTION 2   **STUDY GUIDE**

Exploration 3: Repeating Decimals

GOAL

Repeating and Terminating Decimals

A decimal in which a digit or a sequence of digits keeps repeating is a **repeating decimal**. A bar is written over the digits that repeat.

repeating decimal:
$1.236363636\ldots = 1.2\overline{36}$

A decimal that stops is a **terminating decimal**.

terminating decimal: 1.267

You can write the decimal equivalent of a fraction by dividing the numerator by the denominator.

Example

Write $\frac{4}{5}$ and $\frac{2}{3}$ as decimals.

■ Sample Response ■

$\frac{4}{5} = 4 \div 5 = 0.8$ $\leftarrow$ terminating decimal

$\frac{2}{3} = 2 \div 3 = 0.666\ldots$ or $0.\overline{6}$ $\leftarrow$ repeating decimal

When finding $4 \div 5$ using long division, there is no remainder. When finding $2 \div 3$ using long division however, the difference at each stage of the division is the same, 2, as shown at the right. For repeating decimals, this occurs at some point in the long division.

$$
\begin{array}{r}
0.66 \\
3\overline{)2.00} \\
\underline{1\,8} \\
20 \quad \leftarrow \text{difference: 2} \\
\underline{18} \\
2 \quad \leftarrow \text{difference: 2}
\end{array}
$$

Division with Zero

Zero divided by any non-zero number is always zero, because the product of zero and any non-zero number is always zero.

Example

$0 \div 8 = 0$, because $0 \cdot 8 = 0$.

Division by zero is undefined, because there is no number by which you can multiply zero to produce a non-zero product.

MODULE 4 SECTION 2 | PRACTICE & APPLICATION EXERCISES | STUDY GUIDE

Exploration 1

Find each product. Show your work.

1. (0.049)(3.4)　　　**2.** (23)(2.6)　　　**3.** (7.12)(0.84)　　　**4.** (0.28)(0.16)

5. (425.1)(3.7)　　　**6.** (0.73)(0.08)　　　**7.** (99)(25.61)　　　**8.** (1.03)(2.005)

Exploration 2

Find each quotient. Show your work.

9. $38 \div 2.5$　　　**10.** $0.16 \div 0.05$　　　**11.** $21.28 \div 5.6$

12. $2.52 \div 0.4$　　　**13.** $84 \div 0.0007$　　　**14.** $3.038 \div 3.1$

Exploration 3

Find each quotient. Show your work.

15. $1.5 \div 0.9$　　　**16.** $2.8 \div 0.54$　　　**17.** $98.7 \div 0$

18. $3.2 \div 9$　　　**19.** $0 \div 57.16$　　　**20.** $33.75 \div 0.22$

Write each fraction as a decimal rounded to the nearest hundredth.

21. $\frac{6}{7}$　　　**22.** $\frac{4}{9}$　　　**23.** $\frac{5}{12}$　　　**24.** $\frac{1}{9}$

Spiral Review

For Exercises 25 –30, evaluate each expression.
(Module 4, pp. 241–242)

25. $\frac{2}{5} \cdot \frac{15}{17}$　　　**26.** $8 \div \frac{14}{9}$　　　**27.** $2\frac{4}{7} \cdot 21$

28. $4\frac{1}{3} \div \frac{1}{6}$　　　**29.** $1\frac{2}{3} \div \frac{7}{9}$　　　**30.** $5\frac{1}{4} \cdot \frac{2}{7}$

31. May lives 20 mi due south of Stan. Stan lives 5 mi due north of Bill. Where does Bill live in relation to May? **(Module 1, p. 44)**

Draw an angle with each measure. Then classify each angle as *acute, obtuse, right,* **or** *straight.* (Module 2, p. 83)

32. 90°　　　**33.** 115°　　　**34.** 30°　　　**35.** 180°

MODULE 4 SECTION 3

The Math of Motion   Rotations and Reflections

GOAL   **LEARN HOW TO:** • rotate a figure
                          • describe a rotation
                          • identify rotational symmetries
                          • identify a reflection
                          • identify lines of symmetry

    AS YOU: • study designs used in artwork
                • explore mirror images in art

Exploration 1: Rotations and Symmetry

Rotations

A **rotation** turns a figure about a fixed point, called the **center of rotation**,
a certain number of degrees either clockwise or counterclockwise. The
new figure is the **image** of the original figure.

> **Example**
>
> Draw the image of △*ABC* after a 120° clockwise
> rotation about point *P*.
>
>
>
> **Sample Response**
>
> Since *P* is the center of rotation, use a protractor
> to lightly sketch ∠*APA′* measuring 120° clockwise
> from ray *PA*. Locate point *A′* at a distance from
> *P* so that *AP = PA′*. Repeat this step for ∠*BPB′* and
> ∠*CPC′* to locate points *B′* and *C′*, respectively.
> Connect the points to form △*A′B′C′*, the image
> of △*ABC*.
>
>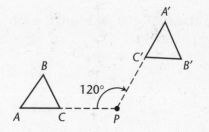

Rotational Symmetry

A figure that fits exactly on itself after being rotated less than
360° about a point has **rotational symmetry.** For example,
the figure at the right has rotational symmetries of 90°, 180°,
and 270°.

MODULE 4 SECTION 3   **STUDY GUIDE**

Exploration 2: Reflections and Symmetry

Reflections

A **reflection** flips a figure across a line. The line is the **line of reflection**. Each point on the original figure and its image are the same distance from the line of reflection. If you connect a point and its image with a segment, the segment will intersect the line of reflection at a right angle. The original figure and its image are **congruent**, since they are the same size and shape.

Each point on a triangle is called a **vertex of the triangle**.

Example

Tell whether each diagram shows a reflection of the original figure across the line.

a.
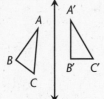

b.
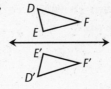

■ Sample Response ■

a. No, the figure is not a reflection across the line. If $\overline{AA'}$ is drawn, it does not form a right angle with the given line.

b. Yes, the figure is a reflection across the line. If segments are drawn between the corresponding vertices of the two triangles, each of these segments would form a right angle with the given line.

Line Symmetry

A figure has **line symmetry** if one half of the figure is the reflection of the other half across a line. The line of reflection is a **line of symmetry** for the figure. For example, the figure at the right has two lines of symmetry, as shown.

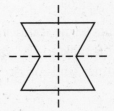

MODULE 4 SECTION 3 | PRACTICE & APPLICATION EXERCISES | STUDY GUIDE

Exploration 1

1. Draw a triangle. Mark and label a point below the triangle to use as the center of rotation. Then draw the image of the triangle after a 160° clockwise rotation.

Determine whether each shape has rotational symmetry. For each shape that has rotational symmetry, find all its rotational symmetries.

2.   **3.**   **4.**   **5.**

Exploration 2

Tell whether each diagram shows a reflection of the original figure across the given line.

6.   **7.** 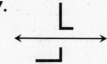 **8.**

Tell whether the figures in each pair are congruent.

9.   **10.** 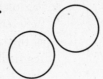 **11.**

Spiral Review

For Exercises 12–14, find each product or quotient.
(Module 4, pp. 255 –256)

12. $(41.6)(0.09)$ **13.** $0.7 \div 10.864$ **14.** $(3.27)(2.139)$

15. Suppose the spinner was spun 30 times. Use the results in the table to find the experimental probability that the spinner lands on A. (Module 1, p. 33)

Event	Total
A	12
B	9
C	9

Find each sum or difference. (Module 2, p. 109)

16. $-18 + 9$ **17.** $45 - (-23)$ **18.** $-4 + (-17) - 9$

MODULE 4 SECTION 4 | **STUDY GUIDE**

Special Effects   Multiplication and Division of Integers

GOAL **LEARN HOW TO:** • multiply and divide integers
• evaluate expressions containing decimals, fractions, and integers

As you: • experiment with reverse motion
• explore how early moviemakers took close-up shots

Exploration 1: Multiplying and Dividing Integers

Properties of Multiplication:

The **commutative property of multiplication** says you can *change the order* of numbers in a multiplication problem and still get the same product.

The **associative property of multiplication** says that you can *change the grouping* when you multiply numbers and still get the same product.

The product or quotient of two integers is:

• *positive* when both integers are positive or when both integers are negative.

$$-5 \cdot (-3) = 15 \qquad -12 \div (-6) = 2$$
$$6 \cdot 4 = 24 \qquad 32 \div 8 = 4$$

• *negative* when one of the integers is positive and the other integer is negative.

$$4 \cdot (-2) = -8 \qquad -18 \div 9 = -2$$

Exploration 2: Evaluating Expressions

You evaluate expressions containing fractions, decimals, or integers the same way you evaluate whole number expressions. Follow the order of operations and evaluate expressions inside grouping symbols first. Remember that a fraction bar is a grouping symbol.

Example

Evaluate the expression $\dfrac{(-3) \cdot 4^2 - 5}{-7 + (-2)}$.

■ **Sample Response** ■

$$\frac{(-3) \cdot 4^2 - 5}{-7 + (-2)} = \frac{(-3) \cdot 16 - 5}{-9}$$
$$= \frac{-48 - 5}{-9} = \frac{-53}{-9} = \frac{53}{9}, \text{ or } 5\frac{8}{9}$$

Name _____   Date _____

MODULE 4 SECTION 4 | PRACTICE & APPLICATION EXERCISES | STUDY GUIDE

Exploration 1

For Exercises 1–9, find each product or quotient.

1. $(-6)(5)$　　　　　　　**2.** $24(-2)$　　　　　　**3.** $-18 \div (-2)$

4. $550 \div (-5)$　　　　　**5.** $(-7)(-4)$　　　　　**6.** $-114 \div 3$

7. $45 \div (-9)$　　　　　　**8.** $(-2)(-2)(-5)$　　**9.** $-63 \div (-7)$

10. James withdrew $15 from his bank account 4 different times this month. What amount must he *add* to his original balance to find his new monthly balance?

Exploration 2

Evaluate each expression.

11. $-3 + (-2)(-1)$　　　**12.** $\left(\dfrac{5}{8} + \dfrac{5}{12}\right) \div \dfrac{5}{6}$　　　**13.** $-3 - (-15) \div (-5)$

For Exercises 14 –16, evaluate each expression when $x = -2$, $y = 0.5$, and $z = 4$.

14. $\dfrac{z}{x}$　　　　　　　**15.** $2y + (-5)x \cdot z$　　　　**16.** $23 - x$

17. Write a word problem that can be solved by evaluating $2x - 3$ for $x = 5$. Then solve the problem.

Spiral Review

Tell whether each figure has *line symmetry*, *rotational symmetry*, or *both*. (Module 4, pp. 270–271)

18. 　　　**19.** 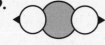　　　**20.**

For Exercises 21–24, solve each equation. Check each answer.
(Module 3, p. 233)

21. $4x = 48$　　　　**22.** $\dfrac{m}{5} = 15$　　　　**23.** $5y = 45$　　　　**24.** $\dfrac{1}{8}b = 8$

25. a. Graph the ordered pairs $(3, 2)$, $(-1, 2)$, $(-4, 0)$, $(-1, -2)$, and $(3, -2)$ in a coordinate plane. (Module 2, p. 95)

　　b. Draw segments to connect the points in the order listed in part (a). Connect the last point to the first point. Name the polygon that is formed.

MODULE 4 SECTION 5

Animation   Translations, Similarity, and Two-Step Equations

GOAL   **LEARN HOW TO:** • use coordinates to describe translations
• locate the image from a translation on a coordinate plane
• stretch or squash a figure on a coordinate plane
• identify similar figures
• solve two-step equations

AS YOU: • explore ways to create animations
• explore ways to make animation more realistic
• explore how to change both the shape and the location of an animated figure

Exploration 1: Translations

Transformations and Translations

A **transformation** is a change in a figure's shape, size, or location. Three types of transformations are reflections, rotations, and translations. Transformations can be described using coordinates. *Left* or *right* are directions used to describe the movement of figures on the horizontal axis, usually called the **x-axis**. *Up* or *down* describes movement on the vertical axis, usually called the **y-axis**.

A **translation** is a transformation that slides a figure to a new location. The image is congruent to the original figure.

Example

The coordinates of the vertices of $\triangle ABC$ are $A(4, 2)$, $B(7, 2)$, and $C(7, 3)$. Draw $\triangle ABC$ on a coordinate plane and translate it 1 unit to the left and 2 units down. Then use coordinates to describe the translation.

■ Sample Response ■

The coordinates of the vertices of the image triangle, $\triangle A'B'C'$, are $A'(3, 0)$, $B'(6, 0)$, and $C'(6, 1)$.

Using coordinates, if the original point is (x, y), then its image is $(x - 1, y - 2)$.

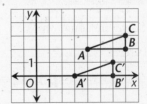

MODULE 4 SECTION 5   **STUDY GUIDE**

Exploration 2: Changing Size and Shape

Transformations that Stretch or Squash

You can stretch or squash a figure horizontally by multiplying the
x-coordinates of all its points by the same factor, or vertically by
multiplying the y-coordinates of all its points by the same factor. A factor
greater than 1 stretches. A factor between 0 and 1 squashes. When you
stretch or squash a figure horizontally and vertically by the same factor,
the image is similar to the original figure. Figures are **similar** if they are
the same shape, but not necessarily the same size.

The figure on the left below shows $\triangle ABC$ with vertices $A(-3, 0)$, $B(-3, 2)$,
and $C(2, 0)$. The middle figure shows two transformations of $\triangle ABC$, a
horizontal stretch where the x-coordinate of every point has been
multiplied by 2 and a vertical squash where the y-coordinate of every
point has been multiplied by $\frac{1}{2}$. The figure on the right shows a third
transformation, one in which both coordinates of every point have been
multiplied by 2. This image triangle is similar to the original triangle.

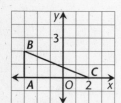 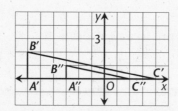 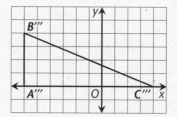

Exploration 3: Solving Two-Step Equations

You solve two-step equations by working backward through the order of
operations using inverse operations.

Example
Solve the equation $5x + 3 = 13$.

■ Sample Response ■

Step 1	Subtract 3 from both sides.	$5x + 3 - 3 = 13 - 3$
Step 2	Simplify both sides.	$5x = 10$
Step 3	Divide both sides by 5.	$\dfrac{5x}{5} = \dfrac{10}{5}$
Step 4	Simplify.	$x = 2$

MODULE 4 SECTION 5 | PRACTICE & APPLICATION EXERCISES | STUDY GUIDE

Exploration 1

Tell whether each diagram shows a translation of the original figure. If not, explain why not.

1.

2.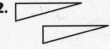

3.

For Exercises 4 and 5, describe each translation using coordinates.

4. 8 units to the left, 1 unit down   **5.** 5 units to the right, 3 units up

6. Draw a rectangle on a coordinate plane. Then draw its image after the translation $(x + 4, y - 3)$.

Exploration 2

7. Tell which figures are similar.

A.   **B.**   **C.**   **D.**

8. Draw a rectangle on a coordinate plane. Then draw its image using the transformation $\left(2x, \dfrac{y}{2} \right)$.

Exploration 3

Solve each equation. Check each solution.

9. $3t + 8 = 32$ **10.** $\dfrac{m}{5} - 2 = -12$ **11.** $30 - 7x = 9$

Spiral Review

Evaluate each expression. (Module 4, p. 282)

12. $12 + 8 \cdot 2\dfrac{3}{5}$ **13.** $0.45 \div 0.9 - 0.3$ **14.** $\left(\dfrac{2}{3} - \dfrac{5}{12} \right) \cdot 3 \div \dfrac{1}{2}$

Replace each __?__ with the number that makes the statement true. (Table of Measures, p. 596)

15. $120 \text{ min} = \underline{\ ?\ } \text{ h}$ **16.** $480 \text{ s} = \underline{\ ?\ } \text{ min}$ **17.** $5 \text{ h} = \underline{\ ?\ } \text{ min}$

Replace each __?__ with >, <, or =. (Module 3, p. 190)

18. $\dfrac{29}{42} \underline{\ ?\ } \dfrac{5}{6}$ **19.** $\dfrac{5}{18} \underline{\ ?\ } \dfrac{2}{9}$ **20.** $\dfrac{7}{12} \underline{\ ?\ } \dfrac{11}{18}$

MODULE 5

Rubber Band Stretch Experiment

(Use with Question 14 on page 331.)

Directions

First

Hook the rubber band onto both paper clips. Then attach the plastic bag to the small paper clip.

Next

Tape the notebook paper to the wall. The lines on the paper should be vertical. Be sure the paper is level.

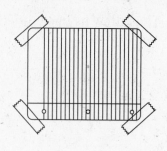

Then

Tape the large paper clip to the wall just above the notebook paper. The bottom of the rubber band should reach the top edge of the paper.

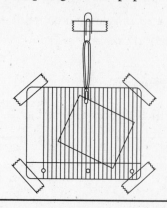

Rubber Band Stretch Graph

(Use with Questions 17–19 on page 332.)

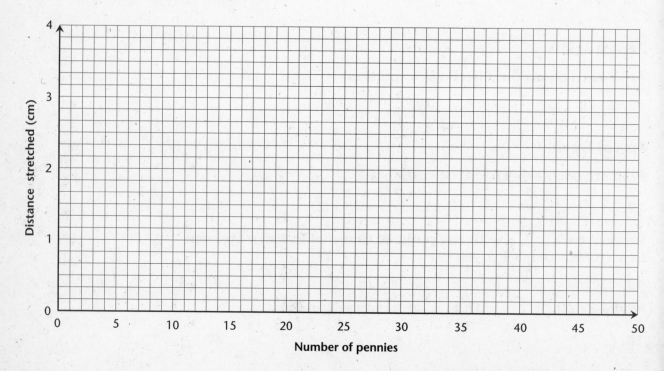

MODULE 5   **LABSHEET** **2B**

Box-and-Whisker Plot (Use with Questions 21–25 on
pages 334–335.)

Directions Plot the winning number of skips for each year from
1969–1984 (except 1981) on the line plot below the box-and-whisker
plot. The first three values in the table have been plotted for you.

Mackinac Island Stone Skipping Tournament 1969–1984

Year	Winning number of skips	Year	Winning number of skips
1969	15 ✔	1977	24
1970	13 ✔	1978	18
1971	13 ✔	1979	17
1972	10	1980	15
1973	9	1981	(not available)
1974	19	1982	22
1975	24	1983	15
1976	23	1984	20

Mackinac Island Stone Skipping Tournament 1969–1984*

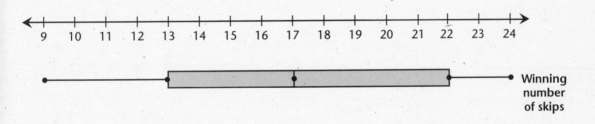

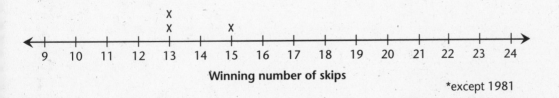

Winning number of skips

*except 1981

MODULE 5   LABSHEET **3A**

Estimating Percents (Use with Question 5 on page 345.)

Directions Complete the exercises below to learn how to use
a percent bar model to estimate the percent rating represented
by the fraction $\frac{17}{30}$.

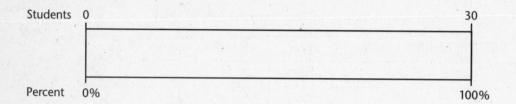

Students 0   30

Percent   0%   100%

a. Use vertical segments to divide the bar into five sections of equal size.

b. What "nice" fractions do the vertical segments you drew in part (a)
represent?

c. Below the bar, write the percent that each vertical segment represents.

d. Across the top of the bar, write the number of students represented by
each vertical segment.

e. Draw a segment for 17 students about where you think it should be
located on the percent bar model. Shade the bar from 0 to 17.

f. Estimate the percent equivalent of $\frac{17}{30}$.

| MODULE 5 | REVIEW AND ASSESSMENT LABSHEET |

Bridge Length Graph (Use with Exercise 15 on page 375.)

Directions
• Plot the lengths of the bridges on the coordinate plane below.

• Draw a fitted line along the points on the graph.

Name of the Bridge	Location	Length (ft)	Length (m)
Golden Gate	California, U.S.A.	4200	1280
Forth Road	Queensferry, Scotland	3300	1006
Longview	Washington, U.S.A.	1200	366
Howrah	Calcutta, India	1500	457
Sydney Harbor	Sydney, Australia	1670	509
Zdákov	Czech Republic	1244	380
Tatara	Ehime, Japan	2920	890
Skarnsundet Bridge	Trondheim, Norway	1739	530
Dartford	Dartford, England	1476	450
Graf Spee	Germany	839	256
Amizade	Foz do Iguassu, Brazil	951	290
Fiumarella	Catanzaro, Italy	758	231

Some Notable Modern Bridges

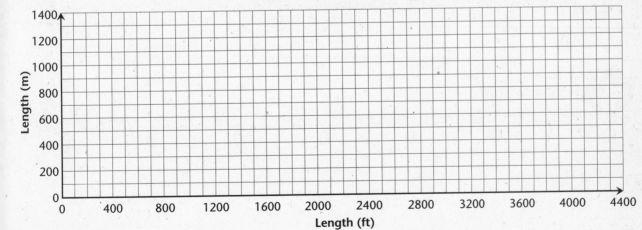

a. About how many meters long is a 500-foot bridge?

b. About how many feet are in a meter?

Name _____   Problem _____

| TEACHER | ASSESSMENT SCALES |

The star indicates that you excelled in some way.

 Problem Solving

❶   ❷   ❸   ❹   ❺

You did not understand the problem well enough to get started or you did not show any work.

You understood the problem well enough to make a plan and to work toward a solution.

You made a plan, you used it to solve the problem, and you verified your solution.

 Mathematical Language

❶   ❷   ❸   ❹   ❺

You did not use any mathematical vocabulary or symbols, or you did not use them correctly, or your use was not appropriate.

You used appropriate mathematical language, but the way it was used was not always correct or other terms and symbols were needed.

You used mathematical language that was correct and appropriate to make your meaning clear.

 Representations

❶   ❷   ❸   ❹   ❺

You did not use any representations such as equations, tables, graphs, or diagrams to help solve the problem or explain your solution.

You made appropriate representations to help solve the problem or help you explain your solution, but they were not always correct or other representations were needed.

You used appropriate and correct representations to solve the problem or explain your solution.

 Connections

❶   ❷   ❸   ❹   ❺

You attempted or solved the problem and then stopped.

You found patterns and used them to extend the solution to other cases, or you recognized that this problem relates to other problems, mathematical ideas, or applications.

You extended the ideas in the solution to the general case, or you showed how this problem relates to other problems, mathematical ideas, or applications.

 Presentation

❶   ❷   ❸   ❹   ❺

The presentation of your solution and reasoning is unclear to others.

The presentation of your solution and reasoning is clear in most places, but others may have trouble understanding parts of it.

The presentation of your solution and reasoning is clear and can be understood by others.

Content Used: _____   **Computational Errors:**   Yes   No

Notes on Errors: _____

STUDENT | **SELF-ASSESSMENT SCALES**

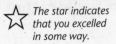 If your score is in the shaded area, explain why on the back of this sheet and stop.

The star indicates that you excelled in some way.

 ## Problem Solving

❶   ❷   ❸   ❹   ❺   ☆→

❶ I did not understand the problem well enough to get started or I did not show any work.

❸ I understood the problem well enough to make a plan and to work toward a solution.

❺ I made a plan, I used it to solve the problem, and I verified my solution.

 ## Mathematical Language

❶   ❷   ❸   ❹   ❺   ☆→

❶ I did not use any mathematical vocabulary or symbols, or I did not use them correctly, or my use was not appropriate.

❸ I used appropriate mathematical language, but the way it was used was not always correct or other terms and symbols were needed.

❺ I used mathematical language that was correct and appropriate to make my meaning clear.

 ## Representations

❶   ❷   ❸   ❹   ❺   ☆→

❶ I did not use any representations such as equations, tables, graphs, or diagrams to help solve the problem or explain my solution.

❸ I made appropriate representations to help solve the problem or help me explain my solution, but they were not always correct or other representations were needed.

❺ I used appropriate and correct representations to solve the problem or explain my solution.

 ## Connections

❶   ❷   ❸   ❹   ❺   ☆→

❶ I attempted or solved the problem and then stopped.

❸ I found patterns and used them to extend the solution to other cases, or I recognized that this problem relates to other problems, mathematical ideas, or applications.

❺ I extended the ideas in the solution to the general case, or I showed how this problem relates to other problems, mathematical ideas, or applications.

 ## Presentation

❶   ❷   ❸   ❹   ❺   ☆→

❶ The presentation of my solution and reasoning is unclear to others.

❸ The presentation of my solution and reasoning is clear in most places, but others may have trouble understanding parts of it.

❺ The presentation of my solution and reasoning is clear and can be understood by others.

MODULE 5 SECTION 1   **PRACTICE AND APPLICATIONS**

For use with Exploration 1

1. Write each rate as a unit rate.

   a. $\dfrac{68 \text{ min}}{8 \text{ mi}}$ **b.** $\dfrac{138 \text{ mi}}{6 \text{ gal}}$ **c.** $\dfrac{\$8.40}{3 \text{ lb}}$

   d. $\dfrac{48 \text{ servings}}{6 \text{ pans}}$ **e.** $\dfrac{\$.28}{4 \text{ min}}$ **f.** $\dfrac{\$2.67}{3 \text{ bunches}}$

   g. $\dfrac{32 \text{ min}}{5 \text{ mi}}$ **h.** $\dfrac{\$18}{4 \text{ lb}}$ **i.** $\dfrac{52.2 \text{ gal}}{9 \text{ min}}$

   j. $\dfrac{30 \text{ servings}}{3 \text{ pans}}$ **k.** $\dfrac{\$7.77}{3 \text{ bunches}}$ **l.** $\dfrac{48 \text{ servings}}{4 \text{ pans}}$

   m. $\dfrac{224 \text{ mi}}{8 \text{ gal}}$ **n.** $\dfrac{\$25.50}{2 \text{ h}}$ **o.** $\dfrac{188 \text{ km}}{8 \text{ L}}$

2. A single grizzly bear may eat 55 pounds of berries per day. Copy and complete the proportion below to show how many pounds of berries a grizzly bear may eat in one week.

$$\frac{55 \text{ lb}}{1 \text{ day}} = \frac{? \text{ lb}}{7 \text{ days}}$$

3. The total area of the district of Columbia is about 68 mi². The total population of the District of Columbia is about 600,000 people. Find the population density, or unit rate of people per square mile, for the District of Columbia.

4. To train for a cross country ski race, Frank wants to ski a total of 120 mi at an average rate no slower than 8 min/mi.

   a. Copy and complete the table below to show the distance covered and cross country skiing times for a rate of 8 min/mi.

Time (min)	?	8	?	80	?
Distance (mi)	0.5	1	5	?	120

   b. How many hours would it take Frank to cross country ski 120 mi at a rate of 8 min/mi?

5. Suppose Erin runs at the rates shown in the table below.

   a. Copy and complete the table for 30 s and 60 s.

Time (s)	1	5	20	30	50
Distance (ft)	6	30	120	?	?

   b. How far would you expect Erin to run in 50 s?

(continued)

| MODULE 5 SECTION 1 | PRACTICE AND APPLICATIONS |

For use with Exploration 2

6. The table shows the number of minutes 20 students in Mr. Clement's class spent reading one night.

Student	Number of minutes	Student	Number of minutes
Jim	89	Doreen	94
Tim	76	Mary	88
Ralph	100	Bob	83
Keisha	85	Nick	79
Arnold	92	Matt	91
Barney	99	Liza	100
Alicia	89	Marty	89
Francine	88	Rosa	86
Buster	83	Janice	92
Arthur	90	Carter	96

a. Make a stem-and-leaf plot to show the number of minutes the students in Mr. Clement's class spent reading one night. Be sure to include a title and a key for your plot.

b. Use the stem-and-leaf plot to find the range, the mean, the median, and the mode of the number of minutes the students in Mr. Clement's class spent reading.

c. What would you consider an average time for the number of minutes the students in Mr. Clement's class spent reading?

For use with Exploration 3

7. The histogram shows the number of minutes students spent on their homework at Alta Junior High School.

a. How many minutes are included in each interval?

b. About how many students spend from 21–30 minutes on homework?

c. Is the number of students who spend more than one half hour on homework greater than, equal to, or less than the number of students who spend less than one half hour on homework?

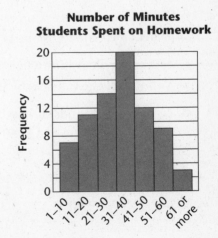

Number of Minutes
Students Spent on Homework

MODULE 5 SECTION 2 — PRACTICE AND APPLICATIONS

For use with Exploration 1

1. How many grams of protein are contained in 680 g of yogurt if 170 g of yogurt contain 7 g of protein?

2. How many grams of carbohydrate are contained in 448 g of pasta if 56 g of pasta contain 40 g of carbohydrate?

3. A horse eats about 75 lb of hay every 4 days. How many pounds of hay would you expect it to eat in 28 days?

4. Solve each proportion.

   a. $\dfrac{8}{15} = \dfrac{28}{x}$

   b. $\dfrac{7}{n} = \dfrac{112}{384}$

   c. $\dfrac{12}{76} = \dfrac{b}{171}$

   d. $\dfrac{36}{45} = \dfrac{y}{15}$

   e. $\dfrac{m}{24} = \dfrac{51}{72}$

   f. $\dfrac{3}{x} = \dfrac{24}{40}$

   g. $\dfrac{5}{12} = \dfrac{w}{30}$

   h. $\dfrac{16}{c} = \dfrac{56}{105}$

   i. $\dfrac{5}{9} = \dfrac{4.5}{t}$

   j. $\dfrac{4.5}{x} = \dfrac{18}{48}$

   k. $\dfrac{5}{9} = \dfrac{z}{72}$

   l. $\dfrac{14}{k} = \dfrac{56}{34}$

   m. $\dfrac{4}{18} = \dfrac{10}{x}$

   n. $\dfrac{8}{14} = \dfrac{12}{n}$

   o. $\dfrac{9}{15} = \dfrac{b}{75}$

5. A selection of the Morningside Café's breakfast menu is shown at the right with the average quantity of the items the restaurant usually uses in two days.

   Morningside Café Breakfast Menu

Item	Amount
bacon	35 lb
eggs	40 dozen
whole wheat bread	50 loaves
white bread	85 loaves
pancake mix	75 lb
maple syrup	12 lb
orange juice	15 gal

   a. How many pounds of pancake mix would you expect the Morningside Café to use in 7 days?

   b. How many gallons of orange juice would you expect the Café to use in 14 days?

   c. How many loaves of whole wheat bread would you expect the Café to use in 30 days?

   d. How many pounds of maple syrup would you expect the Café to use in 60 days?

(continued)

Name _____   Date _____

For use with Exploration 2

6. Two real estate agents made the scatter plots below to show the relationship between the living area and selling prices of houses in a selected area. Choose the letter of the scatter plot that you think shows the better fitted line. Explain your choice.

A.
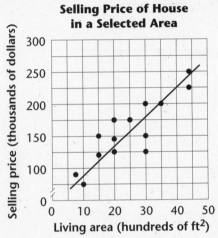

B.
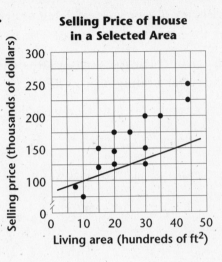

7. Use the scatter plot you chose in Exercise 6.

a. About what do you think the selling price of a 3500 ft^2 house in the selected area would be?

b. There are two houses with a living area of 3000 ft^2. One sells for $125,000 and the other sells for $150,000. Why do you think the selling prices are different?

For use with Exploration 3

8. Use the box-and-whisker plot shown.

a. Estimate the greatest amount of money a shopper spent at the grocery store.

b. Estimate the least amount of money a shopper spent at the grocery store.

c. Estimate the median amount of money a shopper spent at the grocery store.

d. Estimate the range in the amounts of money the shoppers spent at the grocery store.

Amount of Money Spent by 75 Shoppers in a Grocery Store

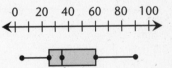

MODULE 5 SECTION 3 | **PRACTICE AND APPLICATIONS**

For use with Exploration 1

1. It is estimated that 9 out of 14 teenagers enrolled in Riviera Middle School play soccer. Estimate the percent of teenagers in Riviera Middle School who play soccer.

2. In a marketing survey of a new cereal, 8 out of every 17 people who responded gave the new cereal a rating of 9 or 10 on a scale of 1 to 10.

   a. What "nice" fraction can you use to estimate the percent of people who gave the cereal a rating of 9 or 10?

   b. Estimate the percent of people who gave the cereal a rating of 9 or 10.

3. Estimate the percent equivalent of each ratio.

   a. $\frac{9}{11}$ b. $\frac{11}{32}$ c. $\frac{7}{18}$

   d. $\frac{24}{35}$ e. $\frac{10}{24}$ f. $\frac{42}{85}$

   g. $\frac{17}{21}$ h. $\frac{42}{98}$ i. $\frac{34}{99}$

   j. $\frac{4}{19}$ k. $\frac{6}{49}$ l. $\frac{11}{45}$

For use with Exploration 2

4. Set up and solve a proportion to find the actual percent for Exercises 1 and 2. Round each answer to the nearest percent.

5. Write each ratio as a percent. Round each answer to the nearest tenth of a percent.

   a. $\frac{10}{12}$ b. $\frac{54}{135}$ c. $\frac{72}{96}$

   d. $\frac{75}{120}$ e. $\frac{21}{30}$ f. $\frac{45}{96}$

   g. $\frac{40}{150}$ h. $\frac{52}{160}$ i. $\frac{12}{72}$

   j. $\frac{28}{36}$ k. $\frac{25}{80}$ l. $\frac{14}{70}$

6. Of the 2628 new books purchased by the library, 525 were for teenagers. What percent of the new books were for teenagers?

(continued)

| MODULE 5 SECTION 3 | PRACTICE AND APPLICATIONS |

For use with Exploration 3

7. Suppose 44% of students at a school do not like classical music. If 198 students do not like classical music, how many students are there in the school? Explain your reasoning.

8. Find each unknown number.

   a. 35% of a number is 17.5.

   c. 68% of a number is 578.

   e. 18% of a number is 32.4.

   g. 45% of a number is 117.

   i. A number is 30% of 120.

   k. 61% of a number is 91.5.

   m. A number is 40% of 40.

   o. 75% of a number is 84.

   q. 56 is 25% of a number.

   s. 48% of a number is 172.8.

   u. 60% of a number is 18.

   w. A number is 55% of 300.

   b. 42 is 70% of a number.

   d. A number is 34% of 75.

   f. A number is 23% of 16.

   h. A number is 70% of 560.

   j. 25% of a number is 21.

   l. 60 is 48% of a number.

   n. 5% of a number is 25.

   p. 63% of a number is 56.7.

   r. A number is 4% of 75.

   t. A number is 71% of 120.

   v. 30% of a number is 45.

   x. A number is 82% of 70.

9. A book costs $5.95. The tax on the book is 8% of the cost. What is the total cost of the book?

10. Jerry and Nadine had dinner at a Chinese restaurant. They left a 15% tip that was $2.70. How much did the meal cost before the tip?

11. An aerobics instructor maintains a strict diet of 2000 Calories per day. An 8 oz container of yogurt provides the instructor with 12% of her daily Calories. How many Calories does the yogurt provide?

12. In a school election, 285 students voted for Bill for the Student Council President. If 47.5% of the students voted for Bill, how many students voted in the election?

MODULE 5 SECTION 4   PRACTICE AND APPLICATIONS

For use with Exploration 1

1. Write each ratio as a fraction in lowest terms, a decimal, and a percent.

a. $2:3$ **b.** $18:36$ **c.** $12:20$

d. $9:25$ **e.** $3:9$ **f.** $28:40$

g. $27:36$ **h.** $37:100$ **i.** $9.5:10$

For use with Exploration 2

2. Write each ratio, fraction, or decimal in percent form.

a. $7:50$ **b.** $\dfrac{3}{4}$ **c.** 0.6

d. $38:50$ **e.** $\dfrac{7}{8}$ **f.** 0.485

g. $\dfrac{30}{80}$ **h.** $\dfrac{4}{25}$ **i.** $\dfrac{45}{125}$

3. Use mental math to write each fraction as a percent.

a. $\dfrac{3}{20}$ **b.** $\dfrac{17}{25}$ **c.** $\dfrac{5}{20}$

d. $\dfrac{1}{9}$ **e.** $\dfrac{32}{100}$ **f.** $\dfrac{222}{333}$

g. $\dfrac{42}{84}$ **h.** $\dfrac{3.5}{50}$ **i.** $\dfrac{16}{32}$

4. To help the school dietician plan lunch menus, some students at a middle school took a survey of a random sample of their classmates to determine the top favorite lunch foods at their school. About 30% of the students surveyed chose pizza as their favorite lunch food. About 25% of the students surveyed chose sandwiches as their favorite lunch food. About 15% of the students surveyed chose pasta as their favorite lunch food. Suppose 600 students attend the school. How many of them would you expect to choose each food listed below?

A. pizza   **B.** sandwiches   **C.** pasta

5. About 79% of American households have a microwave oven. Estimate the number of households that have a microwave oven in a population of 600,000 people.

(continued)

MODULE 5 SECTION 4   **PRACTICE AND APPLICATIONS**

For use with Exploration 3

6. Consider the experiment of flipping a coin and rolling a 6-sided die.
Shade a grid to find the probability of each event.

    a. heads and the number 3

    c. tails and an even number

    e. heads and a 5 or 6

    b. tails and a number less than 4

    d. heads and a number greater than 1

    f. tails and a number less than 5

7. A bag contains one green marble and three yellow marbles. Three
marbles are removed from the bag one after another. After each
marble is removed, its color is recorded and the marble is put back
into the bag before the next marble is removed.

Copy and complete the tree diagram at the right to show the
outcomes of this experiment. Label each branch of the tree
with the probability.

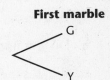

First marble

8. Use the tree diagram from Exercise 7 to find the probability of each
event. Round answers to the nearest tenth of a percent.

    a. drawing three green marbles

    c. drawing a green, a yellow,
and a green marble

    e. drawing exactly two yellow marbles

    g. drawing at least one yellow marble

    b. drawing three yellow marbles

    d. drawing a yellow, a yellow,
and a green marble

    f. drawing exactly two green marbles

    h. drawing at least one green marble

9. Suppose the probability that it will snow in Yellowstone this week is
$\frac{3}{8}$ each day.

    a. What is the probability that it will not snow on a given day?

    b. Make a tree diagram to find all the possible outcomes for two
consecutive days.

    c. Use a grid to find the probability of snow on two consecutive
days.

    d. What is the probability that it will not snow on two consecutive
days?

    e. What is the probability it will snow the first day and *not* snow the
second day?

| **MODULE 5 SECTIONS 1–4** | **PRACTICE AND APPLICATIONS** |

For use with Section 1

1. Write each rate as a unit rate.

a. $\dfrac{46 \text{ min}}{5 \text{ mi}}$

b. $\dfrac{243 \text{ mi}}{9 \text{ gal}}$

c. $\dfrac{\$.64}{8 \text{ min}}$

d. $\dfrac{176.4 \text{ km}}{6 \text{ L}}$

e. $\dfrac{38 \text{ min}}{4 \text{ mi}}$

f. $\dfrac{\$15}{4 \text{ lb}}$

g. $\dfrac{\$58.40}{4 \text{ h}}$

h. $\dfrac{\$4.08}{6 \text{ bunches}}$

i. $\dfrac{45 \text{ min}}{6 \text{ mi}}$

2. To celebrate her fiftieth birthday, Beatrice ran a 50 mile race. Her time for the race was about 14 h. Represent Beatrice's running pace as a unit rate. Round your answer to the nearest tenth.

3. Use the stem-and-leaf plot showing the spelling test scores for one class.

   a. Do you notice any gaps or clusters in the data? Explain?

   b. What is the range of the spelling test scores in the stem-and-leaf plot?

   c. Find the median and mode of the data.

Spelling Test Scores

```
 6 | 9
 7 |
 8 | 0 0 2 5 6 7 8 8 9
 9 | 0 1 1 1 2 2 3 4 5 8
10 | 0
```

8 | 7 means 87

For use with Section 2

4. Solve each proportion.

a. $\dfrac{m}{8} = \dfrac{4.2}{2.4}$

b. $\dfrac{24}{18} = \dfrac{38.4}{s}$

c. $\dfrac{6}{y} = \dfrac{21}{52.5}$

d. $\dfrac{14}{5} = \dfrac{70}{c}$

e. $\dfrac{a}{20} = \dfrac{24}{96}$

f. $\dfrac{9}{p} = \dfrac{45}{18}$

g. $\dfrac{5}{16} = \dfrac{17.5}{t}$

h. $\dfrac{16}{20} = \dfrac{4}{x}$

i. $\dfrac{36}{54} = \dfrac{v}{40.5}$

j. $\dfrac{c}{3} = \dfrac{24}{48}$

k. $\dfrac{33}{15} = \dfrac{w}{45}$

l. $\dfrac{7}{25} = \dfrac{1.4}{r}$

5. A dog eats about 12 lb of dog food every 15 days. How many pounds of dog food would you expect it to eat in 60 days?

(continued)

| MODULE 5 SECTIONS 1–4 | PRACTICE AND APPLICATIONS |

For use with Section 3

6. Estimate the percent equivalent of each ratio.

   a. $\dfrac{38}{79}$ **b.** $\dfrac{1}{9}$ **c.** $\dfrac{41}{52}$

   d. $\dfrac{21}{80}$ **e.** $\dfrac{63}{81}$ **f.** $\dfrac{22}{50}$

7. Write each ratio as a percent. Round each answer to the nearest tenth of a percent.

   a. $\dfrac{28}{60}$ **b.** $\dfrac{17}{85}$ **c.** $\dfrac{32}{128}$

   d. $\dfrac{11}{20}$ **e.** $\dfrac{23}{25}$ **f.** $\dfrac{42}{78}$

8. Find each unknown number.

   a. 25% of a number is 30.   **b.** 105 is 75% of a number.

   c. 60% of a number is 54.   **d.** A number is 42% of 65.

   e. A number is 36% of 150.   **f.** A number is 15% of 60.

9. Members of a running club had lunch at the Whole Grain Burger Palace. They left a 15% tip that totaled $9.30. How much did the meal cost?

For use with Section 4

10. Use mental math to write each fraction as a percent.

   a. $\dfrac{13}{20}$ **b.** $\dfrac{22}{25}$ **c.** $\dfrac{6}{24}$

11. About 76% of American households have a washing machine. Estimate the number of households that have a washing machine in a population of 200,000 people.

12. A box contains 1 red marker and 4 blue markers. Without looking, Danny reaches into the box and pulls out the first marker he touches. He puts the marker back into the box and then his sister Megan reaches into the box, without looking, and pulls out the first marker that she touches. What is the probability that both Danny and Megan pull out blue markers?

MODULE 5 SECTION 1   STUDY GUIDE

Run for Your Life   Ratios and Data Displays

GOAL **LEARN HOW TO:** • find unit rates
 • set up proportions
 • make and interpret stem-and-leaf plots
 • interpret histograms

 AS YOU: • explore running times
 • examine the results of a race

Exploration 1: Ratio and Proportions

Rates, Ratios, and Proportions

A **ratio** is a comparison of two quantities by division. A ratio can be written in any of the three forms shown at the right.

12 ft to 3 s $\dfrac{12 \text{ ft}}{3 \text{ s}}$ 12 ft : 3 s

A **rate** is a ratio that compares quantities measured in different units.

> ### Examples
>
> **a.** The ratio $\dfrac{35 \text{ mi}}{2 \text{ gal}}$ compares miles to gallons by division, so it is a rate.
>
> **b.** The ratio $\dfrac{3 \text{ min}}{60 \text{ min}}$ compares minutes to minutes, so it is *not* a rate.

A **proportion** is an equation stating that two ratios are equivalent. A **unit rate** is the rate for one unit of a given quantity.

> ### Example
>
> Write $\dfrac{\$4.50}{6 \text{ cans}}$ as a unit rate.
>
> ### ■ Sample Response ■
>
> Use a proportion to find the unit rate; that is, find the price for just 1 can.
>
> $$\dfrac{\$4.50}{6 \text{ cans}} = \dfrac{x}{1 \text{ can}}$$
>
> *Think*: What number must you divide the numerator and denominator by to change 6 cans to 1 can?
>
> $$\dfrac{\$4.50 \div 6}{6 \text{ cans} \div 6} = \dfrac{\$.75}{1 \text{ can}}$$
>
> The unit rate is $.75/can.

MODULE 5 SECTION 1   STUDY GUIDE

Exploration 2: Stem-and-Leaf Plots

Displays of Data

The **median** is the middle item when you order a data set from least to greatest. The **mode** is the item that appears most often in a set of data. The **range** of a data set is the difference between the greatest data value and the least data value.

Stem-and-leaf plots can be used to organize and display data. Stem-and-leaf plots show each data value. The *ones digit* of a data value is a *leaf*. The remaining digit or digits of the number form the *stem* for that leaf. The stems are written vertically in order from least to greatest. The leaves are then written horizontally next to the appropriate stem in order from least to greatest.

Medals Won by the Top 20 Countries in 1996 Olympics

```
 1 | 5 5 5 5 7 7 9
 2 | 0 1 2 3 5 7
 3 | 5 7
 4 | 1
 5 | 0
 6 | 3 5
 7 |
 8 |
 9 |
10 | 1
```

6 | 3 represents 63 medals.

> ### Example
>
> Find the mode, the median, and the range of the data shown in the stem-and-leaf plot above.
>
> ### ■ Sample Response ■
>
> The mode is 15, because 15 occurs most often (4 times).
>
> There are 20 data values in order in the plot. The median is the average of the 10th and 11th values found by counting from the first row of the plot. So, the median is $(22 + 23) \div 2$, or 22.5.
>
> The greatest value is 101 and the least value is 15, so the range is $101 - 15$, or 86.

Exploration 3: Histograms

Frequency tables and **histograms** display frequencies in given intervals. A histogram is a bar graph with no spaces between the bars.

Weight of Puppies Sold at a Pet Store	
Weight (lb)	**Frequency**
0.1–2.0	23
2.1–4.0	25
4.1–6.0	15
6.1–8.0	9
8.1–10.0	5

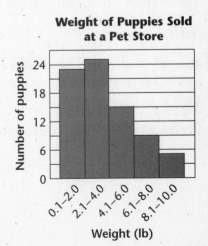

Weight of Puppies Sold at a Pet Store

MODULE 5 SECTION 1 | **PRACTICE & APPLICATION EXERCISES** | **STUDY GUIDE**

Exploration 1

For Exercises 1–4, write each rate as a unit rate.

1. $\dfrac{\$13.80}{3 \text{ boxes}}$ **2.** $\dfrac{135 \text{ mi}}{5 \text{ gal}}$ **3.** $\dfrac{25¢}{4 \text{ min}}$ **4.** $\dfrac{3 \text{ mi}}{25 \text{ min}}$

5. A typical shower uses 4 gal of water per minute. How many gallons of water are used during a 15 min shower?

6. Long distance company X charges $2.70 for a 15 min call. Company Y charges $4.50 for a 27 min call. Which phone company has the best rates for its customers?

Exploration 2

7. a. This list gives the ages of the people enrolled in art classes at the museum: 15, 23, 18, 45, 63, 70, 34, 15, 28, 65, 65, 67, 19. Make a stem-and-leaf plot to show these ages. Be sure to include a title and a key for your plot.

b. State the range, the median, and the mode of the data.

Exploration 3

Use the histogram at the right.

8. Is the number of students who read more than 3 hours per week *greater than, equal to,* or *less than* the number of students who read 3 hours or less per week?

9. How many students read at least 2 hours each week?

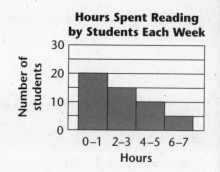

Spiral Review

Solve each equation. Check each solution. (Module 4, p. 300)

10. $3x + 5 = 26$ **11.** $6 + \dfrac{t}{3} = -3$ **12.** $\dfrac{y}{9} - 7 = 8$

Use mental math to find a reasonable estimate for the cost of each purchase. (Toolbox, pp. 582–583)

13. 2.5 lb of candy at $5.95 for 3 lb   **14.** 12 apples at $.39 per apple

Write each fraction in lowest terms. (Module 3, p. 170)

15. $\dfrac{24}{88}$ **16.** $\dfrac{9}{39}$ **17.** $\dfrac{20}{90}$ **18.** $\dfrac{6}{45}$

MODULE 5 SECTION 2 | **STUDY GUIDE**

Just for Fun   Proportions and Plots

GOAL **LEARN HOW TO:** • solve proportions using cross products
• make a scatter plot
• fit a line to a scatter plot
• interpret box-and-whisker plots

AS YOU: • explore the riders' experience on a roller coaster
• examine how much a rubber band stretches
• examine stone-skipping data

Exploration 1: Cross Products

You can use **cross products** to solve a proportion. Cross products are found by multiplying the numerator of one ratio in the proportion times the denominator of the other ratio.

The cross products of the proportion $\frac{1}{3} = \frac{4}{12}$ are $1 \cdot 12$ and $3 \cdot 4$.

Example

Solve the proportion $\frac{4}{5} = \frac{x}{15}$.

■ **Sample Response** ■

$$\frac{4}{5} = \frac{x}{15}$$

$4 \cdot 15 = 5 \cdot x$ ← Use cross products to write an equation.

$60 = 5x$

$\dfrac{60}{5} = \dfrac{5x}{5}$ ← Divide both sides by 5.

$12 = x$

Exploration 2: Scatter Plots

Scatter Plots and Fitted Lines

A **scatter plot** is a good way to explore how two sets of data are related. If the data values lie along a line, you can use a **fitted line** to make predictions.

For example, the fitted line on the scatter plot at the right can be used to predict that about 25 trees will be sold at $125 each.

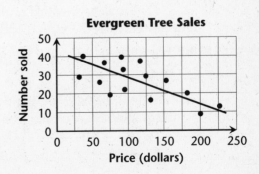

Evergreen Tree Sales

MODULE 5 SECTION 2   **STUDY GUIDE**

Exploration 3: Box-and-Whisker Plots

Box-and-whisker plots are useful for displaying a set of data. There are five important points represented in a box-and-whisker plot.

- The whisker on the left is called the *lower whisker*. The dot at the left end of the lower whisker represents the least value (the *lower extreme*).

- The whisker on the right is the *upper whisker* and the dot at its right end represents the greatest value (the *upper extreme*).

- The box between the two whiskers is divided into two parts by a vertical line. This vertical line represents the *median of the entire data set* (50% of the data are less than this value and 50% is greater).

- The point represented by the left end of the box is the median of the lower half of the data values. This point is called the *lower quartile* value.

- The point represented by the right end of the box is the median of the upper half of the data values. This point is called the *upper quartile* value.

Also, each of the whiskers and each part of the box contain approximately 25% of the values in the data set.

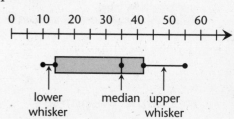

Example

Refer to the box-and-whisker plot above.

a. What is the greatest data value of the data set? the least data value?

b. What is the range of the data?

c. What is the median of the data?

d. About what percent of the data are greater than 14?

■ Sample Response ■

a. 55 (The value represented by the right end of the upper whisker.); 10 (The value represented by the left end of the lower whisker.)

b. 55 – 10, or 45

c. 35

d. Since 14 is the value represented by the lower end of the box, approximately 75% of the data values are greater than 14.

Name _____ Date _____

Exploration 1

Solve each proportion.

1. $\dfrac{8}{22} = \dfrac{g}{33}$

2. $\dfrac{4}{k} = \dfrac{6}{21}$

3. $\dfrac{18}{24} = \dfrac{c}{40}$

4. $\dfrac{5}{12} = \dfrac{3.5}{x}$

Exploration 2

The scatter plots below shows the relationship between the monthly normal temperatures and the average precipitation for Boston, Massachusetts.

A.
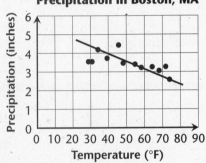

B.
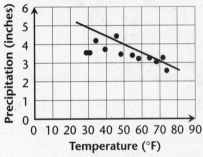

5. Choose the letter of the scatter plot that you think shows the better fitted line. Explain your choice.

6. About how many inches of precipitation would you expect in Boston when the temperature averages 50°?

Exploration 3

Use the box-and-whisker plot at the right.

7. What is the age of the youngest swimmer?

8. About half of the swimmers are under what age?

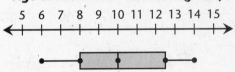

Spiral Review

Write each rate as a unit rate. (Module 5, p. 319)

9. $\dfrac{\$210}{3 \text{ books}}$

10. $\dfrac{75 \text{ min}}{5 \text{ pages}}$

11. $\dfrac{\$29}{2 \text{ dinners}}$

Write each product in exponential form. (Module 1, p. 20)

12. $6 \cdot 6$

13. $2 \cdot 2 \cdot 2 \cdot 2 \cdot 2$

14. $7 \cdot 7 \cdot 7 \cdot 7 \cdot 7 \cdot 7 \cdot 7$

Write each fraction in lowest terms. (Module 3, p. 170)

15. $\dfrac{16}{44}$

16. $\dfrac{5}{90}$

17. $\dfrac{34}{85}$

18. $\dfrac{39}{60}$

MODULE 5 SECTION 3   STUDY GUIDE

You Be the Critic   Percent

GOAL   **LEARN HOW TO:** • estimate percents
                              • find percents
                              • find a missing part or a whole

   AS YOU: • analyze movie ratings
               • find audience approval ratings
               • find how many people rated a movie

Exploration 1: Estimating Percents

Percent Bar Model

When solving problems involving percent, "nice" fractions can be used to
help estimate solutions. "Nice" fractions are fractions that can be
converted to percents easily. $\frac{1}{5}, \frac{1}{2}, \frac{3}{4}$, and $\frac{7}{10}$ are examples of "nice" fractions.

Example
Estimate the percent equivalent of 21 out of 40.

Sample Response

$\frac{21}{40}$ is slightly greater than the "nice" fraction $\frac{1}{2}$.

Since $\frac{1}{2} = 50\%$, $\frac{21}{40}$ is a little more than 50%.

Exploration 2: Finding Percent

Proportions and Percents

You can find the percent equivalent for a ratio by using a proportion.

Example
Write the ratio $\frac{21}{40}$ as a percent.

Sample Response

$$\frac{21}{40} = \frac{x}{100}$$

$$40 \cdot x = 21 \cdot 100$$

$$40x = 2100$$

$$x = 52.5 \qquad \text{So, } \frac{21}{40} = 52.5\%.$$

Name _____   Date _____

Exploration 3: Finding Parts or Wholes

You can use proportions to find a missing part or whole.

Example

Set up and solve a proportion to find the number that is 35% of 70.

■ Sample Response ■

$$
\begin{array}{c}
\textbf{Percent} \qquad \textbf{Number} \\
\text{Part} \rightarrow \dfrac{35}{100} = \dfrac{x}{70} \leftarrow \text{Part} \\
\text{Whole} \rightarrow \phantom{\dfrac{35}{100}} \phantom{\dfrac{x}{70}} \leftarrow \text{Whole}
\end{array}
$$

Now solve the proportion.

$$\frac{35}{100} = \frac{x}{70}$$

$$35 \cdot 70 = 100 \cdot x \qquad \leftarrow \text{Use the cross products.}$$

$$2450 = 100x$$

$$\frac{2450}{100} = \frac{100x}{100} \qquad \leftarrow \text{Divide both sides by 100.}$$

$$24.5 = x$$

So, 35% of 70 is 24.5.

Example

36 is 45% of some number. Use a proportion to find the number.

■ Sample Response ■

$$
\begin{array}{c}
\textbf{Percent} \qquad \textbf{Number} \\
\text{Part} \rightarrow \dfrac{45}{100} = \dfrac{36}{y} \leftarrow \text{Part} \\
\text{Whole} \rightarrow \phantom{\dfrac{45}{100}} \phantom{\dfrac{36}{y}} \leftarrow \text{Whole}
\end{array}
$$

Now solve the proportion.

$$\frac{45}{100} = \frac{36}{y}$$

$$45 \cdot y = 100 \cdot 36 \qquad \leftarrow \text{Use the cross products.}$$

$$45y = 3600$$

$$\frac{45y}{45} = \frac{3600}{45} \qquad \leftarrow \text{Divide both sides by 45.}$$

$$y = 80$$

So, 36% of 45 is 80.

| MODULE 5 SECTION 3 | PRACTICE & APPLICATION EXERCISES | STUDY GUIDE |

Exploration 1

For Exercises 1–4, estimate the percent equivalent of each ratio.

1. $\frac{11}{23}$

2. $\frac{6}{21}$

3. $\frac{14}{17}$

4. $\frac{25}{26}$

5. A librarian estimated that 5 out every 13 library patrons ask the resource librarian a question. Estimate the percent of patrons who ask the resource librarian a question.

Exploration 2

For Exercises 6–9, write each ratio as a percent. Round each answer to the nearest tenth.

6. $\frac{40}{60}$

7. $\frac{15}{25}$

8. $\frac{11}{50}$

9. $\frac{7}{9}$

10. In Marta's class, 8 out of 28 students got 100% on a science exam. What percent of the class did *not* get 100%?

Exploration 3

Find each unknown number.

11. 13% of a number is 7.28.

12. A number is 27% of 44.

13. A number is 40% of 120.

14. 98% of a number is 98.

15. 80% of a number is 20.

16. A number is 75% of 150.

Spiral Review

Solve each proportion. (Module 5, p. 336)

17. $\frac{4}{5} = \frac{x}{25}$

18. $\frac{t}{7} = \frac{30}{280}$

19. $\frac{3}{m} = \frac{20}{100}$

Find the absolute value of each integer. (Module 2, p. 91)

20. −99

21. 58

22. −8

23. −1145

Write each fraction in lowest terms. (Module 3, p. 170)

24. $\frac{36}{180}$

25. $\frac{21}{35}$

26. $\frac{12}{15}$

27. $\frac{38}{44}$

Make Every Shot Count   Percent and Probability

GOAL   **LEARN HOW TO:** • write a fraction as a decimal or percent
                    • estimate percents using "nice" fractions and mental math
                    • use percents to make predictions
                    • find theoretical probabilities for a multiple-stage experiment

As you: • test your free-throw ability
            • examine basketball statistics
            • analyze repeated free throws

Exploration 1: Fractions, Decimals, and Percents

Fraction-Decimal-Percent Equivalents

A ratio can be represented as a fraction, as a decimal, and as a percent.

> ### Example
>
> Write 24 out of 50 in ratio, fraction, decimal, and percent form.
>
> | Ratio form | Fraction form | Decimal form | Percent form |
> |---|---|---|---|
> | 24 to 50 or 24 : 50 | $\frac{24}{50}$ | 0.48 | 48% |

Exploration 2: Predicting Using Percents

Percents can be used to predict future outcomes.

> ### Example
>
> John has hit the bull's-eye of a target with a dart on 15 of 65 throws. How many bull's-eyes can he expect to get in his next 10 throws?
>
> ### ■ Sample Response ■
>
> original fraction: $\frac{15}{65} = \frac{3}{13}$ →   " nice" fraction: $\frac{3}{12} = \frac{1}{4}$
>
> So, $\frac{15}{65} \approx \frac{1}{4} = 25\%$.
>
> Since 25% of 10 = 0.25 • 10, or 2.5, John can expect to hit the bull's-eye 2 or 3 times in his next 10 throws.

MODULE 5 SECTION 4

Exploration 3: Multi-stage Experiments

Probability and Multi-stage Experiments

A **multi-stage experiment** consists of doing two or more events one after the other. You can find the probability of the outcomes of a multi-stage experiment by shading a grid or constructing a tree diagram.

Example

A spinner has three equal sectors numbered 1–3. If the spinner is spun twice, what is the probability that a 3 is spun both times?

■ Sample Response ■

There is a 1 in 3 chance of spinning a 3 on any spin.

Method 1: Use a 3×3 grid.

Start on the left and shade $\frac{1}{3}$ of the columns (1 column)
to show the probability that a 3 is spun on the first spin.

Start at the top and shade $\frac{1}{3}$ of the rows (1 row) to
show the probability that the second spin is a 3.

The probability that the first and the second spins will both be
a 3 is represented by the region of the grid that was shaded twice.
So, the probability is $\frac{1}{9}$.

Method 2: Use a tree diagram.

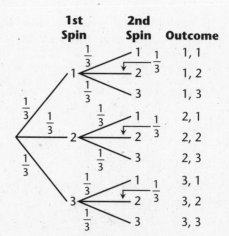

From the diagram, $P(3, 3) = \frac{1}{3} \cdot \frac{1}{3} = \frac{1}{9}$.

MODULE 5 SECTION 4 | PRACTICE & APPLICATION EXERCISES | STUDY GUIDE

Exploration 1

For Exercises 1–8, write each ratio as a fraction, as a decimal, and as a percent.

1. 2 : 5　　　　**2.** 12 : 36　　　　**3.** 8 : 40　　　　**4.** 18 : 100

5. 25 : 500　　　　**6.** 5.4 : 21　　　　**7.** 18 : 24　　　　**8.** 25.8 : 200

9. About 30% of 66 students during the first lunch period chose pizza over hamburgers. If a school enrolls 580 students, how many can they expect to eat pizza?

Use mental math to write each fraction as a percent.

10. $\frac{11}{33}$　　　　**11.** $\frac{8}{32}$　　　　**12.** $\frac{24}{400}$　　　　**13.** $\frac{16}{24}$

Exploration 2

14. Thelma has earned an A on 24% of all her math tests so far this year. There will be 20 more math tests this year. Estimate the number of A's she can expect to earn on these remaining tests.

15. Petra ran 23 out of 35 cross country races in less than 18 min. Based on these results, how many times in the next 15 races would you expect him to finish in less than 18 min?

Exploration 3

16. A bag contains 4 green chips and 5 red chips. Two chips are removed from the bag one after another. After each chip is removed, its color is recorded and the chip is put back into the bag before the next chip is removed.

  a. Draw a 9 × 9 grid. Shade it to find the probability of drawing a green chip on the first pick and a red chip on the second pick.

  b. Draw a tree diagram to show the possible outcomes of this experiment. Label each branch of the diagram with the probability of the outcome represented by it.

  c. Use the tree diagram from part (b) to find the probability of drawing 2 red chips.

Spiral Review

Solve each proportion. (Module 5, p. 352)

17. $\frac{14}{36} = \frac{35}{m}$　　　　**18.** $\frac{y}{100} = \frac{7}{25}$　　　　**19.** $\frac{3}{t} = \frac{8}{48}$　　　　**20.** $\frac{3}{11} = \frac{x}{231}$

MODULE 6   **CENTIMETER GRID PAPER**

(Use with Section 2, Exploration 2.)

MODULE 6   LABSHEET **2A**

Circle (Use with Question 24 on page 402.)

Directions

• Cut out the circle.

• Cut apart the eight sectors and arrange them to form the figure
  shown below.

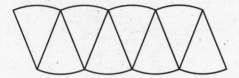

• Tape the figure to a sheet of paper.

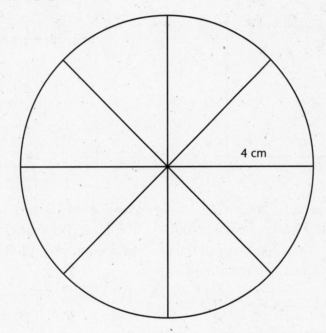

4 cm

MODULE 6   PROJECT LABSHEET **A**

Create a Wild Wing

(Use with Project Question 1 on page 408 and Project Question 4 on page 433.)

Step 1 Draw a line 2 in. from the top of an $8\frac{1}{2}$ in. by 11 in. sheet of paper. This will be the tail of your Wild Wing.

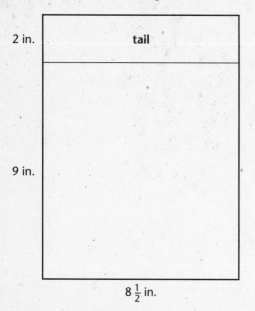

Step 2 Bring the bottom edge of the paper up to meet the line you drew. Fold and crease the paper. Repeat this step three more times.

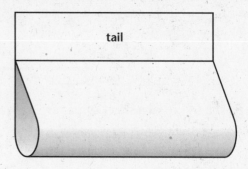

Step 3 To create a rectangular Wild Wing, fold the paper in fourths. Here is one way to do this: first, fold the paper in half, next, open the paper, and then fold each side into the middle.

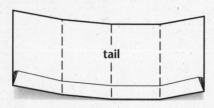

Step 4 Bring the ends together and tape the seam. The folded edge should be in the interior of your Wild Wing.

rectangular Wild Wing

To create a triangular Wild Wing, fold the paper in thirds.

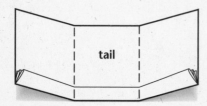

triangular Wild Wing

MODULE 6 LABSHEET **3A**

Curtiss Jennys (Use with Questions 4–7 on pages 411–412.)

Directions
• Carefully cut out each airplane along the solid lines. Include the tabs on the sides and bottom of the plane. Be careful not to bend the drawings.

• Fold back the tabs along the dotted lines. Align the side tabs evenly with the bottom tab and tape them together. Do this carefully so both planes stand up straight.

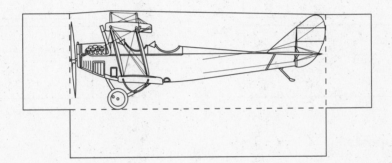

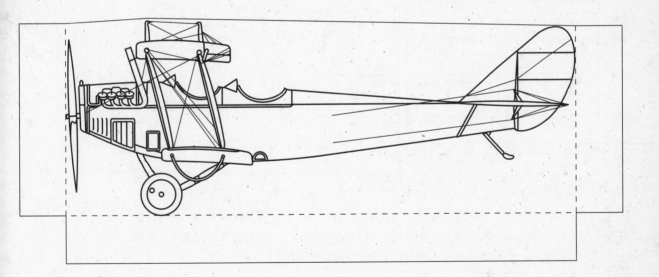

MODULE 6   **LABSHEET** **4A**

Build a Wing
(Use with Question 2 on page 423 and Question 13 on page 426.)

Construct the bases.

First Cut out two $1\frac{1}{2}$ in. × 5 in. bases.

Then Draw support lines at 1 in. intervals on both bases.

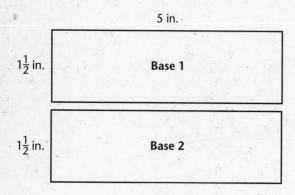

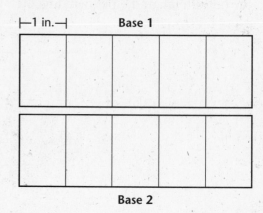

Construct the supports.

First Cut out four $1\frac{1}{2}$ in. × 2 in. supports.

Then Fold $\frac{1}{4}$ in. tabs on each support.

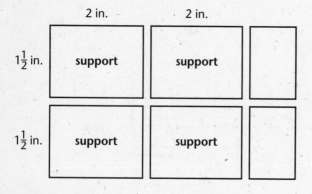

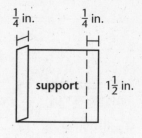

Construct Wing 1.

First Tape one end of a support to a support line on Base 1. Wrap tape around the tab and the base to secure the support. Repeat for the other three supports

Then Tape the free ends of the supports to Base 2.

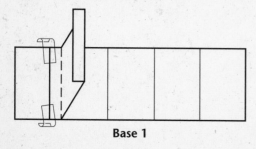

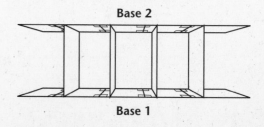

Draw a Transversal   (Use with Questions 9 and 10 on page 425.)

Directions

• Draw a transversal. Then label the angles formed by the parallel lines
  and the transversal as ∠1, ∠2, ∠3, ∠4, ∠5, ∠6, ∠7, and ∠8.

• Measure each angle and record the measurements in the table.

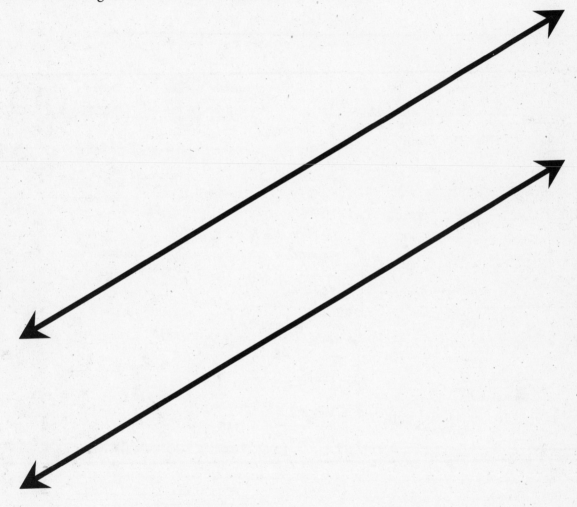

Angle	Measure	Angle	Measure
∠1		∠2	
∠3		∠4	
∠5		∠6	
∠7		∠8	

Map of the Central Region of the United States

(Use with the Extended Exploration on page 435.)

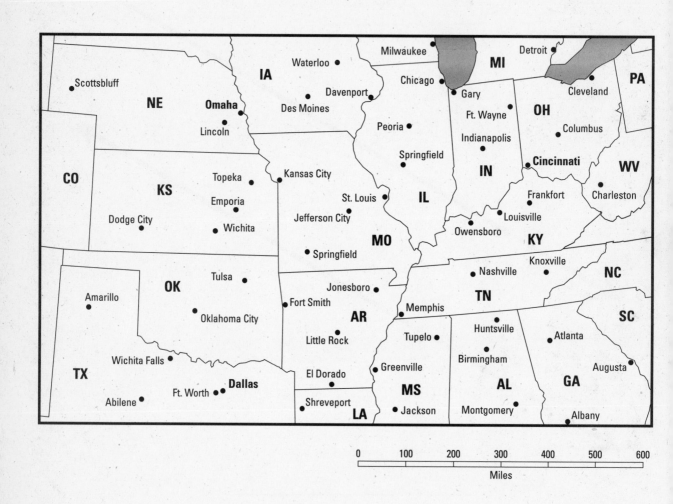

MODULE 6

Combined International Routes

(Use with Question 25 on page 443.)

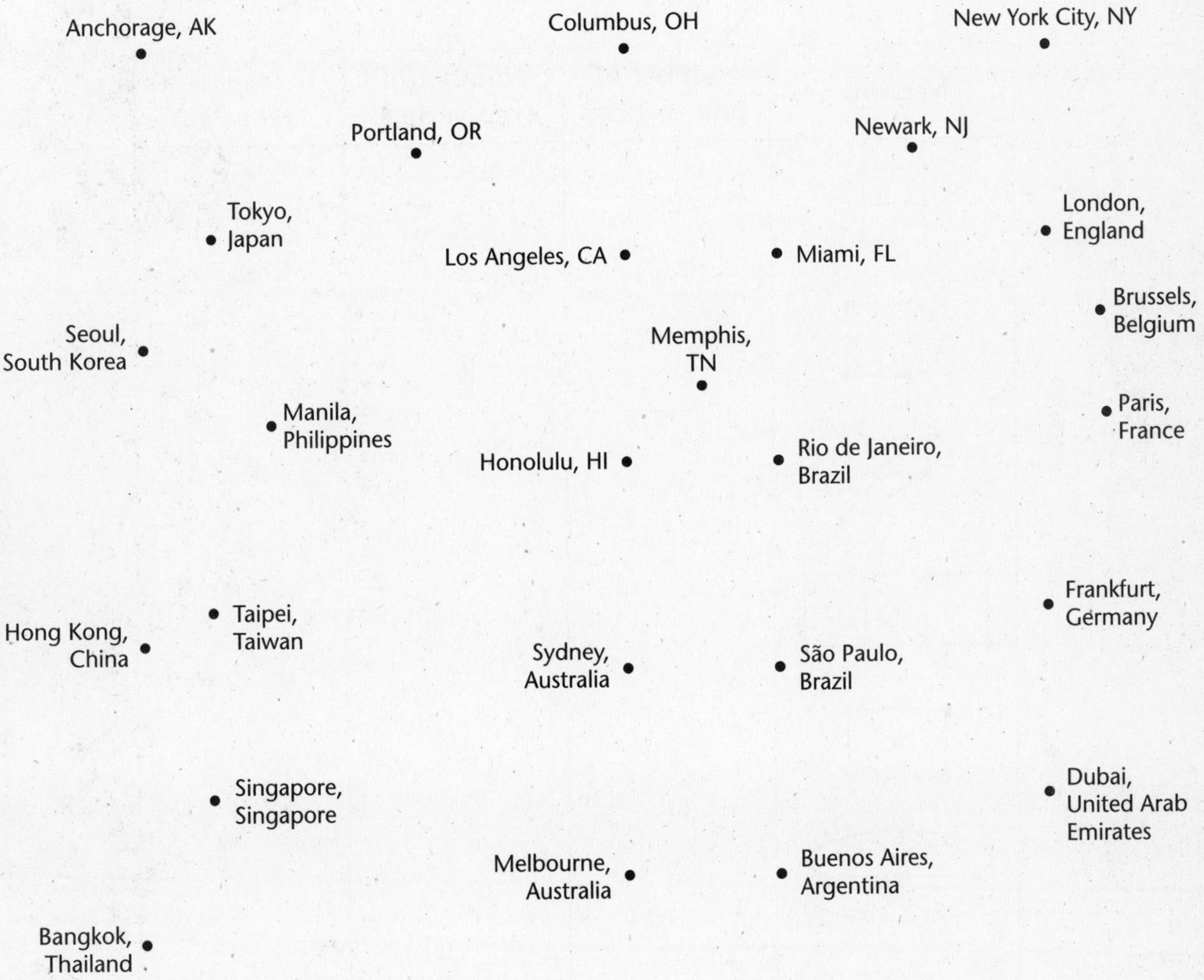

Anchorage, AK
•

Columbus, OH
•

New York City, NY
•

Portland, OR
•

Newark, NJ
•

Tokyo,
• Japan

London,
• England

Los Angeles, CA •

• Miami, FL

Brussels,
• Belgium

Seoul,
South Korea •

Memphis,
TN
•

Paris,
• France

Manila,
• Philippines

Honolulu, HI •

Rio de Janeiro,
• Brazil

Frankfurt,
• Germany

Hong Kong,
China •

Taipei,
• Taiwan

Sydney,
Australia •

São Paulo,
• Brazil

Singapore,
• Singapore

Dubai,
• United Arab
Emirates

Melbourne,
Australia •

Buenos Aires,
• Argentina

Bangkok,
Thailand •

Testing for Traversability (Use with Exercise 36 on page 449.)

Directions
Complete the table.

An odd vertex is a vertex at which an odd number of arcs meet.

An even vertex is a vertex at which an even number of arcs meet.

Network	Number of odd vertices	Number of even vertices	Traversable? (*yes* or *no*)

a. Make a conjecture about when a network is traversable and when a network is not traversable.

b. Test your conjecture by drawing and testing a network fitting each description.

- 0 odd vertices   • 2 odd vertices   • 4 odd vertices   • 6 odd vertices

c. Did your conjecture work in every case you tested? Explain.

Name _____   Problem _____

 The star indicates that you excelled in some way.

Problem Solving

①   **②**   **③**   **④**   **⑤**

① You did not understand the problem well enough to get started or you did not show any work.

③ You understood the problem well enough to make a plan and to work toward a solution.

⑤ You made a plan, you used it to solve the problem, and you verified your solution.

Mathematical Language

①   **②**   **③**   **④**   **⑤**

① You did not use any mathematical vocabulary or symbols, or you did not use them correctly, or your use was not appropriate.

③ You used appropriate mathematical language, but the way it was used was not always correct or other terms and symbols were needed.

⑤ You used mathematical language that was correct and appropriate to make your meaning clear.

Representations

①   **②**   **③**   **④**   **⑤**

① You did not use any representations such as equations, tables, graphs, or diagrams to help solve the problem or explain your solution.

③ You made appropriate representations to help solve the problem or help you explain your solution, but they were not always correct or other representations were needed.

⑤ You used appropriate and correct representations to solve the problem or explain your solution.

Connections

①   **②**   **③**   **④**   **⑤**

① You attempted or solved the problem and then stopped.

③ You found patterns and used them to extend the solution to other cases, or you recognized that this problem relates to other problems, mathematical ideas, or applications.

⑤ You extended the ideas in the solution to the general case, or you showed how this problem relates to other problems, mathematical ideas, or applications.

Presentation

①   **②**   **③**   **④**   **⑤**

① The presentation of your solution and reasoning is unclear to others.

③ The presentation of your solution and reasoning is clear in most places, but others may have trouble understanding parts of it.

⑤ The presentation of your solution and reasoning is clear and can be understood by others.

Content Used: _____   Computational Errors: Yes   No

Notes on Errors: _____

Name _____   Problem _____

STUDENT | SELF-ASSESSMENT SCALES

▬ *If your score is in the shaded area, explain why on the back of this sheet and stop.*

☆ *The star indicates that you excelled in some way.*

Problem Solving

①   **②**   **③**   **④**   **⑤** ☆→

I did not understand the problem well enough to get started or I did not show any work.

I understood the problem well enough to make a plan and to work toward a solution.

I made a plan, I used it to solve the problem, and I verified my solution.

Mathematical Language

①   **②**   **③**   **④**   **⑤** ☆→

I did not use any mathematical vocabulary or symbols, or I did not use them correctly, or my use was not appropriate.

I used appropriate mathematical language, but the way it was used was not always correct or other terms and symbols were needed.

I used mathematical language that was correct and appropriate to make my meaning clear.

Representations

①   **②**   **③**   **④**   **⑤** ☆→

I did not use any representations such as equations, tables, graphs, or diagrams to help solve the problem or explain my solution.

I made appropriate representations to help solve the problem or help me explain my solution, but they were not always correct or other representations were needed.

I used appropriate and correct representations to solve the problem or explain my solution.

Connections

①   **②**   **③**   **④**   **⑤** ☆→

I attempted or solved the problem and then stopped.

I found patterns and used them to extend the solution to other cases, or I recognized that this problem relates to other problems, mathematical ideas, or applications.

I extended the ideas in the solution to the general case, or I showed how this problem relates to other problems, mathematical ideas, or applications.

Presentation

①   **②**   **③**   **④**   **⑤** ☆→

The presentation of my solution and reasoning is unclear to others.

The presentation of my solution and reasoning is clear in most places, but others may have trouble understanding parts of it.

The presentation of my solution and reasoning is clear and can be understood by others.

MODULE 6 SECTION 1   **PRACTICE AND APPLICATIONS**

For use with Exploration 1

1. Write an inequality to represent each statement. Then graph the inequality on a number line.

   a. x is less than 5.

   b. b is greater than or equal to 7.

   c. h is greater than 6 and less than or equal to 14.

   d. 2 is less than p, and p is less than 9.

   e. a is greater than 3.

   f. k is less than or equal to 6.

   g. r is greater than 2 and less than 5.

   h. s is greater than 4 and less than 17.

   i. 4 is less than t, and t is less than or equal to 16.

   j. b is greater than 8 and less than or equal to 10.

2. Use the graph below.

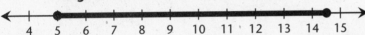

Lengths of North American Owls (in inches)

   a. One of the smallest owls in North America is the elf owl. Estimate its length.

   b. Estimate the range of sizes of the owls represented in the graph.

For use with Exploration 2

3. Tell whether each quadrilateral is a parallelogram. If a quadrilateral is not a parallelogram, explain why not.

   a.

   b.

   c.

4. Classify each polygon as concave or convex.

   a.

   b.

   c.

5. Draw two 6-sided polygons, one that is convex and one that is concave.

(continued)

MODULE 6 SECTION 1   **PRACTICE AND APPLICATIONS**

For use with Exploration 3

6. Find the probability that a small object dropped on each figure will land on the shaded target.

a.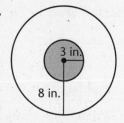

b.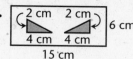

c.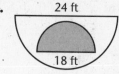

d.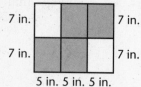

e.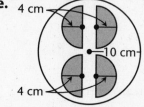

f.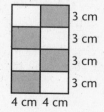

7. Suppose the probability that an object dropped onto the square shown at the right will land inside the shaded star is $\frac{3}{4}$.

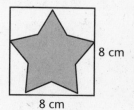

   a. What is the probability that the object will land in the unshaded area?

   b. What is the area of the star?

8. A small object is tossed onto a game board. If the object lands on the shaded area, Player I wins. If not, Player II wins.

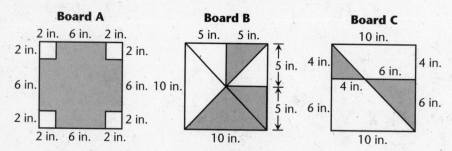

   a. Which game board is fair to both players, that is, makes their chances of winning equal?

   b. If you want Player I to have a greater chance of winning, which game board should you choose?

MODULE 6 SECTION 2   PRACTICE AND APPLICATIONS

For use with Exploration 1

1. Show that each number is a perfect square.

    a. 49   **b.** 900   **c.** 225

2. Find each square root.

    a. $\sqrt{144}$ **b.** $\sqrt{36}$ **c.** $\sqrt{0}$

    d. $\sqrt{169}$ **e.** $-\sqrt{16}$ **f.** $-\sqrt{100}$

    g. $\sqrt{400}$ **h.** $-\sqrt{121}$ **i.** $-\sqrt{81}$

    j. $-\sqrt{196}$ **k.** $\sqrt{324}$ **l.** $-\sqrt{256}$

    m. $\sqrt{289}$ **n.** $-\sqrt{25}$ **o.** $-\sqrt{1}$

    p. $\sqrt{64}$ **q.** $-\sqrt{0}$ **r.** $\sqrt{361}$

3. Give two consecutive whole numbers that each principal square root lies between. Then estimate each square root to the nearest tenth.

    a. $\sqrt{18}$ **b.** $\sqrt{46}$ **c.** $\sqrt{115}$

    d. $\sqrt{30}$ **e.** $\sqrt{7}$ **f.** $\sqrt{140}$

4. Estimate each square root to the nearest tenth.

    a. $\sqrt{72}$ **b.** $\sqrt{160}$ **c.** $\sqrt{28}$

    d. $\sqrt{230}$ **e.** $\sqrt{56}$ **f.** $\sqrt{415}$

    g. $\sqrt{80}$ **h.** $\sqrt{39}$ **i.** $\sqrt{249}$

    j. $\sqrt{50}$ **k.** $\sqrt{130}$ **l.** $\sqrt{260}$

    m. $\sqrt{20}$ **n.** $\sqrt{110}$ **o.** $\sqrt{61}$

    p. $\sqrt{136}$ **q.** $\sqrt{209}$ **r.** $\sqrt{42}$

5. A square playground in the center of a park has an area of 784 ft^2. Karen wants to walk along one side of the playground. How far does she walk?

(continued)

MODULE 6 SECTION 2   PRACTICE AND APPLICATIONS

For use with Exploration 2

6. Use the prism shown.

    a. What kind of prism is this?

    b. How many faces, vertices, and edges does this prism have?

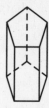

7. Use the prism shown.

    a. What kind of prism is this?

    b. How many faces, vertices, and edges does this prism have?

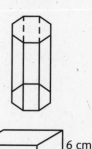

8. Use the rectangular prism shown.

    a. Sketch a net for the prism.

    b. Find the surface area of the prism.

6 cm
8 cm
12 cm

9. A box of macaroni and cheese is 7 in. tall, 4 in. long, and 2 in. wide. What is the surface area of the box?

For use with Exploration 3

10. Use π to write an expression for the exact area of each circle. Then use 3.14 or the [π] key on a calculator to find the approximate area to the nearest hundredth.

a.

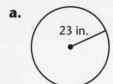

23 in.

b.

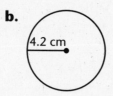

4.2 cm

c.

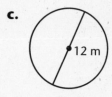

12 m

d.

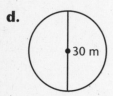

30 m

e.

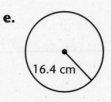

16.4 cm

f.

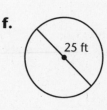

25 ft

11. A circular window has a diameter of 18 in. What is the area of the window?

MODULE 6 SECTION 3

For use with Exploration 1

1. Tell whether the polygons in each pair are *similar, congruent,* or *neither.* If the polygons are similar or congruent, write a statement that can be used to identify the corresponding parts.

a.

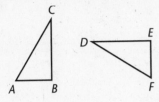

b.

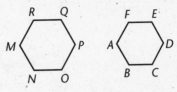

c.

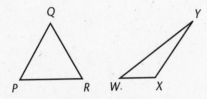

d.

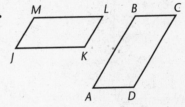

2. A scale drawing of a tree is shown at the right. Each centimeter on the drawing corresponds to 120 cm on the tree. Estimate each measurement of the tree in meters.

   a. height

   b. width of trunk

   c. center width of foliage

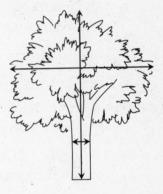

3. A magnifying glass makes an object appear larger. The amount of magnification can be described by using a scale. For each scale, how long does a 6 mm long ant appear to be when seen through the magnifying glass?

   a. 2 : 1   **b.** 5 : 1   **c.** 10 : 1

   d. 15 : 1   **e.** 18 : 1   **f.** 20 : 1

4. On a map, two cities are 3.5 in. apart. The scale of the map is 1 in. : 60 mi. What is the actual distance between the two cities?

(continued)

MODULE 6 SECTION 3   **PRACTICE AND APPLICATIONS**

For use with Exploration 2

5. Classify each triangle as *acute*, *obtuse*, or *right*.

a.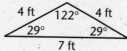
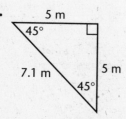

b.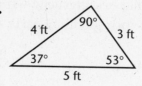

c.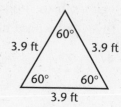

d.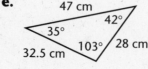

e.

6. △MNO is similar to △PQR.

   a. $\overline{OM}$ corresponds to $\overline{RP}$. What segments correspond to $\overline{MN}$ and $\overline{NO}$?

   b. Find the measures of ∠QPR, ∠PRQ, and ∠RQP.

   c. Find the lengths of $\overline{NM}$ and $\overline{MO}$.

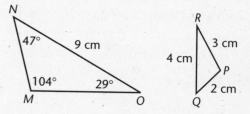

7. Use the similar polygons shown at the right.

   a. $\overline{AB}$ corresponds to $\overline{ZW}$. What angle corresponds to ∠ABC and what is its measure?

   b. Find the measures of ∠WXY, ∠YZW, and ∠XYZ.

   c. Which segment corresponds to $\overline{XY}$? What is its length?

   d. Find the lengths of $\overline{AB}$ and $\overline{AD}$.

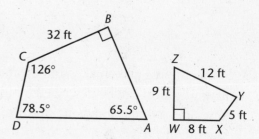

8. Rectangle ABCD is similar to rectangle QRST. The length of one side of rectangle ABCD is three times the width of the rectangle. The length of rectangle QRST is half the length of rectangle ABCD. What is the length of rectangle QRST if the width of rectangle ABCD is 6 cm?

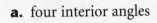

MODULE 6 SECTION 4　　　　　　　　　PRACTICE AND APPLICATIONS

For use with Exploration 1

1. The figure below shows two parallel lines, *c* and *d*, cut by transversal *t*. Name the angles or the pairs of angles that fit each description.

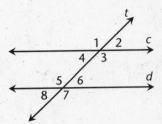

   a. four interior angles

   b. four exterior angles

   c. two pairs of alternate interior angles

   d. two pairs of alternate exterior angles

   e. two pairs of vertical angles

   f. two pairs of corresponding angles

2. Use the figure in Exercise 1. Find the measure of each angle if the measure of ∠8 is 53°.

   a. ∠1　　　　　　　　**b.** ∠2　　　　　　　　**c.** ∠3

   d. ∠4　　　　　　　　**e.** ∠5　　　　　　　　**f.** ∠6

3. Use the figure below. The figure shows two parallel lines, *a* and *b*. Tell whether each statement is *True* or *False*.

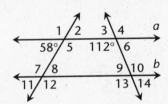

   a. $m\angle 2 = 58°$　　　　　**b.** $m\angle 5 = 122°$　　　　　**c.** $m\angle 6 = 58°$

   d. $m\angle 5 + m\angle 8 = 180°$　　**e.** $m\angle 7 = m\angle 10$　　　　**f.** $m\angle 9 = 68°$

   g. $m\angle 14 = 112°$　　　　**h.** $m\angle 3 = m\angle 9$　　　　**i.** $m\angle 4 = 112°$

   j. $m\angle 1 = m\angle 12$　　　　**k.** $m\angle 8 = 58°$　　　　**l.** $m\angle 11 = m\angle 13$

(continued)

MODULE 6 SECTION 4   **PRACTICE AND APPLICATIONS**

For use with Exploration 2

4. Find the unknown angle measure in each triangle or quadrilateral.

a.

b.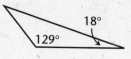

c.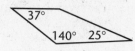

d.

e.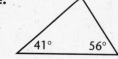

f.

g.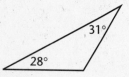

h.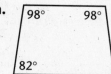

i.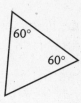

j.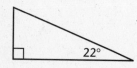

k.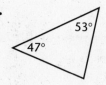

l.

5. The measures of two of the angles of a triangle are given. Find the measure of the third angle of each triangle, and tell whether the triangle is *acute*, *obtuse*, or *right*.

a. 15° and 65°

b. 42° and 54°

c. 46° and 69°

d. 118° and 41°

e. 72° and 26°

f. 32° and 58°

g. 38° and 14°

h. 59° and 27°

i. 11° and 90°

j. 73° and 29°

k. 21° and 36°

l. 47° and 62°

6. A window is in the shape of a triangle. One of the angles of the triangle measures 32°. The other two angles of the triangle have the same measure. Find each angle measure.

| **MODULE 6 SECTION 5** | **PRACTICE AND APPLICATIONS** |

For use with Exploration 1

1. Find the volume of each prism.

a.

2.5 cm
6 cm
1.5 cm

b.

18 ft
7 ft 6 ft

c.

3.5 m
4.1 m
3.2 m

d.

15 m²
4.8 m

e.

22 in.²
6.5 in.

f.

36 cm²
9 cm

g.

3.2 cm
7 cm
1.8 cm

h.

8 m
16 m
6 m

i.

10 in.
12 in.
5 in.

2. a. Suppose blocks like the one at the right are being manufactured for pedestals. What is the volume of one pedestal?

b. How many pedestals can be cut out of a block of wood that is a rectangular prism 6 in. × 20 in. × 9 in.?

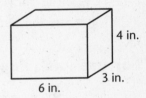

4 in.
6 in. 3 in.

3. a. If the area of the base of a rectangular prism is 24 cm² and its volume is 144 cm³, what is the height of the prism?

b. If the height of a rectangular prism is 8 cm and its volume is 128 cm³, what is the area of the base of the prism?

c. What is the length of each side of the base of the rectangular prism in part (b) if the base is a square?

(continued)

Name _____ Date _____

For use with Exploration 2

4. Replace each ___?___ with the number that makes the statement true.

a. 24 kg = ___?___ g

b. 55,000 m = ___?___ km

c. 0.0028 km = ___?___ m

d. 3500 L = ___?___ kL

e. 6.4 kL = ___?___ L

f. 283 mL = ___?___ L

g. 4.71 L = ___?___ mL

h. 0.8 kg = ___?___ g

i. 0.6 L = ___?___ cm^3

j. 19 kg = ___?___ g

k. 4.3 kL = ___?___ mL

l. 31 mL = ___?___ cm^3

m. 63 L = ___?___ mL

n. 59 g = ___?___ kg

o. 85 L = ___?___ kL

5. The dimensions of a salt water tank at a city aquarium are 2.5 m × 3.4 m × 1.2 m.

a. What is the volume of the tank in cubic centimeters?

b. What is the capacity of the tank in liters?

c. If the tank were completely filled with water, what would be the mass of the water in kilograms?

6. The capacity of a can of juice is 185 mL. The empty can has a mass of 12 g. If the can is filled with water, what is the combined mass of the water and the can in grams?

For use with Exploration 3

7. This network shows approximate road distances in miles between some cities in Canada.

a. Find the length of the path from Nipigon to Montreal that goes through Sault Ste. Marie, North Bay, and Ottawa.

b. Find the length of the path Ottawa-North Bay-Cochrane-Hearst-Geraldton.

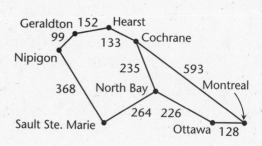

c. How much longer is the path Hearst-Cochrane-Montreal than the path Hearst-Cochrane-North Bay-Ottawa-Montreal?

d. Do you think the network is drawn to scale? Explain.

MODULE 6 SECTIONS 1–5   PRACTICE AND APPLICATIONS

For use with Section 1

1. Tell whether each quadrilateral is a parallelogram. If a quadrilateral is not a parallelogram, explain why not.

a.

b.

c.

2. Classify each polygon as concave or convex.

a.

b.

c.

For use with Section 2

3. Use π to write an expression for the exact area of each circle. Then use 3.14 or the ⌈ π ⌉ key on a calculator to find the approximate area. Round approximate answers to the nearest hundredth.

a.

5.5 in.

b.

8.3 cm

c.

42 m

For use with Section 3

4. Tell whether the polygons in each pair are *similar, congruent,* or *neither.* If the polygons are similar or congruent, write a statement that can be used to identify the corresponding parts.

a.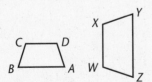

b.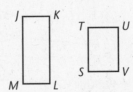

5. On a map, two cities are 4 in. apart. The scale of the map is 1 in. : 75 mi. What is the actual distance between the two cities?

(continued)

For use with Section 3

6. The scale 5000 : 1 describes the setting for the magnification on an electron microscope. How long does a 0.003 mm long speck of asbestos appear to be when seen through the electron microscope?

7. Trapezoid *ABCD* is similar to trapezoid *EHGF*.

   a. Find the measures of ∠*FGH*, ∠*GHE*, and ∠*HEF*.

   b. Find the lengths of $\overline{AD}$, $\overline{AB}$, and $\overline{DC}$.

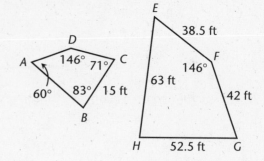

For use with Section 4

8. The figure below shows parallel lines $\overleftrightarrow{AB}$ and $\overleftrightarrow{CD}$ cut by transversal $\overleftrightarrow{SW}$. Find the measure of each named angle.

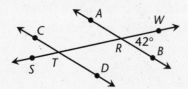

   a. ∠*ART*   **b.** ∠*DTR*   **c.** ∠*STD*

   d. ∠*CTR*   **e.** ∠*CTS*   **f.** ∠*ARW*

For use with Section 5

9. The network shown below gives road distances in miles between several U.S. cities.

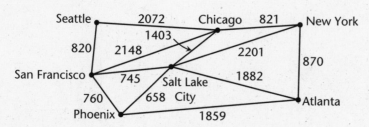

   a. Find the length of the path Seattle-San Francisco-Phoenix.

   b. Find the length of the path San Francisco-Salt Lake City-Atlanta.

   c. Find the shortest path from San Francisco to New York.

   d. Find the shortest path from Seattle to Atlanta.

Will It Fly?   Inequalities, Polygons, and Probability

GOAL **LEARN HOW TO:** • write and graph inequalities
• find the areas of polygons
• use areas to find theoretical probabilities
• find the probabilities of complementary events

AS YOU: • investigate how wing design makes flight possible
• study the wing of an albatross
• simulate skydiving competition

Exploration 1: Inequalities

A mathematical sentence that contains one or more of the symbols
$>$, $<$, $\geq$, or $\leq$ is an **inequality**.

Example

Write an inequality to represent each statement. Then graph the inequality.

a. y is less than 5.

b. 3 is less than or equal to x, and x is less than or equal to 6.

■ Sample Response ■

a. $y < 5$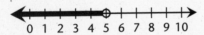

The open circle means 5 is not included.

b. $3 \leq x \leq 6$

The solid circles mean 3 and 6 are included.

Exploration 2: Areas of Polygons

Polygons

A **polygon** is a simple, closed, flat figure made of segments.
A polygon can be either **convex** or **concave**. If a polygon is
convex, every line that contains two of its vertices passes
through the interior of the polygon. For a concave polygon,
there is at least one line containing two vertices that does not
pass through the interior of the polygon. In a **regular** polygon,
all the segments are the same length and all the angles are
equal in measure.

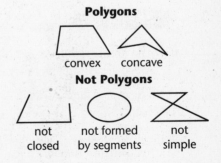

MODULE 6 SECTION 1   STUDY GUIDE

A polygon that has *four sides* is a **quadrilateral**. A **parallelogram** is a quadrilateral that has *two pairs of parallel sides*.

Quadrilateral   **Parallelogram**

The area of a parallelogram is the product of the length of its base and its height. The area of a triangle is half the length of its base times its height.

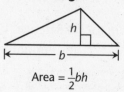

Parallelogram

Area = bh

You can find the area of some polygons by separating them into triangles and parallelograms.

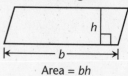

Triangle

Area = $\frac{1}{2}bh$

Exploration 3: Geometric Probability

A probability that is based on lengths, areas, or volumes of figures is a **geometric probability**.

> ### Example
>
> Find the probability that a point selected at random on $\overline{PR}$ is on $\overline{QR}$.
>
>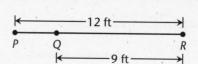
>
> ### ■ Sample Response ■
>
> The probability that a point which is on $\overline{PR}$ is located on $\overline{QR}$ is:
>
> $$\frac{\text{length of } \overline{QR}}{\text{length of } \overline{PR}} = \frac{9}{12} = \frac{3}{4}, \text{ or } 75\%.$$

Two events are **complementary events** if one or the other must occur, but they cannot both happen at the same time. The sum of the probabilities of two complementary events is 1.

> ### Example
>
> The events *rolling an even number* and *rolling an odd number* when a number cube is rolled are complementary events.
>
> The events *landing heads* and *landing tails* when a coin is flipped are complementary events.
>
> When selecting a card at random from a standard deck of cards, the events *drawing a red card* and *drawing a black card* are complementary events.

Name _____ Date _____

Exploration 1

Write an inequality to represent each statement. Then graph the inequality on a number line.

1. w is greater than 5.

2. j is less than or equal to 13.

3. 1 is less than y, and y is less than 4.

4. r is greater than 3 and less than or equal to 7.

Exploration 2

Tell whether each quadrilateral is a parallelogram. If a quadrilateral is not a parallelogram, explain why not.

5.

6.

Classify each polygon as *convex* **or** *concave*.

7.

8.

Exploration 3

9. Suppose a point on $\overline{XZ}$ is selected at random. Find the probability that the point is on $\overline{XY}$.

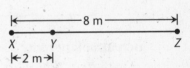

10. Find the probability that a small object dropped on the parallelogram will land on the shaded region.

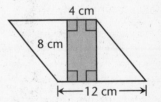

Spiral Review

Use mental math to write each fraction as a percent.
(Module 5, p. 366)

11. $\frac{11}{26}$

12. $\frac{39}{51}$

13. $\frac{41}{83}$

14. $\frac{27}{90}$

Find the prime factorization of each number. (Module 3, p. 156)

15. 20

16. 45

17. 50

18. 130

Write each power in standard form. (Module 1, p. 21)

19. 3^2

20. 4^2

21. 7^2

22. 8^2

MODULE 6 SECTION 2   **STUDY GUIDE**

Go Fly a Kite!   Square Roots, Surface Area, and Area of a Circle

GOAL **LEARN HOW TO:** • find square roots of perfect squares
• estimate square roots to the nearest tenth
• identify prisms and their parts
• draw a net for a prism
• find the surface area of a prism
• find the area of a circle

AS YOU: • investigate the design of a parawing
• investigate box kites
• investigate kite designs

Exploration 1: Square Roots

One of two equal factors of a number is a **square root** of that number.
If $A = s^2$, then s is a square root of A. Every positive number has two
square roots.

Example

Find the square roots of 400.

Sample Response

Since $(20)^2 = 400$ and $(-20)^2 = 400$, the square roots of 400 are 20 and −20.

The **principal square root** of a *positive* number, indicated by $\sqrt{}$, is the
positive square root. A number is a **perfect square** if its principal square
root is a whole number.

Example

a. $\sqrt{625} = 25$, so 625 is a perfect square, and 25 is the principal square root of 625.

b. $\sqrt{114} \approx 10.58$, so 114 is not a perfect square. The approximation 10.58 is the
principal square root of 114.

Exploration 2: Surface Areas of Prisms

Prisms and Surface Area

A **prism** is a space figure that has flat surfaces or **faces** shaped like
polygons. Two of the faces, the **bases**, are parallel and congruent.
The other faces are parallelograms. Pairs of faces meet in segments
called **edges**, and the edges meet in points called **vertices**.

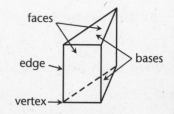

The **surface area** of a prism is the sum of the areas of all its faces.
You can use a net to help find the surface area of a prism.

Example

a. Name the prism at the right. Tell how many faces,
how many vertices, and how many edges it has.

b. Draw a net for the prism and use it to find the surface area.

1 cm
1 cm
3 cm

▪ Sample Response ▪

a. This is a right rectangular prism. It has 6 faces, 8 vertices, and 12 edges.

b.

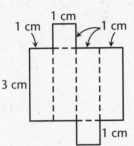

1 cm
1 cm
1 cm
3 cm
1 cm

Each square has an area of 1 cm^2.
Each rectangle has an area of 3 cm^2.
$1 + 1 + 3 + 3 + 3 + 3 = 14$

The surface area of the prism is 14 cm^2.

Exploration 3: Area of a Circle

The area, A, of a circle is equal to πr^2, where r is the radius of the circle.
Recall that the radius of a circle is half its diameter and that π is a constant
approximated by 3.14.

Example

Find the area of a circle with diameter 2.4 cm.

▪ Sample Response ▪

Since the diameter of the circle is 2.4 cm, the radius is $\frac{1}{2}(2.4)$, or 1.2 cm.

$A = \pi r^2$
$\quad = \pi (1.2)^2$
$\quad = 1.44\pi$

The exact area of the circle is 1.44π cm^2.

To find a numerical approximation for the area, substitute 3.14 for π or use the π key.

$A \approx 3.14 \cdot 1.44 = 4.5216$

An approximate area of the circle is 4.52 cm^2.

MODULE 6 SECTION 2 | PRACTICE & APPLICATION EXERCISES | STUDY GUIDE

Exploration 1

Find each square root. If the square root is not a whole number, find the two consecutive integers it is between.

1. $\sqrt{121}$ **2.** $\sqrt{81}$ **3.** $-\sqrt{36}$ **4.** $\sqrt{150}$

Estimate each square root to the nearest tenth.

5. $\sqrt{7}$ **6.** $\sqrt{43}$ **7.** $\sqrt{20}$ **8.** $\sqrt{155}$

Exploration 2

For Exercises 9 and 10, use the prism shown at the right.

9. What kind of prism is this?

10. How many faces, vertices, and edges does this prism have?

11. Use the right rectangular prism shown.

   a. Sketch a net for the prism.

   b. Find the area of each face.

   c. Find the surface area of the prism.

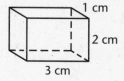

Exploration 3

Use π to write an expression for the exact area of each circle. Then use 3.14 or the π key on a calculator to find the approximate area.

12. radius: 4 mm **13.** diameter: 5.4 ft **14.** radius: 3.1 cm

Spiral Review

Write an inequality to represent each statement. (Module 6, p. 388)

15. x is greater than or equal to 6. **16.** r is less than 8.

Use division to write each fraction as a decimal. (Module 4, p. 256)

17. $\frac{3}{8}$ **18.** $\frac{4}{5}$ **19.** $\frac{9}{20}$ **20.** $\frac{21}{32}$

Write each fraction in lowest terms. (Module 3, p. 170)

21. $\frac{6}{8}$ **22.** $\frac{6}{16}$ **23.** $\frac{20}{25}$ **24.** $\frac{15}{55}$

| **MODULE 6 SECTION 3** | **STUDY GUIDE** |

Barnstorming   Triangles and Similarity

GOAL   **LEARN HOW TO:** • identify similar and congruent polygons
• find the scale of a drawing or model
• classify triangles by the measures of their angles
• find unknown measures of similar figures

As you: • learn about the Curtiss Jenny airplane used by barnstormers
• use scale drawings of a Curtiss Jenny

Exploration 1: Scale Drawings and Similarity

Similar and Congruent Figures

Similar figures have the same shape but not necessarily the same size. Parts
of similar figures that match are called **corresponding parts**. In similar
polygons, the measures of the corresponding angles are equal and the
ratios of the lengths of the corresponding sides are equal.

Example

In the figure at the right, $\triangle ABC$ is similar
to $\triangle DEF$.

a. $\overline{AB}$ corresponds to $\overline{DE}$. What segments
correspond to $\overline{BC}$ and $\overline{AC}$?

b. Find the measures of $\angle D$, $\angle E$, and $\angle F$, and
the lengths of $\overline{EF}$ and $\overline{DF}$.

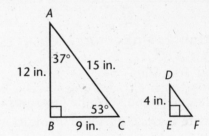

■ Sample Response ■

a. $\overline{EF}$ corresponds to $\overline{BC}$, and $\overline{DF}$ corresponds to $\overline{AC}$.

b. $m\angle D = 37°$, $m\angle E = 90°$, and $m\angle F = 53°$

Since $\dfrac{AB}{DE} = \dfrac{12}{4} = 3$, each side of $\triangle ABC$ is 3 times as long as the corresponding side
of $\triangle DEF$.

So, $DE = 9 \div 3$, or 3 in., and $DF = 15 \div 3$, or 5 in.

Similar figures that have the same shape and the same size are *congruent*.
The lengths of corresponding sides and the measures of corresponding
angles of congruent polygons are equal.

Name _____   Date _____

The **scale of a model or drawing** is the ratio of a length on the model or drawing to the length of the corresponding part on the actual object.

Example

An architect has built a model of a new office building she has designed. The model was built using a scale of 1 in. = 15 ft. If the height of the model is 6.25 in., what will be the height of the actual building?

■ Sample Response ■

Use a proportion.

$$\frac{1 \text{ in.}}{15 \text{ ft}} = \frac{6.25 \text{ in.}}{x \text{ ft}}$$

$$x = 6.25(15)$$

$$= 93.75$$

The building will be 93.75 ft tall.

Exploration 2: Unknown Measures in Similar Figures

Classifying Triangles

Triangles can be classified by the measures of their angles. A triangle that has only acute angles is an **acute triangle**. An **obtuse triangle** has one obtuse angle. A **right triangle** has one right angle.

Example

Classify each triangle as *acute*, *obtuse*, or *right*.

a. 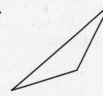   **b.**   **c.**

■ Sample Response ■

a. obtuse   **b.** acute   **c.** right

MODULE 6 SECTION 3 — PRACTICE & APPLICATION EXERCISES — STUDY GUIDE

Exploration 1

Trapezoid *ABCD* is similar to trapezoid *EFGH*.

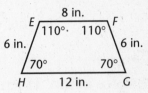

1. $\overline{AB}$ corresponds to $\overline{EF}$. Which segments correspond to $\overline{BC}$, $\overline{CD}$, and $\overline{AC}$, respectively?

2. Find the measures of $\angle A$, $\angle B$, $\angle C$, and $\angle D$.

3. Find the lengths of $\overline{BC}$, $\overline{CD}$, and $\overline{AD}$.

The amount of magnification under a microscope is given. For each scale, how long does a 2 mm long cell appear to be when seen through a microscope?

4. $15 : 1$

5. $100 : 1$

6. $200 : 1$

Exploration 2

Classify each triangle as *acute*, *obtuse*, or *right*.

7.

8.

9.

Spiral Review

Find the surface area of each prism. (Module 6, p. 404)

10.

11.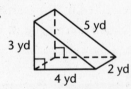

Find each difference. (Module 3, p. 183)

12. $4\frac{3}{8} - 2\frac{3}{4}$

13. $6\frac{4}{5} - 3\frac{4}{5}$

14. $2\frac{1}{2} - 1\frac{1}{3}$

For each angle, find the measure of a supplementary angle.
(Module 2, p. 83)

15. $36°$

16. $45°$

17. $125°$

18. $179°$

MODULE 6 SECTION 4   **STUDY GUIDE**

Winging It   Parallel Lines and Angles of Polygons

GOAL **LEARN HOW TO:** • find relationships among angles formed
by parallel lines and a transversal
• find the sum of the measures of the angles
of triangles and quadrilaterals

AS YOU: • make a model wing
• experiment with ways to make your wing more rigid

Exploration 1: Angles Formed by a Transversal

Parallel Lines and Transversals

A line that intersects two lines is a **transversal**. When a transversal
intersects two parallel lines, the measures of the eight angles formed are
related. Four of the angles are **exterior angles** because they are outside of
the parallel lines. The other four angles are called **interior angles** because
they are on the inside of, or between, the parallel lines.

A pair of nonadjacent exterior angles found on opposite sides of the
transversal are called **alternate exterior angles**. Nonadjacent pairs of
interior angles found on opposite sides of the transversal are called
alternate interior angles. Angles that have the same position on the two
lines cut by a transversal are called **corresponding angles**. There are also
four pairs of **vertical angles** formed by the intersecting lines. These angle
pairs are directly opposite each other at the intersection of the transversal
and one of the other two lines.

When the two lines intersected by the transversal are parallel, each of the
angle pairs mentioned above is congruent. Recall that congruent angles
have the same measure.

Example

In the figure at the right, line *l* intersects parallel lines
m and *n*. Name all the congruent pairs of angles and
tell why they are congruent.

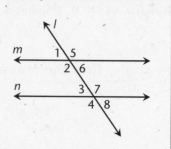

MODULE 6 SECTION 4   **STUDY GUIDE**

Sample Response

∠1 ≅ ∠3 since corresponding angles are congruent.
∠1 ≅ ∠6 since vertical angles are congruent.
∠1 ≅ ∠8 since alternate exterior angles are congruent.
∠2 ≅ ∠4 since corresponding angles are congruent.
∠2 ≅ ∠5 since vertical angles are congruent.
∠2 ≅ ∠7 since alternate interior angles are congruent.
∠3 ≅ ∠6 since alternate interior angles are congruent.
∠3 ≅ ∠8 since vertical angles are congruent.
∠4 ≅ ∠5 since alternate exterior angles are congruent.
∠4 ≅ ∠7 since vertical angles are congruent.
∠5 ≅ ∠7 since corresponding angles are congruent.
∠6 ≅ ∠8 since corresponding angles are congruent.

Exploration 2: Angles of Triangles and Quadrilaterals

Sum of the Angles of a Triangle and of a Quadrilateral

The sum of the measures of the angles of a triangle is 180°.

The sum of the measures of the angles of a quadrilateral is 360°.

A **diagonal** of a polygon is a segment whose endpoints are two non-consecutive vertices of the polygon.

Example

Use the figure at the right.

a. Find the measure of ∠ABC in △ABC.

b. Find the measure of ∠CDE in quadrilateral ACDE.

c. Name a diagonal of polygon ABCDE.

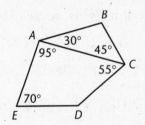

■ Sample Response ■

a. Since the sum of the measures of the angles of a triangle is 180°,

$$m\angle ABC = 180° - (30° + 45°) = 180° - 75° = 105°$$

b. Since the sum of the measures of the angles of a quadrilateral is 360°,

$$m\angle CDE = 360° - (70° + 95° + 55°) = 360° - 220° = 140°$$

c. $\overline{AC}$ is a diagonal of polygon ABCDE.

MODULE 6 SECTION 4 | PRACTICE & APPLICATION EXERCISES | STUDY GUIDE

Exploration 1

The figure at the right shows two parallel lines, *s* and *t*, intersected by transversal *r*. Use this diagram for Exercises 1–12.

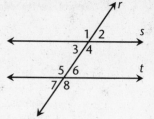

Name the angles or pairs of angles that fit each description.

1. four interior angles

2. four exterior angles

3. two pairs of alternate interior angles

4. four pairs of vertical angles

5. two pairs of alternate exterior angles

6. four pairs of corresponding angles

Find the measure of each angle if the measure of ∠3 is 52°.

7. ∠1

8. ∠2

9. ∠4

10. ∠5

11. ∠6

12. ∠7

Exploration 2

Find the unknown measure in each triangle or quadrilateral.

13.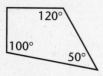

14.

15.

Spiral Review

Classify each triangle as *acute*, *obtuse*, or *right*. (Module 6, p. 417)

16.

17.

18.

Solve each equation. Check each solution. (Module 4, p. 300)

19. $3 + 4x = 7$

20. $5n - 6 = 4$

21. $\frac{t}{3} - 1 = 9$

Find the volume of a cube with each side length. (Module 1, p. 21)

22. 5 mm

23. 3 ft

24. 9 cm

25. 6 in.

MODULE 6 SECTION 5 · **STUDY GUIDE**

A Whale of a Problem Volume of a Prism and Metric Relationships

GOAL **LEARN HOW TO:** • find the volume of a prism
• use the relationships among metric units of volume, capacity, and mass
• use networks

AS YOU: • compare the sizes of Keiko's old and new pools
• investigate how Keiko was shipped
• analyze delivery routes

Exploration 1: Volume of a Prism

The volume V of a prism is the product of the area of a base B and the height h.

> **Example**
>
> Find the volume of this right triangular prism.
>
>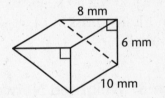
>
> 8 mm
> 6 mm
> 10 mm
>
> ◼ **Sample Response** ◼
>
> Since the bases are triangles, use the area formula for a triangle.
>
> $$\text{area of base} = \frac{1}{2} \times \text{base} \times \text{height}$$
> $$= \frac{1}{2} \cdot 6 \cdot 8$$
> $$= 24$$
>
> $$\text{volume} = \text{area of base} \times \text{height}$$
> $$= 24 \cdot 10$$
> $$= 240$$
>
> The volume of the prism is 240 mm^3.

MODULE 6 SECTION 5   STUDY GUIDE

Exploration 2: Relationships Among Metric Units

Mass, Capacity, and Volume

A container's **capacity** is the amount of fluid it can hold. In the
metric system, mass, capacity, and volume are related as follows:

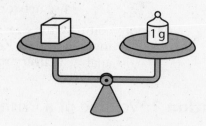

The volume of one **cubic centimeter (cm³)** is equal to ...	the capacity of one **milliliter (mL)** which is equal to ...	the **mass** of one **gram (g)** of water.

One **liter (L)** of liquid will fill a cube measuring 10 cm on each side. There
are 1000 mL in 1 L. The mass of 1 L of water is 1 **kilogram (kg)**. One kg is
equivalent to 1000 g.

Exploration 3: Weighted Networks

Networks

A **network** is a figure made up of points called **vertices** that are connected by
segments or curves called **arcs**. A network in which the arcs are labeled with
numbers representing such things as distances or times is a **weighted network**.

Example

Find the length of the two shortest paths from
vertex *A* to vertex *E* in the network shown
at the right.

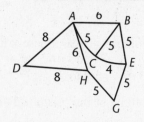

Sample Response

The path *A–C–E* has a length of 5 + 4, or 9.

The path *A–B–E* has a length of 6 + 5, or 11.

The lengths of all the other possible paths from *A* to *E* are greater than 11.

Name _____   Date _____

Exploration 1

Find the volume of each prism.

1.

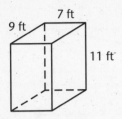

7 ft
9 ft
11 ft

2.

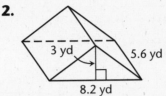

3 yd   5.6 yd
8.2 yd

Exploration 2

Replace each __?__ with the number that makes the statement true.

3. $155 \text{ cm}^3 = $ __?__ mL   **4.** $2.1 \text{ L} = $ __?__ cm^3 **5.** $18 \text{ L} = $ __?__ mL

Exploration 3

Use the network at the right to answer Exercises 6 and 7.

6. Find the length of the shortest path from *A* to *C*.

7. Find the length of the path *A-B-D-E*.

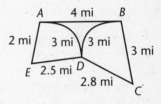

A   4 mi   B
2 mi   3 mi   3 mi   3 mi
E   2.5 mi   D
2.8 mi   C

Spiral Review

Find each unknown angle measure. (Module 6, p. 429)

8.

110°

9.

50°   60°

10.

45°
45°

Use the box-and-whisker plots shown. (Module 5, p. 337)

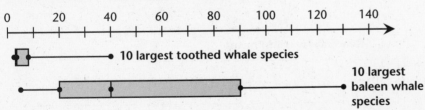

Mass of Largest Whale Species (1000 kg)

0   20   40   60   80   100   120   140

10 largest toothed whale species

10 largest baleen whale species

11. How is the smallest baleen whale represented on the box plot?

12. Estimate the median of both data sets.

Find the area of a circle with each radius. Use 3.14 for π.
(Module 6, p. 405)

13. 1.2 mm   **14.** 8 mm   **15.** 5 ft   **16.** 2.15 cm

MODULE 7   **LABSHEET** (1A)

Changing the Horizontal Scale (Use with Question 17 on page 463.)

Reading for 10 Minutes

Body weight (lb)	Calories burned
75	7.35
100	9.8
150	14.7
200	19.6

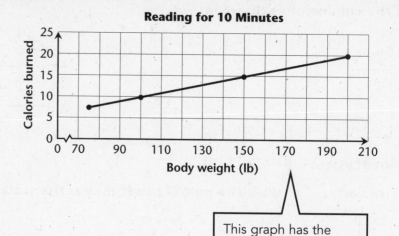

This graph has the original horizontal scale of 10 lb intervals.

Directions

- Write the new scale on the horizontal axis of each graph.
- Plot the data in the table above on each graph.
- Connect the points on each graph.

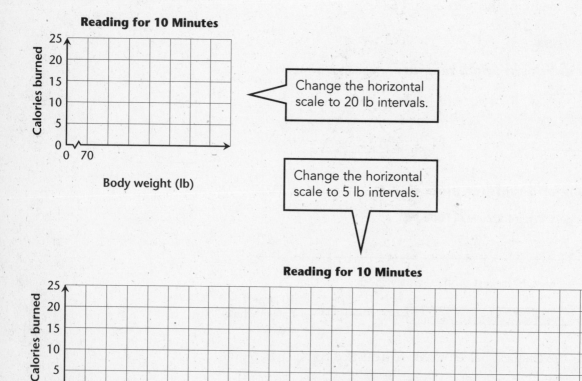

Change the horizontal scale to 20 lb intervals.

Change the horizontal scale to 5 lb intervals.

Three Bicycle Riding Graphs

(Use with Project Questions 1 and 2 on page 469.)

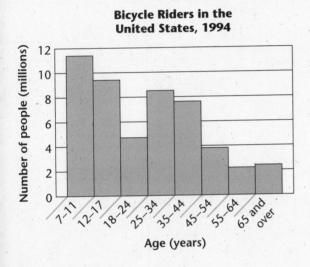

Bicycle Riders in the United States, 1994

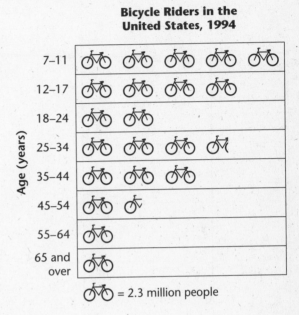

Bicycle Riders in the United States, 1994

= 2.3 million people

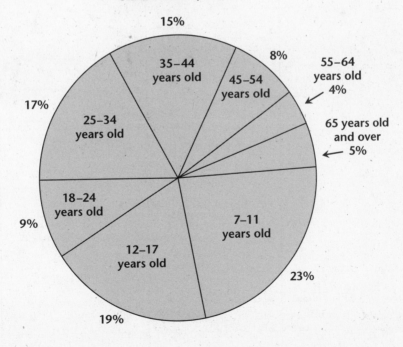

Bicycle Riders in the United States, 1994

MODULE 7   LABSHEET **2A**

Heart Rate Data (Use with Questions 7, 14–16, and 23 on pages 473–475, 477.)

Student	Resting heart rate	Active heart rate	Difference (active − resting)	Percent of increase
1				
2				
3				
4				
5				
6				
7				
8				
9				
10				
11				
12				
13				
14				
15				
16				
17				
18				
19				
20				
21				
22				
23				
24				
25				

MODULE 7   **LABSHEET 3A**

Sugar Contents of 20 Desserts
(Use with Questions 23–26 on pages 491–492.)

Dessert	Sugar (g)
apple pie, deep-dish style	28
brownies	17
carrot cake with frosting	47
cherry cheesecake	28
chocolate chip cookie	4
chocolate fudge cake	20
chocolate ice cream	14
chocolate pudding	19
donut, raspberry filled	17
ice cream cone	23

Dessert	Sugar (g)
caramel custard	20
fruit cocktail	22
gingerbread	20
ice cream sandwich	16
oatmeal cookie	9
pecan pie	45
flavored ice bar	11
pumpkin pie	18
strawberry gelatin	19
vanilla ice cream	13

Ordered List of Amounts of Sugar (g)

Table of Box-and-Whisker Plot Points				
Lower extreme	Lower quartile	Median	Upper quartile	Upper extreme

MODULE 7   LABSHEET **3B**

Comparing Sugar Contents (Use with Questions 27–29 on page 492.)

Directions Follow the directions below to draw a box-and-whisker plot
for the amounts of sugar in some common desserts.

a. On a horizontal line below the number line, plot the points for the
median, the extremes, and the quartiles of the data.

b. Make the box by drawing short vertical segments through the upper
and lower quartiles and then connecting the endpoints of the segments
to form a rectangle.

c. Draw a short vertical segment through the median.

d. Draw whiskers connecting the box to the extremes.

e. Label the box-and-whisker plot you have drawn.

Amount of Sugar in a Serving of a Dessert or a Candy Bar (g)

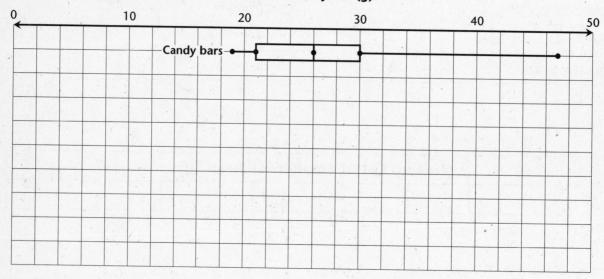

MODULE 7	LABSHEET **3C**

Determining Outliers (Use with Exercise 34 on page 497.)

You will use the *interquartile range*, or IQR, to determine whether 40 g of sugar and 47 g of sugar are outliers. The *IQR* is the difference between the upper and lower quartiles.

IQR = upper quartile – lower quartile

Any data values that are outliers are marked with an asterisk (∗) on the box-and-whisker plot. The whisker is drawn to the next data value that is not an outlier.

Directions Use the partially completed box-and-whisker plot below.

a. What is the interquartile range for the grams of sugar in candy bars?

b. About what percent of the data values are in the IQR?

c. Multiply the IQR by 1.5.

d. Add the result in part (c) to the upper quartile. Any data values that are greater than the sum are outliers.

e. Subtract the result in part (c) from the lower quartile. Any data values that are less than the difference are outliers.

f. Use the table below to determine which of the data values are outliers.

Amounts of Sugar in 26 Candy Bars (g)												
19	20	21	21	21	21	21	21	22	22	23	23	26
26	27	27	27	28	29	30	30	31	33	35	40	47

g. Complete the box-and-whisker plot below to show any outliers.

Amounts of Sugar in 26 Candy Bars (g)

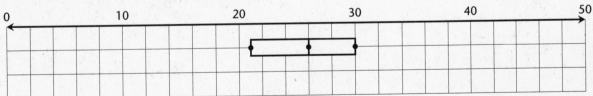

Vacation Days Table (Use with Exercises 12–13 on page 508.)

Paid Vacation Days per Year in 1976														
Bus driver	15	35	20	21	24	26	24	17	20	22	20	30	20	15
Auto mechanic	10	20	18	20	24	26	19	15	14	21	20	20	20	15
Plant manager	20	20	20	24	24	26	28	15	20	22	20	25	27	25
Secretary	10	20	15	20	24	26	23	15	20	20	20	30	24	15

Toronto, Canada — Sydney, Australia — Vienna, Austria — Brussels, Belgium — Copenhagen, Denmark — Paris, France — Dusseldorf, Germany — Dublin, Ireland — Tokyo, Japan — Amsterdam, Netherlands — Oslo, Norway — Madrid, Spain — Stockholm, Sweden — Zurich, Switzerland

Sleep Time Survey (Use with Exercise 14 on page 508.)

		11 years old		12 years old		13 years old		14 years old		15 years old	
		Girls	Boys	Girls	Boys	Girls	Boys	Girls	Boys	Girls	Boys
School night	Bedtime (P.M.)	9:30	9:40	9:45	9:50	10:06	10:28	10:10	10:16	10:24	10:43
	Wake-up time (A.M.)	7:05	7:00	6:55	7:05	6:50	7:00	5:56	6:15	6:05	6:27
Weekend night	Bedtime (P.M.)	10:22	10:50	10:55	11:05	11:20	11:42	11:57	12:06	12:11	12:27
	Wake-up time (A.M.)	8:25	7:45	8:35	8:35	8:45	8:45	9:14	9:12	9:24	9:25

Quadrilateral Sets Game Cards (Use with Question 10 on page 515.)

Directions Cut out each card.
The rest of the cards are on Labsheets 5B and 5C.

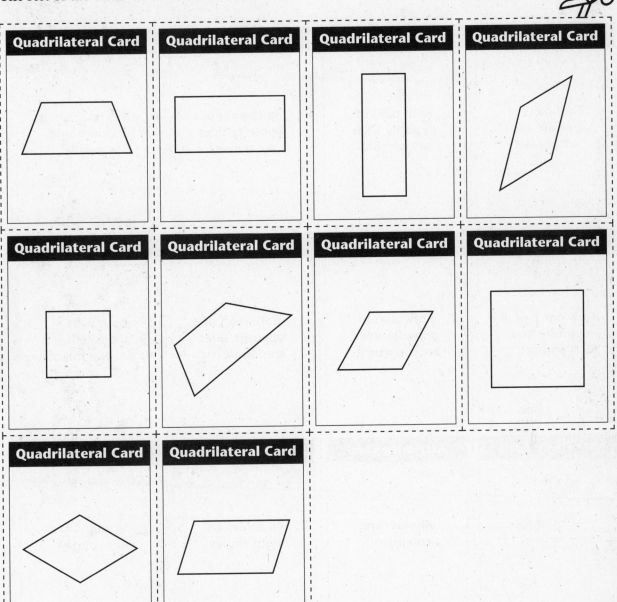

MODULE 7   LABSHEET **5B**

Quadrilateral Sets Game Cards (Use with Question 10 on page 515.)

Directions Cut out each card.
The rest of the cards are on Labsheet 5C.

Attribute Card	Attribute Card	Attribute Card	Attribute Card
Both pairs of opposite sides are parallel.	Both pairs of opposite sides are parallel.	Both pairs of opposite sides are parallel.	Only one pair of opposite sides is parallel.

Attribute Card	Attribute Card	Attribute Card	Attribute Card
Only one pair of opposite sides is parallel.	Both pairs of opposite sides are congruent.	Both pairs of opposite sides are congruent.	Both pairs of opposite sides are congruent.

Attribute Card	Attribute Card	Attribute Card	Attribute Card
All sides are congruent.	All sides are congruent.	All angles are right angles.	All angles are right angles.

MODULE 7

Quadrilateral Sets Game Cards (Use with Question 10 on page 515.)

Name Card	Name Card	Name Card	Name Card
Rhombus	Rhombus	Parallelogram	Parallelogram

Name Card	Name Card	Name Card	Name Card
Rectangle	Rectangle	Trapezoid	Trapezoid

Name Card	Name Card
Square	Square

Trapezoids (Use with Question 12 on page 516.)

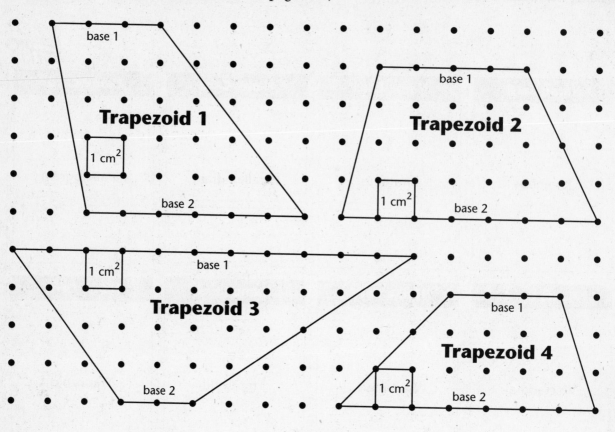

Trapezoid
(Use with Exercise 18 on page 520.)

Polygon
(Use with Exercise 19 on page 520.)

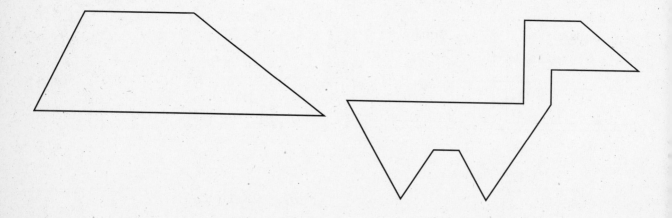

TEACHER ASSESSMENT SCALES

 The star indicates that you excelled in some way.

 Problem Solving

❶ ❷ ❸ ❹ ❺

❶ You did not understand the problem well enough to get started or you did not show any work.

❸ You understood the problem well enough to make a plan and to work toward a solution.

❺ You made a plan, you used it to solve the problem, and you verified your solution.

 Mathematical Language

❶ ❷ ❸ ❹ ❺

❶ You did not use any mathematical vocabulary or symbols, or you did not use them correctly, or your use was not appropriate.

❸ You used appropriate mathematical language, but the way it was used was not always correct or other terms and symbols were needed.

❺ You used mathematical language that was correct and appropriate to make your meaning clear.

 Representations

❶ ❷ ❸ ❹ ❺

❶ You did not use any representations such as equations, tables, graphs, or diagrams to help solve the problem or explain your solution.

❸ You made appropriate representations to help solve the problem or help you explain your solution, but they were not always correct or other representations were needed.

❺ You used appropriate and correct representations to solve the problem or explain your solution.

 Connections

❶ ❷ ❸ ❹ ❺

❶ You attempted or solved the problem and then stopped.

❸ You found patterns and used them to extend the solution to other cases, or you recognized that this problem relates to other problems, mathematical ideas, or applications.

❺ You extended the ideas in the solution to the general case, or you showed how this problem relates to other problems, mathematical ideas, or applications.

 Presentation

❶ ❷ ❸ ❹ ❺

❶ The presentation of your solution and reasoning is unclear to others.

❸ The presentation of your solution and reasoning is clear in most places, but others may have trouble understanding parts of it.

❺ The presentation of your solution and reasoning is clear and can be understood by others.

Content Used: _____

Computational Errors: Yes No

Notes on Errors: _____

STUDENT	SELF-ASSESSMENT SCALES

If your score is in the shaded area, explain why on the back of this sheet and stop.

☆ The star indicates that you excelled in some way.

 ### Problem Solving

①   **②**   **③**   **④**   **⑤**

① I did not understand the problem well enough to get started or I did not show any work.

② I understood the problem well enough to make a plan and to work toward a solution.

⑤ I made a plan, I used it to solve the problem, and I verified my solution.

 ### Mathematical Language

①   **②**   **③**   **④**   **⑤**

① I did not use any mathematical vocabulary or symbols, or I did not use them correctly, or my use was not appropriate.

② I used appropriate mathematical language, but the way it was used was not always correct or other terms and symbols were needed.

⑤ I used mathematical language that was correct and appropriate to make my meaning clear.

 ### Representations

①   **②**   **③**   **④**   **⑤**

① I did not use any representations such as equations, tables, graphs, or diagrams to help solve the problem or explain my solution.

② I made appropriate representations to help solve the problem or help me explain my solution, but they were not always correct or other representations were needed.

⑤ I used appropriate and correct representations to solve the problem or explain my solution.

 ### Connections

①   **②**   **③**   **④**   **⑤**

① I attempted or solved the problem and then stopped.

② I found patterns and used them to extend the solution to other cases, or I recognized that this problem relates to other problems, mathematical ideas, or applications.

⑤ I extended the ideas in the solution to the general case, or I showed how this problem relates to other problems, mathematical ideas, or applications.

 ### Presentation

①   **②**   **③**   **④**   **⑤**

① The presentation of my solution and reasoning is unclear to others.

② The presentation of my solution and reasoning is clear in most places, but others may have trouble understanding parts of it.

⑤ The presentation of my solution and reasoning is clear and can be understood by others.

Name _____   Date _____

For use with Exploration 1

1. Find the volume of each cylinder. Use 3.14 or the [π] key on a
calculator. Round each answer to the nearest hundredth.

a.
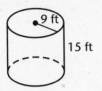
15 ft

b.
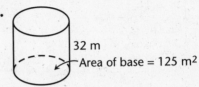
32 m
Area of base = 125 m²

c.
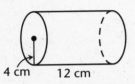
4 cm   12 cm

d.

14 ft
5 ft

e.
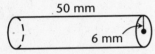
50 mm
6 mm

2. Suppose a 6 in. tall cylindrical can has an inside diameter of 2 in.

  a. What is the volume of the can?

  b. What is the volume of a cylindrical can with the same height and
an inside diameter of 1 in.?

  c. Will a 1 in. diameter cylindrical can with the same height hold
half as much liquid as the cylindrical can with a 2 in. diameter?
Explain.

3. Find the unknown measure for each cylinder. Where necessary,
round answers to the nearest hundredth.

  a. $r = 4$ in., $h = 3$ in., $V = $ __?__ in.³   **b.** $B = 9$ in.², $h = $ __?__ in., $V = 54$ in.³

  c. $B = $ __?__ ft², $h = 4$ ft, $V = 72$ ft³   **d.** $r = $ __?__ cm, $h = 5$ cm, $V = 62.8$ cm³

  e. $r = 3$ cm, $h = 5$ cm, $V = $ __?__ cm³   **f.** $B = 18$ ft², $h = $ __?__ ft, $V = 108$ ft³

  g. $B = $ __?__ ft², $h = 5$ ft, $V = 225$ ft³   **h.** $B = 24$ m², $h = $ __?__ m, $V = 192$ m³

  i. $r = 2$ m, $h = 7$ m, $V = $ __?__ m³   **j.** $B = $ __?__ cm², $h = 39$ cm, $V = 780$ cm³

  k. $r = 8$ ft, $h = 10$ ft, $V = $ __?__ ft³   **l.** $r = $ __?__ cm, $h = 10$ cm, $V = 785$ cm³

  m. $B = 20$ yd², $h = $ __?__ yd, $V = 200$ yd³   **n.** $B = 15$ m², $h = $ __?__ m, $V = 135$ m³

(continued)

MODULE 7 SECTION 1   **PRACTICE AND APPLICATIONS**

For use with Exploration 2

4. Find the slope of each line.

a.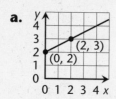

b.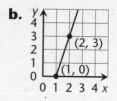

c.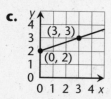

d.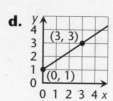

5. Find the slope of a line with each rise and run.

a. rise 8
run 4

b. rise 6
run 2

c. rise 3
run 4

d. rise 5
run 5

e. rise 3
run 1

f. rise 2
run 5

g. rise 3
run 9

h. rise 6
run 12

i. rise 4
run 5

For use with Exploration 3

6. Refer to the graphs shown at the right.

a. About how many words per minute can Clark type?

b. About how many words per minute can Jenny type?

c. Are these graphs misleading? If they are, explain why and redraw them so that they are not misleading.

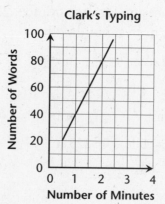

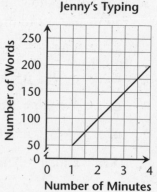

MODULE 7 SECTION 2   **PRACTICE AND APPLICATIONS**

For use with Exploration 1

1. Whitney's resting heart rate is 62 beats per minute. After 2 minutes of exercise, her heart rate is 93 beats per minute. Whitney's active heart rate is what percent of her resting heart rate?

2. Find each percent.

   a. 15 is what percent of 60?   **b.** 27 is what percent of 90?

   c. 44 is what percent of 80?   **d.** 48 is what percent of 64?

   e. 45 is what percent of 50?   **f.** 68 is what percent of 85?

   g. 114 is what percent of 120?   **h.** 25 is what percent of 125?

   i. 209 is what percent of 209?   **j.** 28 is what percent of 80?

   k. 13 is what percent of 10?   **l.** 51 is what percent of 60?

   m. 38 is what percent of 20?   **n.** 154 is what percent of 140?

   o. 12 is what percent of 80?   **p.** 18 is what percent of 40?

   q. 30 is what percent of 24?   **r.** 125 is what percent of 50?

   s. 165 is what percent of 100?   **t.** 70 is what percent of 35?

   u. 35 is what percent of 25?   **v.** 78 is what percent of 65?

   w. 120 is what percent of 75?   **x.** 7 is what percent of 4?

   y. 180 is what percent of 80?   **z.** 69 is what percent of 46?

3. Tom's active heart rate is 180% of his resting heart rate. If his resting heart rate is 65 beats per minute, what is his active heart rate?

4. Carrie's resting heart rate is 70 beats per minute. She wants to increase her heart rate by 30%. What should her active heart rate be?

5. Tracy's active heart rate is 140% of her resting heart rate. If her resting heart rate is 70 beats per minute, what is her active heart rate?

(continued)

MODULE 7 SECTION 2

PRACTICE AND APPLICATIONS

For use with Exploration 2

6. Find each percent of change.

a. original value: 24
final value: 36

b. original value: 64
final value: 16

c. original value: 60
final value: 69

d. original value: 70
final value: 42

e. original value: 180
final value: 405

f. original value: 84
final value: 63

g. original value: 32
final value: 28

h. original value: 12
final value: 20

i. original value: 75
final value: 225

j. original value: 60
final value: 20

k. original value: 45
final value: 90

l. original value: 72
final value: 126

m. original value: 60
final value: 111

n. original value: 80
final value: 68

o. original value: 46
final value: 23

p. original value: 80
final value: 96

7. Greg's heart rate increased from 65 to 91 beats per minute. What is the percent of change in his heart rate?

8. Muriel's heart rate decreased from 84 to 63 beats per minute. What is the percent of change in her heart rate?

9. Last year's fundraisers for the school sold 520 magazines. This year 702 magazines were sold. What is the percent of increase in the number of magazines sold from last year to this year?

10. John makes wreaths to sell at crafts fairs. Each wreath costs $12 to make. If he sells the wreaths for $21 each, what is the percent increase?

11. A furniture store marks down all rocking chairs that originally sold for $450 to $297. What is the percent decrease?

| MODULE 7 SECTION 3 | PRACTICE AND APPLICATIONS |

For use with Exploration 1

1. Replace each __?__ with the number that makes each a true statement.

   a. 4 fl oz = __?__ tbsp

   c. $\frac{1}{2}$ gal = __?__ qt

   e. 3 pt = __?__ fl oz

   g. $1\frac{1}{2}$ c = __?__ tbsp

   i. $\frac{3}{4}$ gal = __?__ c

   k. 3 qt = __?__ gal

   b. 32 fl oz = __?__ pt

   d. $\frac{1}{2}$ qt = __?__ pt

   f. $1\frac{1}{2}$ gal = __?__ pt

   h. 4 pt = __?__ qt

   j. 6 c = __?__ qt

   l. $2\frac{1}{2}$ c = __?__ fl oz

2. The directions on a 6 fl oz can of concentrated soup say to add 4 cans of milk.

   a. How many fluid ounces of milk should be added?

   b. How many cups of milk should be added?

   c. About how many fluid ounces of soup will there be?

   d. About how many cups of soup is that?

3. A recipe for vegetable soup calls for 2 qt of water.

   a. How many cups of water are needed to make the soup?

   b. Suppose the recipe is tripled. How many gallons of water would be needed to make the soup?

   c. Suppose the recipe is halved. How many pints of water would be needed to make the soup?

4. How many gallons of milk are needed to supply a cafeteria with 320 c of milk?

5. Donna drinks 5 pints of water each day in the summer.

   a. How many cups of water does Donna drink each day?

   b. How many fluid ounces of water does Donna drink each day?

(continued)

For use with Exploration 2

6. Solve each inequality.

a. $6x \leq 72$ **b.** $2x > 56$ **c.** $x + 5 < 8$

d. $9x \geq 5$ **e.** $\frac{2}{3}x < 12$ **f.** $-7 + x < 15$

g. $8 \geq 14 + x$ **h.** $6 < 4 + x$ **i.** $8x \leq 80$

j. $\frac{1}{4}x < 11$ **k.** $-3 + x \geq 9$ **l.** $2 < 4 + x$

m. $5x + 1 \geq 6$ **n.** $x + 8 < 4$ **o.** $1 \geq -2 + 3x$

p. $6x < 15$ **q.** $-2 + x > 1$ **r.** $\frac{3}{4}x > 5$

For use with Exploration 3

7. Use the data in the table.

a. Order the data.

b. Find the extremes.

c. Find the median.

d. Find and record the lower quartile.

e. Find and record the upper quartile.

f. Graph the median, the extremes, and
   the quartiles below a number line.
   Then draw the box and whiskers.

Food	Grams of fat
cheese crackers	6
saltine crackers	2
tuna	3
cereal bars	3
graham crackers	5
multigrain bread	2
vanilla wafers	2
raisin bran	1
buttered popcorn (microwave)	5

MODULE 7 SECTION 4   PRACTICE AND APPLICATIONS

For use with Exploration 1

1. Use the circle graph to estimate each percent.

   a. the percent of students who chose green, black, or red as their favorite color

   b. the percent of students who chose green as their favorite color

   c. the percent of students who chose blue as their favorite color

   d. the percent of students who chose black as their favorite color

   e. the percent of students who chose yellow or blue as their favorite color

Favorite Colors of Seventh Graders at Lakeside

2. Find the measure of the central angle for each sector of the circle. Round each measure to the nearest degree.

   a. A   **b.** B

   c. C   **d.** D

   e. E   **f.** F

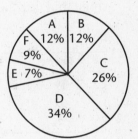

3. One thousand people were asked to identify the main reason they do not exercise. Their responses are summarized in the table.

Main Reason for Not Exercising

Response	Number of people
not enough time	624
too tired	242
too lazy	85
lack of interest	49

   a. Write a percent to tell what part of the group gave each response. Round answers to the nearest whole percent.

   b. Find the measures of the central angles that represent the four reasons on a circle graph. Round each measure to the nearest degree.

(continued)

MODULE 7 SECTION 4 **PRACTICE AND APPLICATIONS**

For use with Exploration 2

4. A county library took a survey of the types of books teenage members prefer to read. The library reports that of its total teenage members, 52% prefer mystery books, 26% prefer science fiction books, 12% prefer fantasy books, and 10% prefer other types of books. Leon decides to make a graph to show these results.

Books Preferred by Teenage Readers

a. Do you think his graph is accurate and effective? Explain.

b. What other type of graph could you use to represent the same results?

5. The table shows the results of a survey of after-school activities of some middle school students.

After–School Activities

Grade	Music lessons	Sports practice	Club meetings
6	28%	64%	12%
7	32%	59%	23%
8	36%	72%	41%

a. What after-school activity is the most popular in grades 6–8?

b. Is there a dramatic difference in participation in each activity among the different grade levels? Explain.

c. Are there any surprising results in this data? Explain.

d. Why is the total participation at each grade level greater than 100%?

e. Choose the best kind of graph to compare the after-school activities in grades 6–8.

f. Draw the graph you have chosen.

g. Write three conclusions you can draw based on your graph.

MODULE 7 SECTION 5	PRACTICE AND APPLICATIONS

For use with Exploration 1

1. Choose the letters of all the figures of each type.

   a. trapezoid   **b.** parallelogram that is   **c.** rhombus
                                          not a rhombus

A.   **B.**   **C.**

D.   **E.**   **F.**

G.   **H.**   **I.**

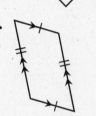

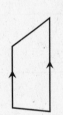
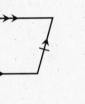

2. Find the area of each rhombus.

   a.   7 m   **b.**   6 ft   **c.**   8 cm
        4 m   5 cm

   d.   **e.**   **f.**   3.8 cm
               1.2 m   2 ft 3.6 ft   9 cm

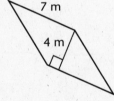

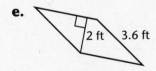
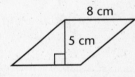
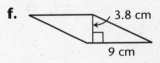

3. Joseph is making a kite in the shape of a rhombus. From a design
book, he knows that the length of one side of the kite is $2\frac{3}{4}$ ft and the
height of the figure is $1\frac{1}{2}$ ft. How many square feet of fabric does
Joseph need to make the kite?

(continued)

Name _____ Date _____

For use with Exploration 2

4. Find the area of a trapezoid with the given measurements.

a. $b_1 = 6$ in., $b_2 = 2$ in., $h = 5$ in.

b. $b_1 = 9$ m, $b_2 = 6$ m, $h = 3$ m

c. $b_1 = 4.3$ m, $b_2 = 6.1$ m, $h = 3.8$ m

d. $b_1 = 3\frac{3}{4}$ in., $b_2 = 2\frac{1}{4}$ in., $h = 5\frac{1}{2}$ in.

e. $b_1 = 2.35$ cm, $b_2 = 4.4$ cm, $h = 5.2$ cm

5. Find the area of each trapezoid.

a.
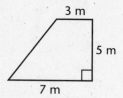
3 m
5 m
7 m

b.
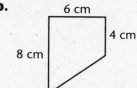
6 cm
4 cm
8 cm

c.
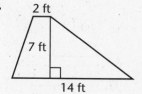
2 ft
7 ft
14 ft

d.
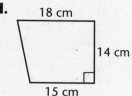
18 cm
14 cm
15 cm

e.
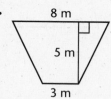
8 m
5 m
3 m

f.
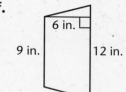
6 in.
9 in.
12 in.

6. For each trapezoid, find the unknown dimension or the area.

a.
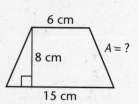
6 cm
8 cm
$A = ?$
15 cm

b.
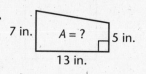
7 in.
$A = ?$
5 in.
13 in.

c.
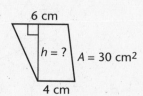
6 cm
$h = ?$
$A = 30$ cm²
4 cm

d.
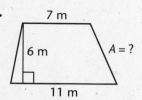
7 m
6 m
$A = ?$
11 m

e.
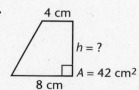
4 cm
$h = ?$
$A = 42$ cm²
8 cm

f.
11 ft
$h = ?$
$A = 80$ ft²
9 ft

7. Mr. Carlisle is building a deck. The floor of the deck is in the shape of a trapezoid. How many square feet of lumber will Mr. Carlisle need if the dimensions of the deck are $b_1 = 12$ ft, $b_2 = 18$ ft, and $h = 15$ ft?

MODULE 7 · SECTIONS 1–5 | PRACTICE AND APPLICATIONS

For use with Section 1

1. Find the unknown measure for each cylinder. Use 3.14 for π. If necessary, round answers to the nearest hundredth.

   a. $r = 3.2$ m, $h = 4.6$ m, $V =$ __?__ m^3

   b. $B = 12$ in.^{2}, $h =$? in., $V = 72$ in.^{3}

   c. $B =$ __?__ ft^2, $h = 8$ ft, $V = 176$ ft^3

   d. $r =$ __?__ cm, $h = 8$ cm, $V = 904$ cm^3

   e. $r = 4$ cm, $h = 16$ cm, $V =$ __?__ cm^3

   f. $B = 38$ ft^2, $h =$ __?__ ft, $V = 266$ ft^3

2. Scanning for insects, a bat sends out 400 pulses of sound per second.

   a. Suppose you make a graph with the number of pulses of sound on the vertical axis and the number of seconds on the horizontal axis. What scale would you use for each axis? Explain.

   b. Draw and label a graph of the data.

3. Find the slope of a line with each rise and run.

   a. rise 6
      run 3

   b. rise 3
      run 4

   c. rise 4
      run 16

For use with Section 2

4. Find each percent of change.

   a. original value: 60
      final value: 75

   b. original value: 80
      final value: 92

   c. original value: 80
      final value: 52

   d. original value: 154
      final value: 294

   e. original value: 85
      final value: 17

   f. original value: 120
      final value: 6

For use with Section 3

5. Replace each __?__ with the number that makes each a true statement.

   a. 12 pt = __?__ gal

   b. 2 gal = __?__ qt

   c. 5 c = __?__ pt

   d. $3\frac{1}{2}$ fl oz = __?__ tbsp

(continued)

MODULE 7 SECTIONS 1–5

For use with Section 4

6. Find the measure of the central angle for each sector of the circle. Round each measure to the nearest degree.

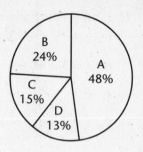

   a. A   **b.** B

   c. C   **d.** D

7. a. List your grades from tests in one subject area for 1 or 2 months.

   b. Choose the best kind of graph to compare your test grades for the time period you selected.

   c. Draw the graph you have chosen.

   d. Write three conclusions you can draw based on your graph.

For use with Section 5

8. Find the area of a trapezoid with the given measurements.

   a. $b_1 = 4$ in., $b_2 = 7$ in., $h = 8$ in.

   b. $b_1 = 9$ cm, $b_2 = 5$ cm, $h = 12$ cm

   c. $b_1 = 2.4$ in., $b_2 = 3.6$ in., $h = 4.3$ in.

9. Find each unknown dimension or the area.

   a. trapezoid   **b.** parallelogram   **c.** trapezoid

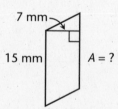
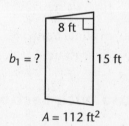

10. An artist is making a frame in the shape of a rhombus. The length of one side of the frame is 9 in. The corners of the frame meet in right angles. How many square inches of fabric will the artist need if he wants to put canvas on the frame?

MODULE 7 SECTION 1 **STUDY GUIDE**

Burning Calories   Cylinders and Graphs

GOAL **LEARN HOW TO:** • find the volume of a cylinder
• choose a scale for a graph
• use formulas to find values and make graphs
• find the slope of a line
• determine how the scale affects the appearance of a graph

As you: • explore the meaning of Calorie
• investigate the number of Calories burned when you exercise
• identify misleading graphs

Exploration 1: Volume of a Cylinder

A circular **cylinder** is a space figure with two
congruent parallel circular bases.

To find the *volume* of a cylinder, multiply the *area of the base, B,*
times the height, h. Since the two bases are congruent circles,
B can be replaced by πr^2.

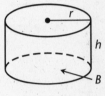

$V = Bh = \pi r^2 h$

Exploration 2: Formulas and Graphs

Choosing a Good Scale for a Graph

The numbers written along the axis of a graph are its **scale**. Usually, the
maximum and the *minimum data values* determine the *range* of the scale.
The size of the *interval* depends on how spread out the data values are.
The two axes can have different scales and intervals.

Finding the Slope of a Line

The **slope** of a line is the ratio of the *rise* to the *run*.

The **rise** is the number of units
the graph rises between two points.

$$\text{slope} = \frac{\text{rise}}{\text{run}}$$

The **run** is the number of units
left or right between the same two points.

MODULE 7 SECTION 1

Example

Find the slope of the line on the graph.

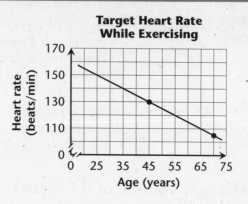

Target Heart Rate While Exercising

▪ Sample Response ▪

At age 70 the target heart rate while exercising is about 105 beats per minute.

At age 45 the target heart rate while exercising is about 130 beats per minute.

$$\text{slope} = \frac{130 - 105}{45 - 70} \quad \begin{matrix} \leftarrow \text{rise} \\ \leftarrow \text{run} \end{matrix}$$

$$= \frac{25}{-25}$$

$$= -1$$

Exploration 3: Misleading Graphs

The scales chosen for a graph will affect the way the data appears.

Example

The graphs below show how the data in the table appear different when the scales on the vertical axes are different.

A	B
1	2
2	4
3	6
4	8
5	10

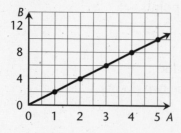

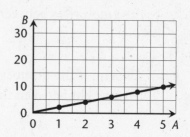

MODULE 7 SECTION 1 | **PRACTICE & APPLICATION EXERCISES** | **STUDY GUIDE**

Exploration 1

Find the unknown measure for each cylinder. Use 3.14 or the π key on a calculator.

1. $r = 4$ cm, $h = 5$ cm, $V = $ __?__ cm^3 **2.** $r = $ __?__ ft, $h = 7$ ft, $V = 87.92$ ft^3

Exploration 2

Find the slope of a line with each rise and run.

3. rise 4   **4.** rise 8   **5.** rise 27   **6.** rise 48   **7.** rise 9
run 8   run 24   run 9   run 6   run 15

Exploration 3

Use the table at the right for Exercises 8 and 9.

8. Make two graphs of the data using different scales on the vertical axes.

9. Explain which graph you would show your employer to help you get a pay raise.

Hourly pay	Month
$5.00	January
$5.15	May
$5.20	September

Spiral Review

Find the volume of each prism. (Module 6, p. 445)

10. 3 ft, 5 ft, 5 ft

11. 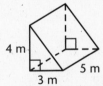 4 m, 3 m, 5 m

12. 8 cm, 6 cm, 7 cm

For each spinner in Exercises 13 and 14, find the theoretical probability of the outcome shown. (Module 1, p. 33)

13. 2, 4, 6

14. 3, 3, 2, 2, 4, 6

15. Suppose each spinner in Exercises 13 and 14 is spun 100 times. For each spinner, about how many times do you expect the outcome to be "3"? (Module 1, p. 33)

Write each ratio in percent form. (Module 5, p. 366)

16. 8 : 10   **17.** 5 : 20   **18.** 45 : 300   **19.** 2 : 10

MODULE 7 SECTION 2

Heart Rates   Percent Equations

GOAL **LEARN HOW TO:** • find percents greater than 100%
• find a percent of increase or decrease

AS YOU: • compare your resting and active heart rates
• examine resting and active heart rates

Exploration 1: Percents Greater Than 100%

Some percent problems involve percents greater than 100%.

Example

36 is what percent of 15?

▪ Sample Response ▪

Think: 36 is greater than 15, so 36 is more than 100% of 15.

$36 = \dfrac{x}{100} \cdot 15$ ← x is the unknown part of 100%.

$36 = \dfrac{15x}{100}$ ← Simplify and solve for x.

$3600 = 15x$

$\dfrac{3600}{15} = \dfrac{15x}{15}$

$240 = x$ So, 36 is 240% of 15.

Exploration 2: Percent of Change

You can find the **percent of change** between two numbers by comparing
the difference of the numbers with the original amount.

Example

Malia's pedaling changed from 10 mi/h to 14 mi/h. What is the percent of change?

▪ Sample Response ▪

First Find the difference in pedaling rates.   → $14 - 10 = 4$

Then Find the percent that this difference is of the original amount.

$4 = \dfrac{x}{100} \cdot 10$ ← 4 is what percent of 10?

$4 = \dfrac{x}{10}$

$40 = x$ So, Malia's pedaling rate increased 40%.

MODULE 7 SECTION 2 | PRACTICE & APPLICATION EXERCISES | STUDY GUIDE

Exploration 1

1. When Jeff begins typing, he types at a rate of 25 words per minute. After several minutes, his rate increases to 30 words per minute. What percent of Jeff's beginning speed is this rate of 30 words per minute?

Find each percent.

2. 18 is what percent of 45?

3. 46 is what percent of 80?

4. 278 is what percent of 139?

5. 81 is what percent of 60?

Exploration 2

For Exercises 6 and 7, find each percent of change.

6. original value: 12
final value: 18

7. original value: 8
final value: 5

8. Betty's active heart rate is 170 beats per minute. After 2 min of rest, her heart rate is down to 130 beats per minute. What is the percent of change in her heart rate?

Spiral Review

Find the slope of a line with each rise and run. (Module 7, p. 464)

9. rise 4
run 2

10. rise 12
run 3

11. rise 1
run 5

12. rise 2
run 4

For Exercises 13 –15, find the product. Write each product in lowest terms. (Module 4, p. 241)

13. $\frac{4}{7} \cdot \frac{5}{8}$

14. $2\frac{5}{6} \cdot \frac{3}{18}$

15. $3\frac{1}{9} \cdot 2\frac{1}{7}$

16. Choose two heart-rate intervals from the table at the right. Write an inequality for each, then graph each inequality on a number line. (Module 6, p. 388)

Human Target Heart Rate (beats per minute)	
20 year old	140–170
25 year old	137–166
30 year old	133–162
35 year old	130–157
40 year old	126–153
45 year old	123–149
50 year old	119–145
55 year old	116–140

MODULE 7 SECTION 3

Healthy Choices Customary Capacity and Inequalities

GOAL

LEARN HOW TO: • convert customary units of capacity
• solve inequalities
• make a box-and-whisker plot

AS YOU: • interpret nutritional labels on food products
• investigate daily nutritional requirements
• examine the amount of sugar in foods

Exploration 1: Customary Units of Capacity

Customary units of capacity for fluids include **fluid ounce (fl oz)**,
tablespoon (tbsp), **cup (c)**, **pint (pt)**, **quart (qt)**, and **gallon (gal)**.

The table shows the relationship among customary units of capacity.

1 tbsp   1 c   1 pt   1 qt   1 gal

Customary Units of Capacity
1 tbsp = 0.5 fl oz
1 c = 8 fl oz
1 pt = 2 c = 16 fl oz
1 qt = 2 pt = 4 c = 32 fl oz
1 gal = 4 qt = 16 c = 128 fl oz

Example

A recipe calls for $2\frac{3}{4}$ c of pumpkin. How many 15 fl oz cans of pumpkin will be needed
to make the recipe? How much will be left?

■ Sample Response ■

Multiply the number of fluid ounces in 1 c by
2 to get the number of fluid ounces in 2 c.

$$
\begin{array}{rcr}
1\,c & = & 8\ \text{fl oz} \\
\times 2 & & \times 2 \\
\hline
2\,c & = & 16\ \text{fl oz}
\end{array}
$$

Now find the number of fluid ounces in $\frac{3}{4}$ c.

$\frac{3}{4}\,c = \frac{3}{4}\,(8)$, or 6 fl oz

So, the number of ounces needed is 16 + 6, or 22 fl oz.

Since 22 > 15, 2 cans of pumpkin will be needed and there will be 2(15) − 22, or
8 fl oz left over.

Exploration 2: Solving Inequalities

When you solve problems that ask for a minimum or maximum amount, you might want to use an inequality.

Example

Solve the inequality $14x + 5 \geq 12$.

■ Sample Response ■

$$14x + 5 \geq 12$$

$14x + 5 - 5 \geq 12 - 5$ ← Subtract 5 from both sides.

$14x \geq 7$ ← Simplify.

$\dfrac{14x}{14} \geq \dfrac{7}{14}$ ← Divide both sides by 14.

$x \geq \dfrac{1}{2}$

Exploration 3: Making Box-and-Whisker Plots

Box-and-Whisker Plots

Box-and-whisker plots show how spread out a set of data values is. This plot is particularly useful when comparing two or more sets of data.

Example

Use the box-and whisker-plot at the right to find the lower and upper extremes, the lower and upper quartiles, and the median of the data.

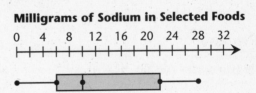

Milligrams of Sodium in Selected Foods

■ Sample Response ■

The left end of the left whisker shows the lower extreme, 0.

The right end of the right whisker shows the upper extreme, 28.

The left end of the box shows the lower quartile value, 6. This value is the median of the lower half of the data.

The right end of the box shows the upper quartile value, 22. This value is the median of the upper half of the data.

The vertical line inside the box shows the median of all the data, 10.

MODULE 7 SECTION 3 | PRACTICE & APPLICATION EXERCISES | STUDY GUIDE

Exploration 1

Replace each ___?___ with the number that makes each statement true.

1. 6 fl oz = ___?___ tbsp

2. $\frac{3}{8}$ gal = ___?___ c

3. 8 tbsp = ___?___ fl oz

4. $2\frac{5}{8}$ pt = ___?___ fl oz

Exploration 2

Solve each inequality.

5. $5x \geq 35$

6. $-4 + x < 10$

7. $7 \leq 9 + x$

8. $\frac{2}{3}x < 16$

9. $6x \geq 9$

10. $12 \leq 18 + 2x$

Exploration 3

11. Use the data in the table at the right.

   a. Order the data.

   b. Find the extremes.

   c. Find the median.

   d. Find the quartiles.

   e. Draw a box-and-whisker plot of the data.

Food	Amount of Sodium per Serving (mg)
jelly	10
beef stew	870
peanut butter	80
bread	150
cereal	210
cake	270
macaroni and cheese	580

Spiral Review

Find each percent. (Module 7, p. 479)

12. 8 is what percent of 5?

13. 40 is what percent of 18?

14. 36 is what percent of 12?

15. 18 is what percent of 4?

Find each square root. (Module 6, p. 404)

16. $\sqrt{49}$

17. $\sqrt{400}$

18. $\sqrt{4}$

Find each amount. (Module 5, p. 353)

19. 12% of 50

20. 50% of 44

21. 70% of 244

Name _____ Date _____

Getting Your ZZZ's   Circle Graphs and Choosing a Graph

GOAL   **LEARN HOW TO:** • make a circle graph
                              • choose an effective visual representation

AS YOU: • conduct a survey on sleep habits
             • perform an experiment on rest

Exploration 1: Circle Graphs

A **circle graph** can be used to compare parts of a data set with the whole, or to display percent data.

A **central angle** is an angle that has its vertex at the center of a circle.

A **sector** is a wedge-shaped region bounded by two radii and an arc of a circle.

Example

Fifty students were asked the question "Do you use a pillow when you are sleeping?" Their answers are shown in the table at the right. Draw a circle graph to represent the results.

Response	Number of people
always	42
sometimes	5
never	3

■ Sample Response ■

First, use the data from the table to find the percent of students who chose each of the three responses.

42 out of 50, or 84% said *always*.
5 out of 50, or 10% said *sometimes*.
3 out of 50, or 6% said *never*.

Use these percents to find the degree measure for each of the three sectors.

84% of 360° = 0.84(360°) = 302.4° ≈ 302°
10% of 360° = 0.10(360°) = 36°
6% of 360° = 0.06(360°) = 21.6° ≈ 22°

On a circle, draw a central angle of measure 36° and label the resulting sector "Sometimes." Then draw a 22°, central angle adjacent to the first sector and label this one "Never." Label the remainder of the circle "Always." Finally, choose a title for the graph. The completed circle graph is shown at the right.

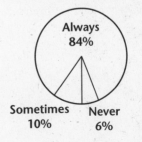

**Students' Use of a
Pillow when Sleeping**

Always
84%

Sometimes
10%

Never
6%

MODULE 7 SECTION 4   STUDY GUIDE

Exploration 2: Choosing a Graph

To make a comparison between data values or sets of data, you can display
the data using a graph. You have learned several ways to display a set of data.

Box-and-whisker plots are good for *comparing two sets of data*.

**Points Scored in Basketball Games
by Teams A and B**

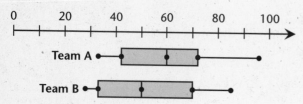

Bar graphs or **histograms** can be used to compare values in a data set. A
frequency table is helpful when you have a large set of data to organize.

**1997 Participation
in Basketball**

Age in years	Number of participants
6–8	50
9–11	60
12–14	75
15–17	50

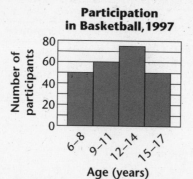

Stem-and-leaf plots display individual values. This type of plot can help
you organize data and see gaps and clusters in the data.

**Number of Long Distance Phone
Calls Made per Month (1997)**

```
0 | 4 5 6 6 7
1 | 0 0 0
2 | 2 5 9
3 | 1
```

2 | 5 represents 25 phone calls

MODULE 7 SECTION 4 | **PRACTICE & APPLICATION EXERCISES** | **STUDY GUIDE**

Exploration 1

Find the measure of the central angle for each sector of the circle. Round each measure to the nearest degree.

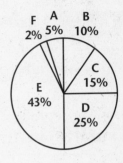

F A B
2% 5% 10%

C 15%

E 43%

D 25%

1. A   **2.** B   **3.** C

4. D   **5.** E   **6.** F

Exploration 2

7. The table at the right shows the price of a cake donut at 20 different bakeries.

Price of cake donuts
25¢ 35¢ 20¢ 25¢ 45¢
50¢ 25¢ 35¢ 30¢ 50¢
65¢ 75¢ 75¢ 60¢ 55¢
28¢ 35¢ 39¢ 39¢ 59¢

a. Choose the best kind of graph to display the data.

b. Draw the graph you chose in part (a).

c. Write three conclusions you can draw based on the graph you made in part (b).

Spiral Review

Replace each __?__ with the number that makes each statement true. (Module 7, p. 493)

8. 10 tbsp = __?__ fl oz

9. 64 fl oz = __?__ qt

10. $\frac{1}{2}$ qt = __?__ pt

11. $1\frac{1}{2}$ gal = __?__ c

Evaluate each expression. (Module 4, p. 284)

12. $\frac{1}{3}(-9) - \frac{1}{3}$

13. $2.4 \div 3 + (-8)$

14. $16 \cdot \frac{5}{6} + (-2)$

Find the area of each figure. (Module 6, p. 383)

15.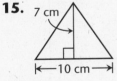
7 cm
10 cm

16.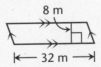
8 m
32 m

17.
5 ft
6 ft
2 ft
3 ft

MODULE 7 SECTION 5 **STUDY GUIDE**

A Thousand Words   Quadrilaterals

GOAL

LEARN HOW TO: • identify trapezoids and rhombuses
• classify quadrilaterals
• find the area of a trapezoid

AS YOU: • play a game
• analyze the Food Guide Pyramid

Exploration 1: Classifying Quadrilaterals

Trapezoids and Rhombuses

A **trapezoid** is a *quadrilateral* that has exactly *one pair of parallel sides*. The sides that are parallel are the **bases of the trapezoid,** b_1 and b_2. The *height* of the trapezoid is the distance between its two bases.

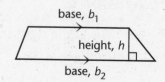

A **rhombus** is a *parallelogram* that has four congruent sides.

Exploration 2: Area of a Trapezoid

The area of a trapezoid can be calculated using the formula $A = \frac{1}{2}(b_1 + b_2)h$, where A is the area, h is the height, and b_1 and b_2 are the lengths of the two bases.

Example

Find the area of the trapezoid shown.

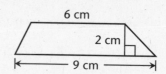

■ Sample Response ■

$A = \frac{1}{2}(b_1 + b_2)h$

$= \frac{1}{2}(6 + 9)2$ ← Substitute 6 for b_1, 9 for b_2, and 2 for h.

$= \frac{1}{2}(15)2$

$= 15$

The area of the trapezoid is 15 cm^2.

MODULE 7 SECTION 5 | PRACTICE & APPLICATION EXERCISES | STUDY GUIDE

Exploration 1

Choose the letters of all the figures of each type.

1. trapezoid

2. parallelogram

3. rhombus

A.

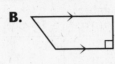
B.

C.

Exploration 2

Find the area of each trapezoid.

4.

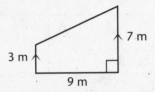
3 m

7 m

9 m

5.

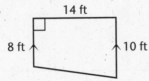
14 ft

8 ft

10 ft

6. ⊢—16 cm—⊣

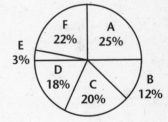
10 cm

12 cm

Find each unknown dimension.

7. trapezoid: $h = 15$ m, $b_1 = 8$ m, $A = 135$ m^2, $b_2 =$ ___**?**___

8. trapezoid: $b_1 = 17$ ft, $b_2 = 21$ ft, $A = 57$ ft^2, $h =$ ___**?**___

Spiral Review

For each sector of the circle graph, find the measure of the central angle. Round to the nearest degree. (Module 7, p. 505)

9. A

10. B

11. C

12. D

13. E

14. F

F 22% | A 25% | E 3% | D 18% | C 20% | B 12%

For Exercises 15 and 16, write an expression that models each situation. (Module 2, p. 129)

15. Maria is 5 years younger than her sister's age. Her sister is x years old. How old is Maria?

16. Julean ran twice as long as Kyle did. If Julean ran r minutes, how long did Kyle run?

17. Draw a tree diagram to represent all the possible outcomes for two spins of a spinner that is divided into three equal sectors colored red, blue, and green. (Module 3, p. 171)

MODULE 8   LABSHEET **1A**

Table of Orders (Use with Questions 8, 9, 12, and 13 on pages 531 and 533.)

Number of cities	Possible orders	Total number of orders	Number of choices for 1st city	Number of choices for 2nd city	Number of choices for 3rd city	Number of choices for 4th city
2 cities						
3 cities						
4 cities	(See tree diagram below.)					

Tree Diagram for Four Cities (Use with Questions 11 and 12 on pages 532–533.)

Directions In the space below or on the back of this labsheet, make a tree diagram to show all the possible orders in which you can visit the four cities chosen by your group. The first column is labeled for you.

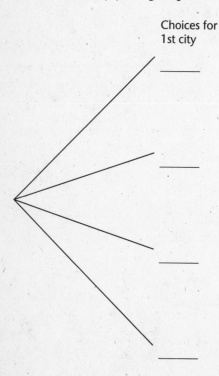

Choices for
1st city

MODULE 8

Pyramid Nets (Use with Question 10 on page 544.)

Directions Cut out each pyramid net. Crease each net along the dashed lines. Then fold each net, tuck in the tabs, and tape the edges together to form two pyramids.

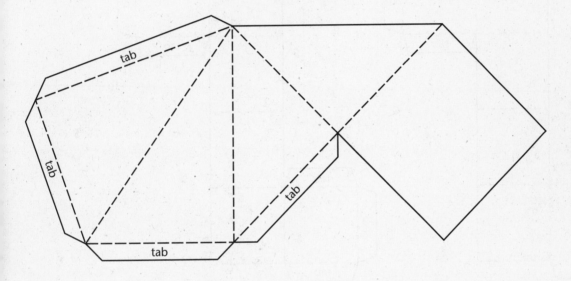

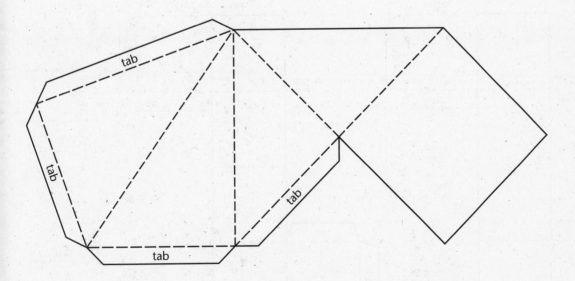

Cube Nets   (Use with Exercise 1 on page 548.)

Directions Cut out each cube net. Crease each net along the dashed lines. Then fold each net, tuck in the tabs, and tape the edges together to form each cube.

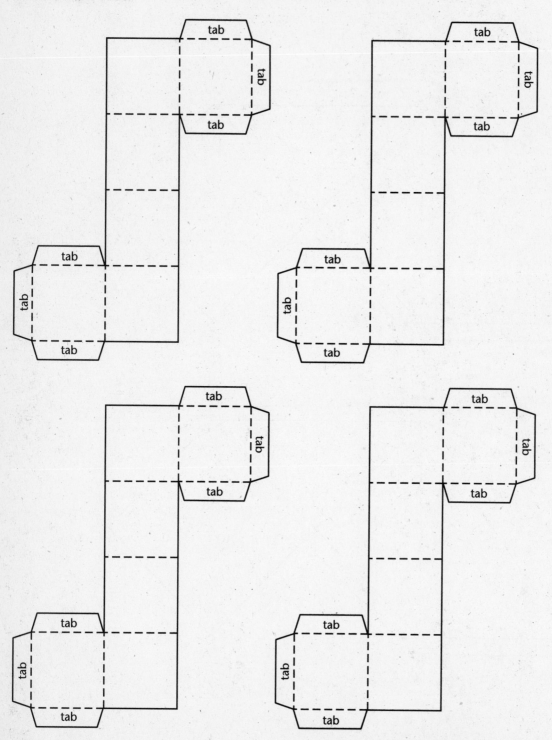

Map of New York City (Middle West Side)
(Use with Questions 1 and 2 on page 553.)

Directions Follow the directions in Questions 1 and 2 on page 553 to mark locations and trace routes on the map below.

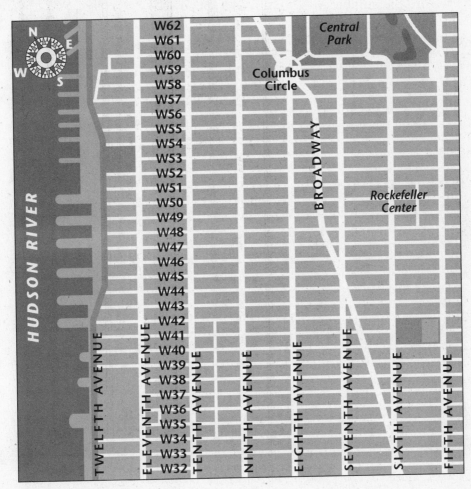

MODULE 8   **LABSHEET 3B**

Street Diagram (Use with Questions 6 and 7 on page 555.)

Directions Find the number of possible shortest paths from intersection X to each of the other intersections. Record the number in the circle at each intersection. A few intersections have been done for you. (*Hint:* Start with the intersections closest to X and work outward. Look for number patterns you can apply from Questions 3–5 on pages 554–555.)

There is only one shortest path from X to this intersection.

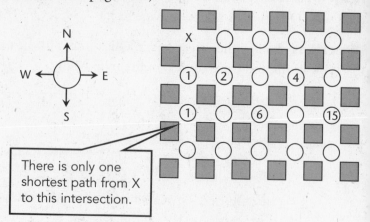

Escape Route Map (Use with Question 8 on page 555.)

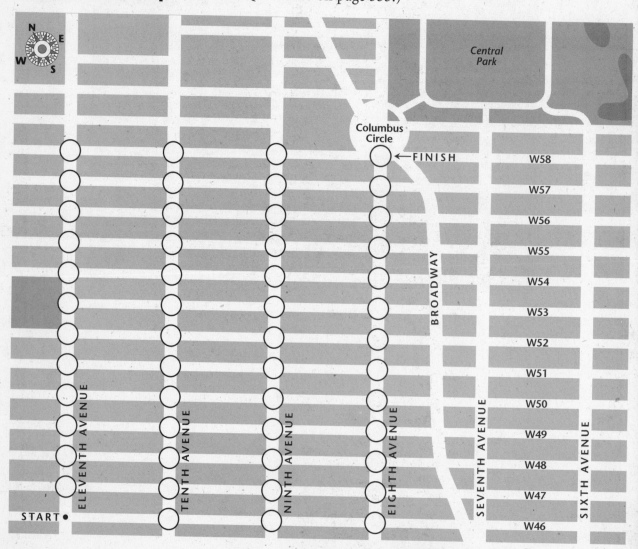

Cone and Cylinder Nets (Use with Question 14 on page 569.)

Directions

a. Cut out the cone and cylinder nets below.

b. Compare the bases of both nets. Are they congruent?
What does this tell you about the areas of the bases?

c. Use tape to join edges A and B on each net. Leave the cone open, but
close one end of the cylinder with tape.

d. Compare the height of the cone to the height of the cylinder.

e. Fill the cone with rice. Then pour that rice into the cylinder.
Repeat this process until the cylinder is full.

f. How many cones of rice does it take to fill the cylinder with rice?

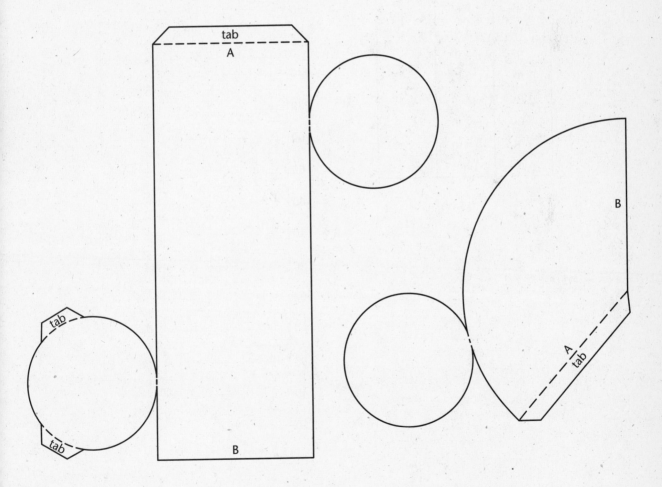

MODULE 8   **LABSHEET 4B**

Comparing Volumes of Cones and Cylinders

(Use with Questions 16 and 17 on page 569.)

Directions

a. Find the volume of each cylinder in the table. Round each volume to the nearest tenth.

b. Graph the radius and the volume of each cylinder.

c. Draw a smooth curve connecting the data points on your graph.

Volumes of Cylinders		
Height	Radius	Volume
1 m	1 m	
1 m	2 m	
1 m	3 m	
1 m	4 m	
1 m	5 m	
1 m	6 m	
1 m	7 m	
1 m	8 m	
1 m	9 m	
1 m	10 m	

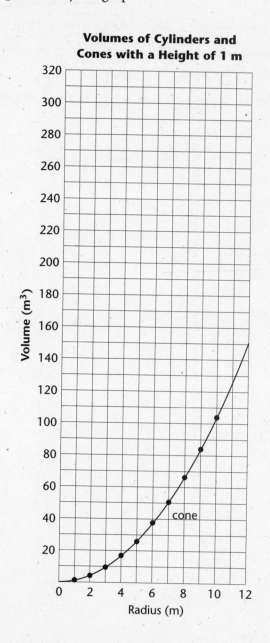

Volumes of Cylinders and Cones with a Height of 1 m

Pattern Block Shapes (Use with Exercise 4 on page 572.)

Name _____

TEACHER ASSESSMENT SCALES

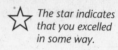
The star indicates that you excelled in some way.

 Problem Solving

❶   ❷   ❸   ❹   ❺

❶ You did not understand the problem well enough to get started or you did not show any work.

❸ You understood the problem well enough to make a plan and to work toward a solution.

❺ You made a plan, you used it to solve the problem, and you verified your solution.

 Mathematical Language x^2

❶   ❷   ❸   ❹   ❺

❶ You did not use any mathematical vocabulary or symbols, or you did not use them correctly, or your use was not appropriate.

❸ You used appropriate mathematical language, but the way it was used was not always correct or other terms and symbols were needed.

❺ You used mathematical language that was correct and appropriate to make your meaning clear.

 Representations

❶   ❷   ❸   ❹   ❺

❶ You did not use any representations such as equations, tables, graphs, or diagrams to help solve the problem or explain your solution.

❸ You made appropriate representations to help solve the problem or help you explain your solution, but they were not always correct or other representations were needed.

❺ You used appropriate and correct representations to solve the problem or explain your solution.

 Connections

❶   ❷   ❸   ❹   ❺

❶ You attempted or solved the problem and then stopped.

❸ You found patterns and used them to extend the solution to other cases, or you recognized that this problem relates to other problems, mathematical ideas, or applications.

❺ You extended the ideas in the solution to the general case, or you showed how this problem relates to other problems, mathematical ideas, or applications.

 Presentation

❶   ❷   ❸   ❹   ❺

❶ The presentation of your solution and reasoning is unclear to others.

❸ The presentation of your solution and reasoning is clear in most places, but others may have trouble understanding parts of it.

❺ The presentation of your solution and reasoning is clear and can be understood by others.

Content Used: _____   **Computational Errors:**   Yes   No

Notes on Errors: _____

_____

Name _____   Problem _____

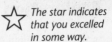

STUDENT   SELF-ASSESSMENT SCALES

 If your score is in the shaded area, explain why on the back of this sheet and stop.

☆ *The star indicates that you excelled in some way.*

 ### Problem Solving

①   ②   ③   ④   ⑤ ☆

① I did not understand the problem well enough to get started or I did not show any work.

② I understood the problem well enough to make a plan and to work toward a solution.

⑤ I made a plan, I used it to solve the problem, and I verified my solution.

 ### Mathematical Language

①   ②   ③   ④   ⑤ ☆

① I did not use any mathematical vocabulary or symbols, or I did not use them correctly, or my use was not appropriate.

② I used appropriate mathematical language, but the way it was used was not always correct or other terms and symbols were needed.

⑤ I used mathematical language that was correct and appropriate to make my meaning clear.

 ### Representations

①   ②   ③   ④   ⑤ ☆

① I did not use any representations such as equations, tables, graphs, or diagrams to help solve the problem or explain my solution.

② I made appropriate representations to help solve the problem or help me explain my solution, but they were not always correct or other representations were needed.

⑤ I used appropriate and correct representations to solve the problem or explain my solution.

 ### Connections

①   ②   ③   ④   ⑤ ☆

① I attempted or solved the problem and then stopped.

② I found patterns and used them to extend the solution to other cases, or I recognized that this problem relates to other problems, mathematical ideas, or applications.

⑤ I extended the ideas in the solution to the general case, or I showed how this problem relates to other problems, mathematical ideas, or applications.

 ### Presentation

①   ②   ③   ④   ⑤ ☆

① The presentation of my solution and reasoning is unclear to others.

② The presentation of my solution and reasoning is clear in most places, but others may have trouble understanding parts of it.

⑤ The presentation of my solution and reasoning is clear and can be understood by others.

MODULE 8 SECTION 1   PRACTICE AND APPLICATIONS

For use with Exploration 1

1. List all the permutations for each situation.

   a. Three friends, Jeff, Kim, and Lyle, are standing in line for movie tickets.

   b. Four books with different colored covers, red, yellow, blue, and green, are set side by side on a shelf.

   c. Two out of three sports balls, a soccer ball, a basketball, and a football, are displayed in the window of a sports store side by side.

   d. Two out of four markers, a red marker, a black marker, a purple marker, and a yellow marker, are set side by side on a table.

2. Every spring, the "Pole-Paddle-Pedal" race is held in Jackson, Wyoming. The competitors in this race ski from the top of a mountain to their bikes, then ride their bikes to the river, and kayak down the river. List all the other possible orders for these three events.

3. The numbers in one of the area codes in Utah are 0, 1, and 8.

   a. List all the possible orders of these digits.

   b. If the numbers 0 and 1 cannot be used as the first digit, how many orders are possible in reality?

4. The numbers in one of the area codes in New York are 1, 7, and 8.

   a. List all the possible orders of these digits.

   b. If the number 1 cannot be used as the first digit, how many orders are possible in reality?

5. Wayne, Vance, and Bart are finalists in the slalom competition at some winter races. The order of their starts in the final ski run will be determined by a random drawing.

   a. List all possible orders in which they might start in the final race.

   b. What is the probability that Wayne will ski first?

   c. Do you think the order in which skiers start in a race matters? Why or why not?

(continued)

MODULE 8 SECTION 1   PRACTICE AND APPLICATIONS

For use with Exploration 2

6. Find how many permutations are possible for each situation.

    a. four children standing in a line

    b. eight students standing in line to practice free throws

    c. the top 2 candidates out of 50 applicants for a job

    d. the four finalists in a math competition of 20 students

    e. the top three spellers out of a spelling bee of 40 students

7. A cafeteria has organized its serving lines for lunch so that people can choose hot sandwiches or cold sandwiches at the first station, soup or salad at the second station, and whole wheat bread, cornbread, or white bread at the third station.

    a. Suppose one item is chosen at each station. Draw a tree diagram to show all the possible meals that could be chosen.

    b. How many meals are possible?

    c. Suppose a fourth station is added that serves apples or bananas. How does this affect the number of possible meals?

8. Use the factorial key [x!] on a calculator to find the total number of permutations for each set of items. Tell whether your answer is approximate or exact.

    a. 5 musical notes   **b.** 7 songs on a cassette tape

    c. 21 pages in a pamphlet   **d.** 30 magazines in a box

9. a. How many permutations are possible when 4 movies are in 4 different theaters?

    b. How many permutations are possible when 4 movies are in 6 different theaters?

10. How many permutations are possible when 3 out of 25 students are called on to recite poems?

11. How many permutations are possible when 2 crayons are selected out of a box of 18 crayons of 18 different colors?

MODULE 8 SECTION 2   **PRACTICE AND APPLICATIONS**

For use with Exploration 1

1. Choose the letter from A to I of the front view and the right-side view for each model building.

a.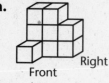
Front   Right

b.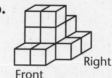
Front   Right

c.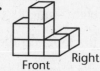
Front   Right

A.

B.

C.

D.

E.

F.

G.

H.

I.

2. a. Draw the front and side views of the model building shown at the right.

b. Copy and complete the base plan for the model building.

c. Suppose the cubes in the model building are centimeter cubes. Find the volume of the model building.

d. Suppose you want to paint the outside of the model building (made from centimeter cubes), including the base. How many cube faces will you need to paint? Recall that this number represents the surface area of the model building in square centimeters.

(continued)

MODULE 8 SECTION 2   **PRACTICE AND APPLICATIONS**

For use with Exploration 2

3. Use the pyramid at the right. Use the letters of the vertices to name each of the following.

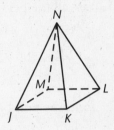

a. the base

b. the other faces

c. the vertex

4. Determine whether each net can be folded to create a pyramid. If so, identify the type of pyramid it will form.

a.
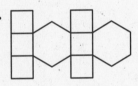

b.
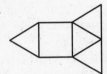

c.
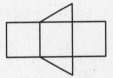

d.

e.

f.

5. Find the volume of each pyramid with the given base area B and height h. Round decimal answers to the nearest tenth.

a. $B = 18$ cm^2
$h = 9$ cm

b. $B = 42$ in.^{2}
$h = 6$ in.

c. $B = 17$ ft^2
$h = 8$ ft

d. $B = 26$ mm^2
$h = 5$ mm

e. $B = 14$ cm^2
$h = 5$ cm

f. $B = 23$ ft^2
$h = 11$ ft

6. a. Paula is making a model of a square pyramid. The lengths of the sides of the square base are 16 cm. The height of the pyramid is 9 cm. What is the volume of the pyramid?

b. Suppose Paula makes a rectangular pyramid with the same height as the square pyramid in part (a). The length of the rectangular base is 15 cm and the width is 17 cm. Which pyramid has the greater volume, the rectangular pyramid or the square pyramid? How much greater?

MODULE 8 SECTION 3   **PRACTICE AND APPLICATIONS**

For use with Exploration 1

1. List all the permutations of the letters in each word.

    a. CAT   **b.** NINE   **c.** SEES

    d. COO   **e.** NUN   **f.** FULL

2. Find the number of permutations of three non-zero digits in a 3-digit number in each case.

    a. All three digits are the same.

    b. Two of the digits are the same.

    c. All three digits are different.

3. Suppose there are eight girl scouts in a girl scout troop. They are assigned to work together in groups of two to sell granola bars. How many different groups of 2 can be selected from the 8 girl scouts?

4. Draw all possible segments connecting four different points on a circle. How many segments are there? (Remember: Only one segment can be drawn between two points.)

5. The twelve members of the cycling club need to elect a president, a secretary, and a treasurer for their club. In how many different ways can three students be selected to hold these positions? Explain.

6. There are 9 students auditioning for the two leads in a school play. In how many ways can the two leads be selected from the group of students auditioning? Explain.

7. Enid has 6 pencils. In how many different ways can she arrange the pencils in a row in her pencil box? Explain.

8. A bookshelf contains 10 books. In how many ways can two books be selected from the 10 books on the shelf? Explain.

(continued)

MODULE 8 SECTION 3   PRACTICE AND APPLICATIONS

For use with Exploration 2

9. Tell whether each is a *permutation* or a *combination*.

   a. Students in a class of 28 are organized into groups of 4.

   b. Four photos out of a group of twelve are used in a yearbook.

   c. Thirty people are forming a line to buy concert tickets.

   d. Three out of 35 members of a fan club are selected to attend a convention.

   e. Five out of 16 sculptures are displayed in a row in a display case.

   f. Four books out of 25 books on a recommended reading list are chosen.

   g. On a field trip, a class of 32 students is organized into groups of 8 to go on a tour.

10. List all the ways four children, Luther, Ariel, Pat, and Nellie, can be matched up in pairs to walk to the park to play.

11. a. How many different groups of four students can be formed from a group of five students?

   b. How many different groups of three students can be formed from a group of five students?

   c. How many different groups of two students can be formed from a group of five students?

   d. Did you find each answer using the idea of a combination or a permutation? Explain.

12. a. Suppose twelve candidates are running for three openings on the student council in their school. How many different groups of 3 candidates can be elected?

   b. Suppose there are ten students on the Student Council. They choose a president and a vice-president from the student council members. How many results are possible?

   c. Which question in parts (a) and (b) is a permutation question? Which is a combination question? Explain your answers.

MODULE 8 SECTION 4   **PRACTICE AND APPLICATIONS**

For use with Exploration 1

1. Trace each polygon below and then create a tessellation with it. Be sure to match up the corresponding sides.

a.

b.

c.

d.

e.

f.

2. Refer to the figures below.

   a. Which of the figures tessellate?

   b. Which two figures can combine to tessellate?

A.

B.

C.

D.

E.

F.

G.

H.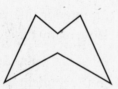

I.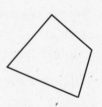

3. Shauna wants to create a tessellation to decorate a posterboard. She is considering the following figures to make the tessellation: an equilateral triangle, a right triangle, a square, a rhombus, a trapezoid, a regular pentagon, and a regular hexagon. Which figure will not tessellate?

(continued)

MODULE 8 SECTION 4   **PRACTICE AND APPLICATIONS**

For use with Exploration 2

4. Find the volume of each cone. Use 3.14 for π. Round answers to the nearest tenth.

a.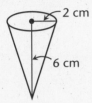
2 cm
6 cm

b.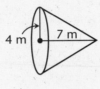
4 m   7 m

c.
9 in.
3 in.

d.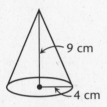
9 cm
4 cm

e. 6 ft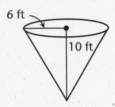
10 ft

f.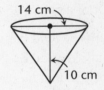
12 mm
5 mm

g.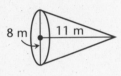
8 m   11 m

h.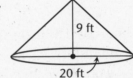
9 ft
20 ft

i.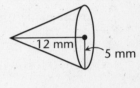
14 cm
10 cm

5. The area of the base of a cone is 16 ft^3. The volume of the cone is 144 ft^3. What is the height of the cone?

6. The height and the diameter of a cone are each 20 cm. What is the volume of the cone? Round your answer to the nearest tenth.

7. A cone and a cylinder have the same height and the same radius. The radius of the base is 4 in. and the height is twice the radius.

  a. Find the volume of the cylinder.

  b. Find the volume of the cone.

8. The volume of a cone is 12.56 in.^{3}. What is the radius of the cone if the height of the cone is 3 in.?

9. Use the dimensions below. Which cones will have the same volume?

  a. $r = 4$ cm
   $h = 9$ cm

  b. $r = 8$ cm
   $h = 16$ cm

  c. $r = 5$ cm
   $h = 16$ cm

  d. $r = 2$ cm
   $h = 25$ cm

  e. $r = 3$ cm
   $h = 16$ cm

  f. $r = 5$ cm
   $h = 4$ cm

MODULE 8 SECTIONS 1–4   PRACTICE AND APPLICATIONS

For use with Section 1

1. Find how many permutations are possible for each situation.

   a. three cyclists riding together

   b. six friends hiking along a trail in a line

   c. the first three finishers in a 15 person race

2. The United States Postal Service has added 4-digit numbers to follow the standard 5-digit ZIP Code.

   a. How many different 4-digit ZIP Codes can the Postal Service create using the digits 1, 2, 3, and 4 if each digit is used only once?

   b. How many different 4-digit ZIP Codes can be created using the digits 0 through 9 if each digit is used only once?

3. How many permutations are possible when 4 marbles are selected out of a bag of 15 marbles?

4. Suppose Reid has a six-period school day. His main subjects are mathematics, English, chemistry, and history. He has an elective in Spanish and he plays the cello in the orchestra. In how many different orders can Reid's classes meet?

For use with Section 2

5. Find the volume of each pyramid with the given base area B and height h. Round answers to the nearest tenth.

   a. $B = 19$ m^2
   $h = 10$ m

   b. $B = 15$ cm^2
   $h = 5$ cm

   c. $B = 30$ ft^2
   $h = 9$ ft

   d. $B = 36$ in.^{2}
   $h = 20$ in.

   e. $B = 27$ cm^2
   $h = 14$ cm

   f. $B = 29$ in.^{2}
   $h = 13$ in.

6. A water tank shaped like a cylinder has a radius of 5 ft and is 24 ft tall. What is the volume of the water tank? Use 3.14 for π.

7. A cylindrical tube has a volume of 148 cm^3. It has a radius of 3.2 cm. What is the height of the tube? Use 3.14 for π. Round your answer to the nearest tenth.

8. Jason makes a cardboard tube in the shape of a cylinder. The height of the tube is 16 in. It has a diameter of 8 in. What is the volume of the tube? Use 3.14 for π. Round your answer to the nearest tenth.

(continued)

MODULE 8 SECTIONS 1–4 **PRACTICE AND APPLICATIONS**

For use with Section 3

9. Find the number of permutations of four non-zero digits in a 4-digit number in each case.

    a. All four digits are the same.

    b. Three of the digits are the same.

    c. Two of the digits are the same.

    d. The four digits are different.

10. Mickey made 5 model airplanes. In how many different ways can he display the model airplanes together in a row on a shelf in his room? Explain.

11. How many different seating arrangements are possible for a family of four if they sit in a row for a family photo?

12. Tell whether each is a *permutation* or a *combination*.

    a. Twelve skiers are lining up preparing for the downhill race.

    b. Two paintings from a collection of 8 paintings are selected for display in a gallery.

For use with Section 4

13. Trace each polygon below and then create a tessellation with it. Be sure to match up the corresponding sides.

a.   **b.**   **c.**

14. Find the volume of each cone. Use 3.14 for π. Round decimals to the nearest tenth.

a. 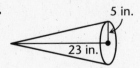 **b.**   **c.**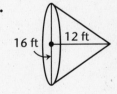

MODULE 8 SECTION 1   **STUDY GUIDE**

Take a Trip   Counting Problems

GOAL **LEARN HOW TO:** • find all possible arrangements of items
• apply tree diagrams to counting problems
• use the counting principle

AS YOU: • plan routes for a trip
• find the number of routes between cities

Exploration 1: Introduction to Permutations

Permutations

The possible arrangements of a group of items in which *order is important*
are called **permutations**. An organized list can help you find permutations.

Example

Jim, Ann, and Terry have been chosen as the three finalists in a science contest. There
will be a first prize and a second prize. Name all the possible ways the prizes could be
awarded.

■ Sample Response ■

Make a table to show the different possibilities.

1st place	2nd place	1st place	2nd place
Jim	Ann	Ann	Terry
Jim	Terry	Terry	Jim
Ann	Jim	Terry	Ann

There are 6 different ways the two prizes could be awarded.

Exploration 2: The Counting Principle

Tree Diagrams and the Counting Principle

A tree diagram can also be used to find permutations.

MODULE 8 SECTION 1

Example

Make a tree diagram to show the possible outcomes of the contest discussed in the Example on the previous page.

■ Sample Response ■

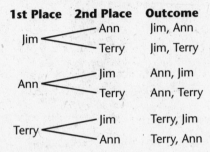

1st Place	2nd Place	Outcome
Jim	Ann	Jim, Ann
	Terry	Jim, Terry
Ann	Jim	Ann, Jim
	Terry	Ann, Terry
Terry	Jim	Terry, Jim
	Ann	Terry, Ann

Again, there are 6 different ways the prizes could be awarded.

If you just want to know the *number* of permutations, you can multiply together the number of options at each point where you make a choice. This is known as the **counting principle**.

Example

Use the counting principle to find the number of ways the prizes for the contest discussed in the Example on the previous page could be awarded.

■ Sample Response ■

Since one person cannot win both prizes, the number of ways to award 2nd prize will be 1 less than the number of ways to award 1st prize.

Number of choices for 1st prize	Number of choices for 2nd prize	Total possible ways for both prizes to be awarded
3	• 2	= 6

This method also shows that there are 6 different ways the prizes could be awarded.

MODULE 8 SECTION 1 | PRACTICE & APPLICATION EXERCISES | STUDY GUIDE

Exploration 1

List all the permutations for each situation.

1. The three numbers 6, 7, and 8 are used to form a 3-digit number, where each digit is different.

2. Three of four people, Mary, Tim, Claire, and Steven, must stand beside each other.

Exploration 2

3. How many permutations are possible when 5 out of 10 students are chosen for parts in the school play?

4. Suppose Susan has 6 days to finish 6 different homework assignments. If she does one each day, how many different ways could she do these assignments?

5. Use the factorial key [x!] on a calculator to find the value of 3! and 4!.

Spiral Review

Find the area of each trapezoid. (Module 7, p. 518)

6.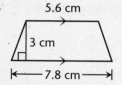
5.6 cm
3 cm
7.8 cm

7.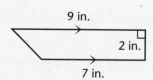
9 in.
2 in.
7 in.

Solve each equation. Check each solution. (Module 4, p. 300)

8. $8 + 3b = 5$

9. $3x - 9 = -21$

10. $\frac{y}{5} + 3 = 7$

11. $m - \frac{4}{7} = \frac{3}{7}$

Find the surface area of a right rectangular prism with the given dimensions. (Module 6, p. 404)

12. 2 cm, 8 cm, 9 cm

13. $2\frac{1}{3}$ yd, $3\frac{1}{3}$ yd, 8 yd

14. 6.4 m, 1.1 m, 0.9 m

15. 9 mm, 11 mm, 1 mm

| MODULE 8 SECTION 2 | STUDY GUIDE |

A Tower of Power   Drawing Views and Finding Volumes

GOAL **LEARN HOW TO:** • draw different views of a space figure
• recognize a pyramid
• find the volume of a pyramid

AS YOU: • create model buildings with centimeter cubes
• build rectangular prisms using pyramid blocks

Exploration 1: Views of a Space Figure

You can use front, top, and side views of a space figure to determine its
surface area and volume. Space figures with the same volume can have
different surface areas.

Example

Find the volume and surface area of each space figure. Then compare the volumes and
surfaces areas.

a.   **b.**

■ Sample Response ■

a. The volume of the figure is 6 cubic units. To find the surface area of the figure,
sketch the various views of it.

front and
back views

two side
views

top and
bottom views

Use the surface area shown in each view to find the total surface area.

Surface Area = 2(6) + 2(3) + 2(3)
= 12 + 6 + 6
= 24 square units

(continued on next page)

MODULE 8 SECTION 2   **STUDY GUIDE**

Example

■ **Sample Response (continued)** ■

b. The volume of the figure is 6 cubic units. To find the surface area of the figure, sketch the various views of it.

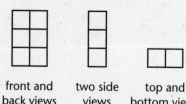

front and
back views

two side
views

top and
bottom views

Use the surface area shown in each view to find the total surface area.

$$\text{Surface Area} = 2(6) + 2(3) + 2(2)$$
$$= 12 + 6 + 4$$
$$= 22 \text{ square units}$$

So, the volumes of the two space figures are the same, but the surface area of the figure in part (a) is 2 square units greater than that of the figure in part (b).

Exploration 2: Volume of a Pyramid

A **pyramid** is a space figure that has one base. All the other faces (called **lateral faces**) are triangles that meet at a single vertex. The height of a pyramid is the perpendicular distance from the base to the vertex opposite it. A pyramid is named for the shape of its base.

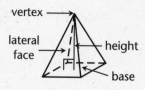

vertex

lateral
face

height

base

square pyramid

The volume V of a pyramid is given by the formula $V = \frac{1}{3}Bh$, where B is the area of the base and h is the height.

Example

Find the volume of an octagonal pyramid whose base area is 50 ft^2 and whose height is 24 ft.

■ **Sample Response** ■

$$V = \frac{1}{3}Bh \qquad \leftarrow \text{Substitute 50 for } B \text{ and 24 for } h.$$
$$= \frac{1}{3}(50)(24) \qquad \leftarrow \text{Simplify.}$$
$$= 400$$

The volume of the pyramid is 400 ft^3.

Name _____ Date _____

Exploration 1

Choose the letter from A to G of the front, top, and right-side views for each model building. (Note: Some letters may be used more than once.)

1.

front   right

2.
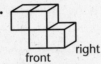
front   right

3.

front   right

A.

B.

C.

D.

E.

F.

G.

Exploration 2

Find the volume of each pyramid with the given base area *B* and height *h*. Round decimal answers to the nearest tenth.

4. $B = 11 \text{ cm}^2$
$h = 9 \text{ cm}$

5. $B = 23 \text{ in.}^2$
$h = 15 \text{ in.}$

6. $B = 33 \text{ ft}^2$
$h = 4 \text{ ft}$

7. $B = 42 \text{ mm}^2$
$h = 10 \text{ mm}$

Spiral Review

Find how many permutations are possible for each situation.
(Module 8, p. 534)

8. 5 rings on 5 fingers

9. 8 cars in 8 parking spaces

Tell whether each set of side lengths *can* or *cannot* form a triangle. If they can, tell whether the triangle is *isosceles*, *equilateral*, or *scalene*. (Module 3, p. 223)

10. 3 ft, 8 ft, 3 ft

11. 5 mm, 6 mm, 7 mm

12. 1 yd, 1 yd, 1 yd

Sketch an example of each shape. Mark parallel sides.
(Module 7, p. 518)

13. a parallelogram that is not a rectangle

14. a quadrilateral that is not a parallelogram

15. a parallelogram that is a rhombus

MODULE 8 SECTION 3   **STUDY GUIDE**

Escape to Central Park   Permutations and Combinations

GOAL   **LEARN HOW TO:** • list and find the number of permutations when items repeat
                  • list and find all the possible combinations
                  • distinguish a combination from a permutation

As you: • find the shortest path between two points on a grid
          • consider ways to group horses

Exploration 1: Permutations

Permutations with Repeated Items

The number of permutations of 3 *different items* is 3 • 2 • 1 = 6.

When some of the items are repeated, the number of permutations is reduced because some of the arrangements are duplicated.

Example

List all the permutations of the letters in the word *see*.

■ Sample Response ■

If all the letters were different, there would be 3 • 2 • 1, or 6 arrangements of the three letters. However, since two of the letters are the same, there are only *half* this number of permutations. The three permutations are *see*, *ese*, and *ees*.

Permutations can be used to find the shortest paths between two points on a grid.

Example

Suppose the letters N and E stand for the map directions north and east. The number of permutations of the letters N, E, and N give 3 possible shortest routes from intersection A to intersection B in the street map below.

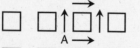

Route 1: N-N-E

Route 2: E-N-N

Route 3: N-E-N

MODULE 8 SECTION 3   STUDY GUIDE

Exploration 2: Combinations

A **combination** is a selection of objects in which *order is not important*.

One way to find all the possible combinations in a situation is to first list all the possible permutations.

An organized list can help you find combinations.

Example

Make a list to show all the possible ways to choose 2 pencils from a group of 5 pencils whose colors are red (r), green (g), blue (b), yellow (y), and white (w). The order in which the two pencils are selected is not important. That is, selecting red and then green is the same result as selecting green and then red.

1st pencil selected	Possibilities for 2nd pencil	Combinations	Number of combinations
r	g b y w	**rg** **rb** **ry** **rw**	4
g	r b y w	gr (duplicate) **gb** **gy** **gw**	3
b	r g y w	br (duplicate) bg (duplicate) **by** **bw**	2
y	r g b w	yr (duplicate) yg (duplicate) yb (duplicate) **yw**	1
w	r g b y	wr (duplicate) wg (duplicate) wb (duplicate) wy (duplicate)	0

There are 4 + 3 + 2 + 1 + 0, or 10 possible ways to choose 2 pencils from a group of 5 pencils. (These 10 combinations are shown in bold type in the third column of the table.)

MODULE 8 SECTION 3 | PRACTICE & APPLICATION EXERCISES | STUDY GUIDE

Exploration 1

For Exercises 1–4, list all the permutations of the letters in each word.

1. FIX   **2.** MOON   **3.** MISS   **4.** MOM

5. Find the number of permutations of five letters in each case.

   a. All five letters are the same.

   b. Four of the letters are the same.

   c. All five of the letters are different.

   d. Three of the letters are the same.

Exploration 2

Tell whether each is a *permutation* or a *combination*.

6. Six of 20 band members have been chosen to perform.

7. Two out of six exercises must be read each day.

8. Two of seven students have been chosen for 1st and 2nd prize.

Spiral Review

Find the volume of a pyramid with the given base area and height. (Module 8, p. 547)

9. Area of base = 40 mm^2
   Height = 9 mm

10. Area of base = 16 yd^2
   Height = $7\frac{1}{2}$ yd

For Exercises 11–14, find each sum or difference. (Module 3, p. 183)

11. $4\frac{3}{5} - 2\frac{3}{10}$ **12.** $1\frac{5}{6} + 2\frac{1}{10}$ **13.** $7\frac{1}{2} - 1\frac{7}{9}$ **14.** $6\frac{5}{8} + 3\frac{5}{7}$

15. The measures of three angles in a quadrilateral are 35°, 111°, and 25°. Find the measure of the fourth angle. (Module 6, p. 429)

STUDY GUIDE

Art in the City   Tessellations and Volumes of Cones

GOAL **LEARN HOW TO:** • create a tessellation using triangles and quadrilaterals
• find the volume of a cone

AS YOU: • examine sculptures

Exploration 1: Tessellations

A **tessellation** is a tiling that uses congruent polygons in a repeating
pattern to cover a plane with no gaps or overlaps. All triangles and
quadrilaterals tessellate. A triangle has been tessellated to make the
pattern shown at the right.

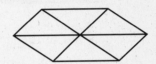

A **vertex of a tessellation** is the point where the vertices of the polygons
meet. The sum of the angles around a vertex is 360°.

Example

Create a tessellation using the quadrilateral at the right.

■ Sample Response ■

Step 1 Copy the figure several times.

Step 2 Flip or rotate the copies to orient them in the right direction.

Step 3 Move the polygons together to create a tessellation.

MODULE 8 SECTION 4

Exploration 2: Volume of a Cone

A space figure with a *circular base* and one *vertex* is a **circular cone**.

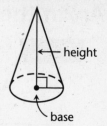

height

base

Example

Name the space figures below.

rectangular prism

cone

cylinder

The *volume* of any cone is given by the formula $V = \frac{1}{3}Bh$, where B equals the area of its base and h equals its height.

Example

The height of a cone is 9 cm and the base has a radius of 3 cm. Find the volume.

■ Sample Response ■

First Find the area of the base.

$A = \pi r^2$ ← The base is a circle.

$\approx (3.14)(3^2)$ ← Substitute 3.14 for π and 3 for r.

$= (3.14)(9)$

$= 28.26$

Then Use the area of the base in the formula for the volume of a cone.

$V = \frac{1}{3}Bh$

$\approx \frac{1}{3}(28.26)(9)$ ← Substitute 28.26 for B and 9 for h.

$\approx \frac{1}{3}(9)(28.26)$ ← Use the associative property of multiplication.

$\approx 3(28.26)$

≈ 84.78

The volume of the cone is about 84.78 cm^3.

MODULE 8 SECTION 4 | **PRACTICE & APPLICATION EXERCISES** | **STUDY GUIDE**

Exploration 1

**Trace each figure below and then create a tessellation with it.
Be sure to match up the corresponding sides.**

1.

2.

3.

Exploration 2

**For Exercises 4 – 6, find the volume of each cone. Round
decimals to the nearest tenth.**

4.

16 in. →

3 in.

5.

5 mm

2 mm

6.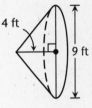

4 ft

9 ft

7. The volume of a cone is 240 ft³. What is the volume of a cylinder
that has the same height and base area as the cone?

Spiral Review

**For Exercises 8 and 9, tell whether each situation is a
permutation or a *combination*. (Module 8, p. 558)**

8. the number of ways to select 3 boxes of cereal from a choice of
5 boxes

9. the number of ways to arrange 8 shirts hanging in a closet

10. a. Plot and label each point in a coordinate plane. Then draw
segments connecting A to B, B to C, C to D, and D to E. Then
connect E to A. **(Module 2, p. 95)**

$A(1, 2)$ $B(3, 1)$ $C(1, -1)$ $D(1, 1)$ $E(-2, 1)$

  b. Use coordinates to describe a transformation that will result in an
image similar to the polygon you plotted in part (a). Then draw
the image after your transformation. **(Module 4, p. 299)**